The Power of Jewelry

Nancy Schiffer

Schiffer
Publishing Ltd

This book is dedicated to
Annchie
for making me aware of nice jewelry.

Title page:
Necklace and earrings of emeralds, rubies,
sapphires and diamonds by Cartier,
London, circa 1955. The central floral
motif of the necklace is detachable and
can be worn as a clip.
Pendant earrings of ruby beads and
circular and baguette diamonds designed
as tassels, circa 1935.

Copyright © 1988 by Nancy Schiffer.
Library of Congress Catalog number: 88-61467.

Printed in the United States of America.
ISBN: 0-88740-135-X
Published by Schiffer Publishing Ltd.
1469 Morstein Road, West Chester, Pennsylvania 19380

This book may be purchased from the publisher.
Please include $2.00 postage.
Try your bookstore first.

Acknowledgments

The huge debt of gratitude I owe to the people who have had a hand in the evolution of this book is shared by many. Each one's contributions have added to the overall content, because projects like this take on a life of their own. One idea prompted several more, and on the web grew entrapping friends, colleagues and perfect strangers who became friends through their ideas. Out of the experience of working with gems and jewelry of great design and powerful significance I have further developed my awareness of the unique place that color and design have in our everyday lives. Because they are rare and hard to obtain, we have acknowledged the color of gems and the designs of the jewelry to be influential in the areas of life that are frightening, which we are otherwise powerless to change, and which we cannot otherwise explain. My associates have shared in this awareness and I gratefully acknowledge their contributions to our readers.

For the many ways he has helped with research, writing, and editing the manuscript I thank Chris Biondi. For their talents and ideas with photography I thank Lyn Kelley, Doug Congdon-Martin, Judy Pyle and Wanda Mack who also did much-needed research. For their assistance with the manuscript I thank Jean Cline, Sue Taylor, Lucy Short, and Skye Alexander.

The jewelry herein represents private collections, the stock of specialized jewelry dealers, and items in the temporal care of auction houses. They represent items of both personal and company ownership, and the pictures were both taken for this volume alone and gleaned from existing negatives. In alphabetical order I thank the people at each collection who helped me: At Anne's Arts in Chestnut Hill, Philadelphia, Loren and Anne Starr. At Asprey & Co., London, Claire Shepard of the Press Office. At Bizarre Bazaar in New York, Nora Lee. At Bentley & Co., London, Miss D. Woolf. Linnet Bolduc. At Bonham's Auctioneers in London, I. Glenney. Marion Carroll of the Black Angus Antique Mall, Adamstown, PA. At Christie's East, Auctioneers in New York, Kathleen Tuttle. At Christie's in London, David Warren and Miranda North Lewis. At Christie's in New York, Sarah Hart Kinney. Dennis Cogdell at the Black Angus Antique Mall in Adamstown, PA. At Elaine Cooper in Chestnut Hill, PA, Helene Huffer. Norman Crider in New York. Sandy DeMaio in Bryn Mawr, PA. Jackie Fleischmann at the Black Angus Antique Mall in Adamstown, PA. Diana Foley at Gray's Mews Antique Mall, London. At Franny's in the Black Angus Antique Mall, Adamstown, PA, Frances Cronan and Frances Detweiler. Patricia Funt in New York. Michael Greenberg in New York. Nicholas Harris in London. John Joseph at Gray's Mews Antique Mall, London. Muriel Karasik in New York. Mim Klein in Philadelphia. Angela Kramer in New York. Maureen McEvoy in London. Nigle Milne in London. Linda Morgan in London. At Phillips Auctioneers in London, Louise C. Goeritz. Leonard Prins at Prins and Volkhardt Jewelers in Strafford, PA. Landra H. Prins. At James Robinson, Inc., New York, Edward, Norma and Joan Munves. Terry Rodgers in New York. At Sotheby's Auctioneers in London and Geneva, Clare Parker. At Wartski, Ltd., London, Geoffrey C. Munn. And certainly not least I thank my publisher, Peter, who is relieved that this book is finally completed.

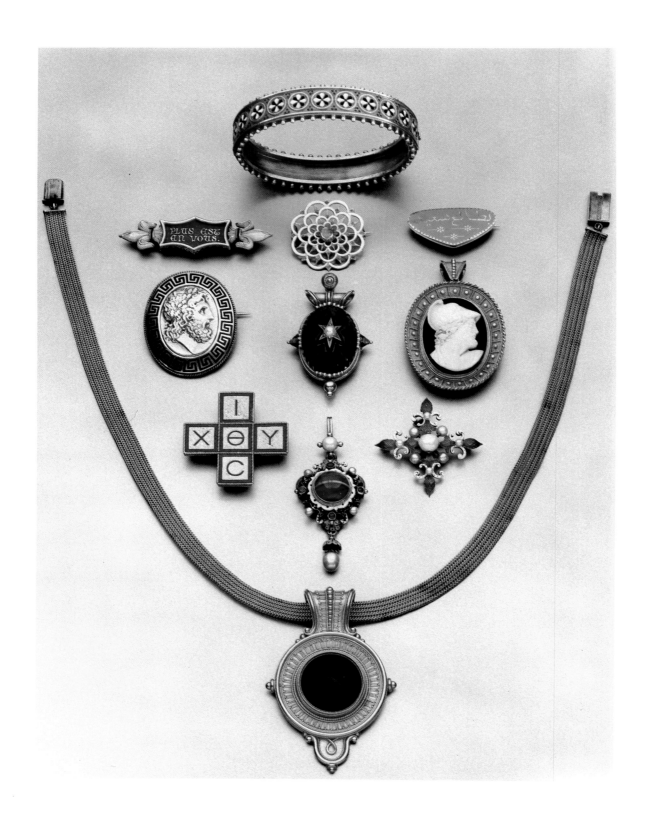

Group of jewelry in the archaeological and neo-Renaissance styles from the middle of the nineteenth century. Top: Bracelet of gold and enamel by Carlo Giuliano, London, circa 1870. Row 1: Pin of gold and enamel by Robert Phillips, Cockspur Street, London, circa 1870. Pin of white and red enamel on gold by Carlo Giuliano, London, circa 1870. Pin of gold and aqua enamel with inscription from the Koran, by Giuliano, circa 1880. Row 2: Pin of gold and enamel with head of a Classical man, patented by Phillips, London, circa 1870. Pendant of gold, carbuncle and pearl by John Brogden, London, circa 1870. Pendant stone cameo in gold of the head of Ajax by John Brogden, London, circa 1870. Row 3: Pin of micro-mosaic and gold by Castellani, Rome, circa 1860. The early Christian derivation for the design is evident in the cross shape of equal arms and the Greek letters spelling ICTHUS, an early reference for "Christ". Pendant of banded agate, pearls, enamel, gems and gold, unsigned, circa 1860. Pin of enamel, pearl and gold by Phillips, London, circa 1860. Bottom: Necklace of gold and agate, unsigned, circa 1860. This "bulla" style originates from Etruscan, Greek and Roman forms which were worn around the necks of young boys as charms.

Contents

The Powers That Be 6

The Power of Gems

AGATE 18

AMBER 24

AMETHYST 26

AQUAMARINE 31

BERYL 34

BLOODSTONE 36

CARNELIAN 38

CAT'S EYE 41

CHALCEDONY 42

CITRINE 44

CORAL 47

CRYSTAL 52

DIAMOND 56

EMERALD 89

GARNET 104

JADE 112

JET 114

LAPIS LAZULI 118

LAVA 121

ONYX 123

OPAL 129

PEARL 135

PERIDOT 150

RUBY 153

SAPPHIRE 171

SHELL 186

TOPAZ 189

TOURMALINE 193

TURQUOISE 195

ZIRCON 201

The Power of Design

ANCHORS & SHIPS 204

ANGELS 205

ANIMALS 209

BIRDS 214

BUTTERFLIES 220

CROSSES 224

FISH 228

FLOWERS 230

HANDS 236

INSECTS 237

MOON, STARS & ARROW 242

PEOPLE 246

SERPENTS 254

PICTURE CREDITS 257

REFERENCES 258

INDEX 269

The Powers That Be

Great gems went with great people . . . gems were the historical perfume of the rich and powerful . . . history was about the rich and the powerful. The gems went along with it . . . Only in the last few hundred years were they (jewels) considered a form of monetary exchange. For most of man's history they were considered to have magical powers.

Richard B. Sapir, *Quest*

The powers which jewelry embodies and reflects about its wearers have been held important to man since primitive times. Anything bright and colorful found in the earth or sea was prized by early man, perhaps because possession of it set the person apart. The possessor could thereby assume powers over his peers and attribute them to the object. Or perhaps it was the object which bestowed its power to the possessor. Up to the present, jewelry has been an individual adornment quick to identify rank, authority, wealth and influence to both those who wear it, and, in its absence, to those who merely observe it.

Jet, shale, amber, ivory, and shell are among the first materials used in the making of personal adornments. Frequent mention of certain gem stones in the Bible attest to the importance of them in early recorded history. The breastplate of the highest priest, for example, contained twelve stones of great value, each engraved with the name of one of the tribes of Israel. Persians, Indians, Phoenicians, Greeks, Romans, and the now extinct civilizations in South America all held precious stones in high esteem with legends concerning their method of formation and their so-called "virtues."

The center of the ancient jewel trade was Alexandria where traders from Athens, Persia, Egypt and Rome gathered. The Romans learned to gather gems from Greek collections which they plundered and brought home. In turn, the Roman soldiers introduced the riches of the East to the West. Cleopatra reputedly entertained Caesar in a banquet hall with porphyry columns, ivory porticoes, onyx pavement, thresholds of tortoise set with emeralds, furniture inlaid with yellow jasper, and couches studded with gems. Julius Caesar learned quickly. He collected many precious stones himself before he declared pearls prohibited from all below a certain rank and forbid any gems to be worn by unmarried women. Among the great Roman collections of old, those of Alexander the Great, Hadrian, Pompey and Augustus remain infamous. Still, the largest collections known are those of Indian princes. In the thirteenth century, Marco Polo recorded previously unknown, and since unmatched, collections in India, China, Burma and Ceylon.

Many of these early collectors believed that precious gems actually lived and were capable of maturing or "ripening." Some thought that tropical heat was necessary for the full development of their forms, and in the seventeenth century Garcilaso de la Vega in South America wrote that emeralds "take their tincture from the nature of the soil from whence they are produced, ripening there with time like fruit in their proper seasons." It was also widely believed in these times that gems were capable of human feelings and passions so that they could express jealousy or shock. For example, as will be seen in the individual sections which follow in this book, pearls, diamonds, turquoise, coral, emeralds and other stones were believed to anticipate the future, respond to their owners' state of health, and express feelings so that they took on the properties of fetishes.

These and the other gems have been credited with occult powers since ancient times. They were first, perhaps, worn as amulets, and later as ornaments. Many astrologers and students of the ancient teachings believe that each stone has its own personality and attributes. Rambam, the great Maimonides, on the other hand, wrote that, "there is no wisdom in a stone, for it is not the property of objects to be wise . . . the only value in a diamond or in any other gem is what man places on it. Otherwise it is no different from the pebble underfoot. A stone can no more make a person wise than it can make him good. A stone has no will of its own, much less power to act on it." Maimonidaes further illustrated his point by asking if a one-qurot diamond made a person somewhat bright and a ten-qurot diamond made him a genius.

People believed these things about stones because life was just too powerful and terrifying without them. People have known since early ages that the great and terrifying things of life are always beyond the absolute control of man.

Dumb Jewels often in their silent kind, More than quick words, do move a woman's mind.
Two Gentlemen of Verona

Necklaces

Among the most ancient forms of jewelry is the necklace, for very old beads of pebbles, bone and shell are known from the earliest traces of mankind. Stone Age teeth strung together into necklaces have been found in cave deposits. Since then, each civilization has contributed its forms of ornamental and revered neckwear. Egyptian necklaces of gold and gem stones from around 2000 B.C. show rounded and polished gems. Greek and Roman strings of beads include the liberal use of agate and more elaborate settings. As new sources of different gems became known, their appearance in the highest levels of societies are seen at each age.

Rings

In prehistoric times rings were probably associated with the sun, which brings warmth, light and life to the earth. One of the oldest and most interesting talismanic rings is known as the Naoratna, the "nine-stone" gem mentioned in old Hindu treatises on gems: Manner of composing the setting of a ring:

In the center	The Sun	The Ruby
To the East	Venus	The Diamond
To the Southeast	The Moon	The Pearl
To the South	Mars	The Coral
To the Southwest	Rahu	The Jacinth
To the West	Saturn	The Sapphire
To the Northeast	Jupiter	The Topaz
To the North	The descending node	The Cat's-eye
To the Northwest	Mercury	The Emerald

Such is the planetary setting.

Later, rings were associated with the magic circle that a magician drew around himself when he summoned spirits and demons to do his bidding. A magic circle helped the magician control his unearthly assistants, just as the legendary Ring of Solomon enabled him to bind all the demons of the world to do his will.

The continuous round shape of a finger ring has continually signified eternity, for we pass through time to eternity. The breaking of a finger ring was ominous. At an early time, people inscribed their names on finger rings and soon found it was necessary to widen and thicken the part of the ring to be so inscribed. This resulted in the formation of signet rings. In the fifteenth century, the German writer Trithemius of Spandau suggested: "Make a ring of gold and silver. Cast it at the hour in the day in which you were born. Inscribe upon it the four letters of the Tetragrammaton [see below]. Place it upon the thumb of your left hand and at once you will be invisible." (The Tetragrammaton is the four letter unspeakable name of God, written "JHVH" and represented in English as "Jehovah" or "Yahweh". Among ancient Jews it was probably a pseudonym intended to keep knowledge of God's true name from sorcerers. In the Middle Ages it was believed to be the source of great power when inscribed on an amulet.)

Finger rings are perhaps the most popular of all amulets. Many people have believed in a connection between the ring and the wearer so that what happens to one affects the other. For many centuries English monarchs gave their faithful followers gold rings known as cramp rings and they were credited with curing mild and serious illness. The material from which a ring was made contributed to its power, whether gold, silver, iron, clay, bone, glass, or horn. It was a Medieval belief that when you, "dream that you have found a ring, great honor will come to thee."

Necklace and earrings of gold, seed pearls,
Jaipur enamel, white sapphire and ruby,
Indian. Earrings of polished emeralds and
diamonds. Bracelet of gold and emeralds,
English, circa 1875. Finger ring of dark
green jade in prong setting.

Necklace, bracelet and pendant of gold, pearl, diamond and enamel, unsigned, circa 1890. Necklace of pink tourmaline, diamond, enamel and gold, unsigned, circa 1900. Pendant of enamel, ruby, diamond, and gold, unsigned, circa 1900. Pin of pink topaz and diamonds, unsigned, circa 1830.

Color

The symbolism of color played an important part in recommending particular stones for special purposes in jewelry. Red stones were generally thought to be remedies for bleeding and inflammatory diseases, to provide a calming influence, and remove anger. Yellow stones were believed to cure bilious disorders and diseases of the liver. Green stones traditionally have been suggested to correct diseases of the eyes. The blue stones both calmed spirits of darkness and brought the aid of light and ensured sure-footedness.

In the East of England, folks say:

> Blue is true; red's brazen;
> Yellow's jealous; white is love;
> Green's forsaken; and black is death.

Elements

An old myth relates the offerings made by the four elements to the deity:

> The Air offered a rainbow to form a halo about the god;
> The Fire offered a meteor to serve as a lamp;
> The Earth offered a ruby to decorate the forehead;
> The Sea offered a pearl to be worn upon the heart.

Seasons of the Year

Gems of Spring
Amethyst
Green diamond
Chrysoberyl
Spinel (rubicelle)
Pink topaz
Olivine (peridot)
Emerald

Gems of Summer
Zircon
Garnet (demantoid)
Chrysoberyl (Alexandrite)
Spinel
Pink topaz
Ruby
Fire opal

Gems of Autumn
Hyacinth
Topaz
Sapphire
Jacinth
Cairngorm
Adamantine spar
Tourmaline
Oriental chrysolite

Gems of Winter
Diamond
Rock-crystal
White sapphire
Turquoise
Quartz
Moonstone
Pearl
Labradorite

Medicine

Besides the medical uses explained in the following sections of this book, gem stones were worn for prevention of diseases and it was important that the different stones were worn on different parts of the body. According to one authority:

> the Jacinth should be worn on the Neck
> the Diamond should be worn on the Left arm
> the Sapphire should be worn on the Ring finger
> the Ruby or turquoise should be worn on the Index or little finger

The indispensable materials which should be in every good pharmacy included the following gem stones:

Jacinth	Coral	Emerald
Sapphire	Jasper	Topaz
Hematite		Pearl

In the sixteenth century, the following gems were used in all tonics prescribed to protect the heart against the effects of poison and the plague:

Sapphire		Emerald
Ruby	Sardonyx	Garnet
Jacinth		Coral

In a German druggist's price list of 1757, the following gems appear:

1 pound rock-crystal, 6 groschen	1 pound ruby, 1 thaler
1 pound emerald, 8 groschen	1 pound lapis-lazuli, 5 thalers
1 pound sapphire, 16 groschen	

Words

In France and England during the eighteenth century, jewelry was often set with gems the first letters of which, combined, formed a motto or expressed a sentiment. Some of the more common ones appear below. In the sentimental late nineteenth century, this practice was repeated, and it is still used by romantics today.

AEI (Greek for "Forever" or "Eternity")
Alexandrite
Emerald
Indicolite (blue Tourmaline)

AMITIE
Alexandrite
Moonstone
Indicolite
Topaz
Idocrase
Emerald

BONHEUR
Beryl
Opal
Nephrite
Hyacinth
Emerald
Uralian emerald
Ruby

CHARITY
Cat's-eye
Hyacinth
Aquamarine
Ruby
Iolite
Tourmaline
Yellow sapphire

DEAREST
Diamond
Emerald
Alexandrite
Ruby
Essonite (Hessonite)
Sapphire
Turquoise

FAITH
Fire opal
Alexandrite
Iolite
Tourmaline
Hyacinth

FOREVER
Fire opal
Opal
Ruby
Emerald
Vermeille
Essonite
Rubellite

FRIENDSHIP
Feldspar
Rock crystal
Idocrase
Emerald
Nephrite
Diamond
Sard
Hematite
Iolite
Pearl

GOOD LUCK
Garnet
Opal
Obsidian
Diamond
Lapis lazuli
Uralian emerald
Cat's-eye
Kunzite

HOPE
Hyacinth
Opal
Pearl
Emerald

LOVE ME
Lapis-lazuli
Opal
Vermeille
Emerald

Moonstone
Emerald

MIZPAH
Moonstone
Indicolite
Zircon
Peridot
Asteria
Hyacinth

REGARD
Ruby
Emerald
Garnet
Amethyst
Ruby
Diamond

SOUVENIR
Sapphire
Opal
Uralian emerald
Vermeille
Emerald
Nephrite
Iolite
Ruby

ZES (Greek, "Mayest thou live")
Zircon
Emerald
Sapphire

Days of the Week

Auspicious times for wearing gemstones grew out of the various beliefs in their powers to do good, and so different gems were designated as lucky on particular days of the week, as follows:

Sunday	Ruby
Monday	Moonstone
Tuesday	Coral
Wednesday	Emerald
Thursday	Cat's-eye
Friday	Diamond
Saturday	Sapphire

Clockwise from top: Pin of gold, pearl and onyx cameo of an African girl wearing ruby and diamond earrings and necklace, circa 1880. Pin of carved agate, enamel, ruby and diamond designed as a blockamoor, 19th century. Pin of enamel and diamond designed as a bow, circa 1900. Pendant of gold and diamonds designed as a crown, circa 1900. Pin of garnet and diamonds, circa 1880; the garnet is carved with an angel child signifying Love. Pin of gold and diamonds designed as a ribbon inscribed Carmen Sylva below the royal cypher of Elizabeth Queen of Roumania, by Resch, circa 1900. Pendant of gold, enamel, pearl and diamonds designed with an allegory of Time, Austrian, circa 1890. Pin/pendant of gold, carbuncle and diamond in the shape of a flower head, unsigned, circa 1890. Center: Pendant of gold, carnelian, and enamel, unsigned, circa 1825; the carnelian is carved with a relief portrait of Napoleon.

Diagonal rows from top left. Left row: Pendant of carbuncle and diamond designed as a cluster of berries, circa 1860. Regimental badge pin of gold, enamel, and diamonds of the English Queen's Own Oxfordshire Hussars, circa 1900. Center row: Earrings and pendant in Holbeinesque style of gold, enamel, carbuncle and gems, circa 1870. Pin/pendant of openwork design with emeralds and diamonds, circa 1880. Pendant of Holbeinesque style in gold with enamel, emerald, diamond and pearls (perhaps added later), circa 1870. Pendant of gold with enamel, ruby, emerald and diamonds, circa 1870. Right row: Finger ring of gold with enamel, onyx, and ruby, circa 1880; a gold bust of a caryatid is mounted on the onyx as a cameo. Pin of gold in a heart shape with enameled landscape and house and diamond border, circa 1900. Pin of gold with opal cameo, enamel and garnets by Carlo Giuliano, London, circa 1870.

Months of the Year

In Poland, many years ago, a tradition grew up of designating particular gems as lucky for people born in each month of the year. This belief probably evolved from the spiritual philosophies of the Jewish wanderers who found asylum in Poland, for the Poles absorbed much of these teachings into their culture.

Besides the gemstones for each month, two ages old poems are quoted in month order below, with a stanza of each divided out for its particular time.

JANUARY: GARNET
No gems save garnets should be worn
By her who in this month is born;
They will insure her constancy,
True friendship and fidelity.

The gleaming garnet holds within its sway
Faith, constancy, and truth to one alway.

FEBRUARY: AMETHYST
The February-born may find
Sincerity and peace of mind,
Freedom from passion and from care,
If she an amethyst will wear.

Let her an amethyst but cherish well,
And strife and care can never with her dwell.

MARCH: JASPER, BLOODSTONE
Who on this world of ours her eyes
In March first opens may be wise,
In days of peril firm and brave,
Wears she a bloodstone to her grave.

Who wears a jasper, be life short or long,
Will meet all dangers brave and wise and strong.

APRIL: DIAMOND, SAPPHIRE
She who from April dates her years
Diamonds should wear, lest bitter tears
For vain repentance flow. This stone
Emblem of innocence is known.

Innocence, repentance—sun and shower—
The diamond or the sapphire is her dower.

MAY: EMERALD
Who first beholds the light of day
In spring's sweet flow'ry month of May,
And wears an emerald all her life,
Shall be a loved and happy wife.

No happier wife and mother in the land
Than she with emerald shining on her hand.

JUNE: AGATE
Who comes with summer to this earth,
And owes to June her hour of birth,
With ring of agate on her hand
Can health, long life, and wealth command.

Thro' the moss-agate's charm, the happy years
Ne'er see June's golden sunshine turn to tears.

JULY: TURQUOISE
The heav'n-blue turquoise should adorn
All those who in July are born;
For those they'll be exempt and free
From love's doubts and anxiety.

No other gem than turquoise on her breast
Can to the loving, doubting heart bring rest.

AUGUST: CARNELIAN
Wear a carnelian or for thee
No conjugal felicity;
The August-born without this stone,
'Tis said, must live unloved, alone.

She, loving once and always, wears, if wise,
Carnelian—and her home is paradise.

SEPTEMBER: CHRYSOLITE
A maid born when September leaves
Are rustling in the autumn breeze,
A chrysolite on brow should bind—
'Twill cure diseases of the mind.

If chrysolite upon her brow is laid,
Follies and dark delusions flee afraid.

OCTOBER: BERYL
October's child is born for woe,
And life's vicissitudes must know;
But lay a beryl on her breast,
And Hope will lull those woes to rest.

When fair October to her brings the beryl,
No longer need she fear misfortune's peril.

NOVEMBER: TOPAZ
Who first comes to this world below
With drear November's fog and snow
Should prize the topaz's amber hue—
Emblem of friends and lovers true.

Firm friendship is November's, and she bears
True love beneath the topaz that she wears.

DECEMBER: RUBY
If cold December give you birth—
The month of snow and ice and mirth—
Place on your hand a ruby true;
Success will bless whate'er you do.

December gives her fortune, love and fame
If amulet of rubies bear her name.

Gems of the Zodiac

Since ancient times gemstones have been considered lucky depending on their associations with the various signs of the constellations in the Zodiac. These are not necessarily the same gems associated with the months of the year, but because the days governed by the constellations overlap the month divisions, some similarities appear. The choice of respective gems for each sign has varied through the ages, with Romans, early Christians, Medieval Jews and Arabs, primarily, all having their own preferred list. The selections below represent what many people believe to be lucky stones of the Zodiac today. The stanzas of poetry relating to each one are from an old and anonymous rhyme.

AQUARIUS * JANUARY 21 to FEBRUARY 21 * GARNET
If you would cherish friendship true,
In Aquarius well you'll do
To wear this gem of warmest hue—
The garnet.

PISCES * FEBRUARY 21 to MARCH 21 * AMETHYST
From passion and from care kept free
Shall Pisces' children ever be
Who wear so all the world may see
The amethyst.

AIRES * MARCH 21 to APRIL 20 * BLOODSTONE
Who on this world of ours his eyes
In Aires opens shall be wise
If always on his hand there lies
A bloodstone.

TAURUS * APRIL 20 to MAY 21 * SAPPHIRE
If on your hand this stone you bind,
You in Taurus born will find
'Twill cure diseases of the mind,
The sapphire.

GEMINI * MAY 21 to JUNE 21 * AGATE
Gemini's children health and wealth command,
And all the ills of age withstand,
Who wear their rings on either hand
Of agate.

CANCER * JUNE 21 to JULY 22 * EMERALD
If born in Cancer's sign, they say,
Your life will joyful be alway,
If you take with you on your way
An emerald.

LEO * JULY 22 to AUGUST 22 * ONYX
When youth to manhood shall have grown,
Under Leo lorn and lone
'Twill have lived but for this stone,
The onyx.

VIRGO * AUGUST 22 to SEPTEMBER 22 * CARNELIAN
Success will bless whate'er you do,
Through Virgo's sign, if only you
Place on your hand her own gem true,
Carnelian.

LIBRA * SEPTEMBER 22 to OCTOBER 23 * CHRYSOLITE
Through Libra's sign it is quite well
To free yourself from evil spell,
For in her gem surcease doth dwell,
The chrysolite.

SCORPIO * OCTOBER 23 to NOVEMBER 21 * BERYL
Through Scorpio this gem so fair
Is that which every one should wear,
Or tears of sad repentence bear,—
The beryl.

SAGITTARIUS * NOVEMBER 21 to DECEMBER 21 * TOPAZ
Who first comes to this world below
Under Sagittarius should know
That their true gem should ever show
A topaz.

CAPRICORN * DECEMBER 21 to JANUARY 21 * RUBY
Those who live in Capricorn
No trouble shall their brows adorn
If they this glowing gem have worn,
The ruby.

Bracelet, Necklace and earrings of gold, ruby, turquoise, seed pearl, diamond and enamel in Egyptian style by Carlo Giuliano, London, circa 1865. Bracelet of gold, enamel, carbuncles and zircon in lattice pierced design, by Carlo Giuliano, circa 1865. Pin of gold, enamel, diamonds and pearls designed as a caduceus (reversed), unsigned, circa 1900.

Five unmounted fancy diamonds ranging in size from approximately 3.3 to 6.3 carats, one unmounted ruby of approximately 2.75 carats, and two unmounted emeralds of approximately 2.2 and 4.90 carats.

The Power of Gems

Agate

Finger ring of gold with agate cameo and grey stone background cut with a double bust portrait of a man's head overlapping a woman's head, circa 1870.

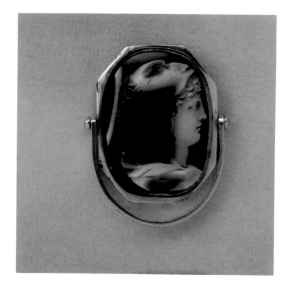

Finger ring of gold with agate double sided cameo hinged to show one side carved as a woman's head with lion headdress in relief, and the reverse of a woman's head and cloth mantle, circa 1870.

Pin of yellow and white gold with a moss agate placque applied with a gold and diamond driving scene surrounded by black onyx and circular diamonds, circa 1920.

Agate is a type of chalcedony found in a variety of different colors and translucencies formed in curved bands or layers. Many types of agate are distinguished due to the variety of shapes and colors which may appear as other minerals infiltrate the stone. Bands in the stone may form an eye agate or a ribbon agate, and often, the shapes of trees, clouds and plants may be discerned on the surface of the "tree agate" or "moss agate" lending a mysterious quality to the stone. The name agate is derived from a Greek word for the River Achates in Sicily. It was first discovered in quantity in this river in about 300 B.C. Agates are currently mined in the United States, India, Brazil and Uruguay.

Interestingly, most commercial agates are cut in the town of Idar-Oberstein in West Germany. The Romans, during Julius Caesar's Gallic Wars discovered quantities of Agate in this small town and set up a major gem-cutting operation which has remained in operation for almost two thousand years. Astrologically, the agate is connected with the death sign, Scorpio, and was wielded to seek divine assistance.

In Egypt, grey agates are worn on the neck to protect against stiff-neck, colic and diarrhoea. The ancient Romans believed the moss agate to have been singled out by the creator to have occult power. The Romans ground the ingredients for medicinal lotions and ointments on moss agate pallets in the belief that the stone could improve vision. The Roman scholar Pliny the Elder found that the Persians attributed to the agates the power to avert storms. All types of agates, powdered in wine, were used by the ancient Greeks and Romans as antidotes for snakebites and scorpion stings. The agates were also strung from the hair of a lion's mane in the belief that they would then bring love, friendship and the favors of the great.

Of all the agates, the strongest talismanic powers have been attributed to the brown agate. With a brown agate in hand, a sick man will soon recover and a poor man may find riches. The brown agate, it was believed, would make the warrior victorious, enhance love, cure poisonous reptile bites, increase intelligence and cause all varieties of good to be bestowed upon the wearer. To quote Orpheus, musician and poet of Greek mythology, "If thou wear a piece of tree agate upon thine hand, the Immortal Gods shall be well pleased with thee; if the same be tied to the harness of thy oxen when ploughing, or about the ploughman's sturdy arm, wheat crowned Ceres shall descend from heaven with full lap upon thy furrows." Agate was also the "fortune stone" of Aeneus, the Trojan hero, who used it as protection in war and on voyages.

In Persia and the Orient, the agate has long been used as a talisman against fever, and to bring good luck and eloquence to the wearer. It also was used to

improve sight, make the wearer friendly and lead to the discovery of treasure. One such talisman, popular in modern times, is a ring of agate on which a verse of the Koran is carved to protect the wearer from sickness and evil. In Italy and in Persia, the agate was held to protect the wearer against the evil eye, and in Syria, a necklace of triangular agates was thought to prevent intestinal troubles. In Byzantine times, the agate was used to soothe inflamed eyes and headaches, and to stave excessive bleeding. The Mohammedans mixed powdered agates with fruit juices to cure insanity and harden tender gums.

Saint Albertus Magnus, thirteenth century German philosopher, theologian and scientist held the agates to be effective against certain skin diseases. In the fourteenth century, the agate was placed in the mouth to quench thirst and reduce fever, and it was also considered to be an effective defense against poisons. This belief accounts for the use of agates in drinking cups and bowls.

William Shakespeare honored the agate in his play *Romeo and Juliet.*

> Who comes in summer to this earth,
> Owing to June his day of birth,
> If wearing Agate on his hand,
> May all the joys of life command. (1.3)

The banded agate, as one of the seven seas gems, was supposed to take away the terrors of the ocean, and to dream of an agate was considered a harbinger of an ocean journey. Many more medicinal powers were ascribed to the agates. The wearer of an agate was believed to develop mental alertness and overcome madness and epilepsy. Agates were also thought to attract solar energy and when an agate was worn as an amulet, it was credited with providing protection against reptiles, scorpions, madness and the evil eye. The owner of an agate was guarded from all dangers and was enabled to vanquish all terrestrial obstacles with a bold heart.

Agate was a popular material for carving bowls and drinking cups. One piece measuring more than twenty-eight inches in diameter was carved from a solid piece of agate. This bowl was taken during the Crusades and rests now in Vienna. Another famous piece of agate is a wine cup that has been traced back to the Roman Emperor Nero. The cup has since changed hands several times. For several centuries, the cup was used during the coronations of French Kings and is now cherished as a relic of French history.

Pendant of gold with agate cameo, diamonds and pearls, English, 1870's.

Necklace of graduated agate beads on knotted black cord, clasp replaced.

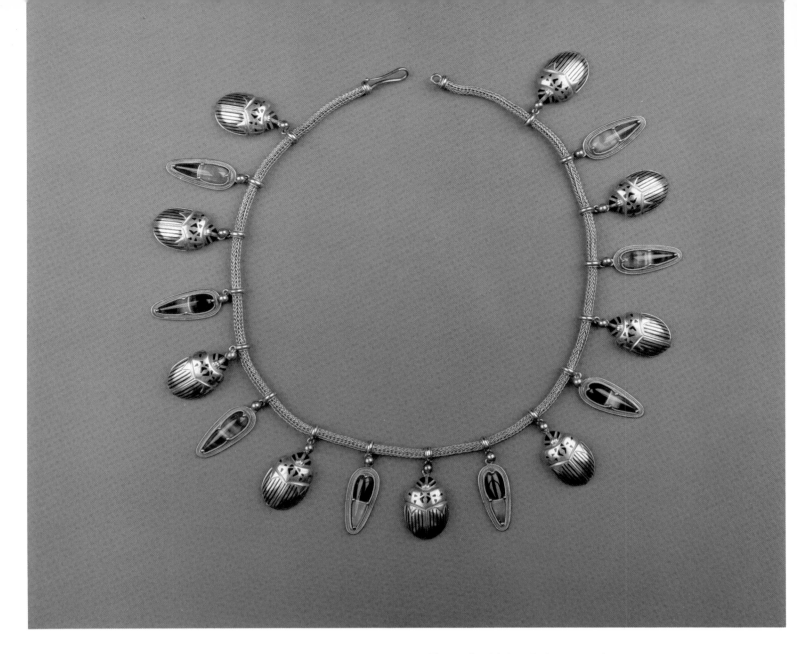

Necklace of gold, banded agate and enamel by Robert Phillips, London, circa 1860; the Egyptian style is expressed by the materials and design with exquisite workmanship in each detail.

Bracelet, pin and earrings of gold with agate cameos, English, circa 1870.

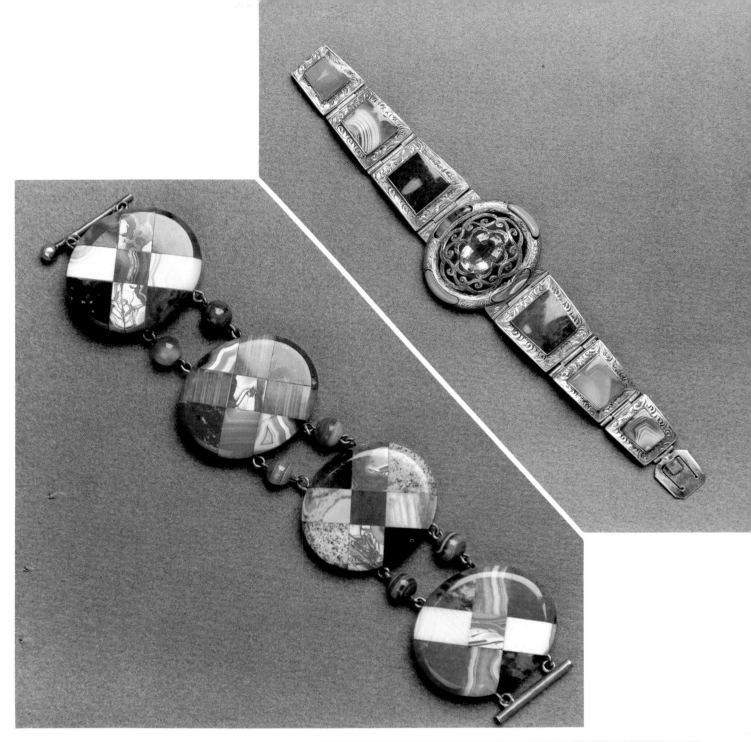

Bracelet of agate and granite with brass fittings and clasp, Scottish, circa 1880.

Bracelet of sterling silver with grey and moss agate, citrine and granite, Scottish, circa 1870.

Pin of gold with three agate cameos, English, circa 1870.

Bracelet of grey agate and gold, circa 1865; and pin of grey agate, cairngorm and gold, circa 1880, both Scottish.

Pin of four banded agate beads cut from one large stone, circa 1870, Scottish.

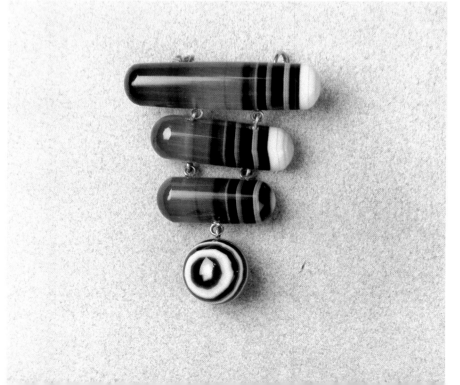

Pendant and chain of sterling silver with banded agate and pearl by Rebajez, Mexico, circa 1945.

Two bracelets of gold and oval agate panels of differing varieties, mid-nineteenth century.

Amber

Pin of sterling silver with amber and amethyst, from Chester, England, 1907.

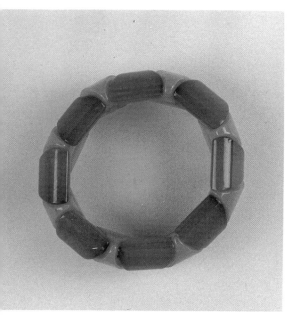

Bracelet of amber beads in two colors linked with an expansion elastic.

Amber is not actually a mineral, but the sixty million year old fossilized resin from an extinct species of pine. Composed chiefly of carbon, amber was often used for incense as it emits a pleasant odor when burned. The color of amber varies from pale yellow to dark brown or red, and depending on the lighting and presence of air bubbles within, it may also appear green, blue or violet. The highest quality amber is found washed up on the shore of the southern Baltic in Poland and East Germany. Pieces found on the beach have broken away from the ocean floor and floated to the surface. This type of amber is also known as seastone or scoopstone. Other mined varieties are found in Sicily, Burma and Rumania.

Amber is very brittle and easily cut by a knife making it suitable for intricate carving. Amber becomes electrified when rubbed and was known to the ancient Greeks as "electron". "Electron" was thought to be pieces of the sun broken away in the ocean at sunset. Many stories and legends have arisen from the confusion surrounding the source of amber. Athenian historian Nicias thought amber to be the perspiration of an overheated earth.

One Greek myth tells that pieces of amber were the tears of sisters who, in their grief at the death of their brother, turned into poplar trees. As the myth relates, Apollo granted his son, Phaethon, his desire of driving the chariot of the sun for a day. Phaethon, however, lost control of the horses and scorched the earth. An angered Jupiter cast a thunderbolt at the boy setting his hair afire. The blazing Phaethon plunged into the river Eridanus as his sisters stood by weeping tears of amber.

The ancient Greeks ground amber and mixed it with honey and rose oil as a cure for deafness, and when mixed properly with attic honey, amber was believed to improve vision. The Chinese word for amber translates to "the soul of the tiger" and it originated from the ancient belief that amber is the mineralized spirit of the tiger. Consequently, amber is symbolic of courage and is said to hold all of the qualities of a fierce tiger. A particular type, known as "blood amber" is used as an aphrodisiac in China.

The Latin word for amber, *succinum*, means juice and was believed, quite accurately, by Pliny the Elder in the first century A.D. to be the hardened sap of certain trees. Pliny also wrote that necklaces of amber were worn by children to ward off evil spirits and witchcraft. The Romans used amber to protect from poisonous drugs, and amber was thought to prevent insanity when worn at the neck or taken in a powdered form. Golden-yellow amber was held to be particularly effective against ague. Amber was also used to prevent teething pain in children and tooth loss in adults.

The mystery of the source of amber continued into the seventeenth century when it was thought to be the product of the urine of the lynx. In 1638 it was written "By the Jesuits rule no physician . . . should make use of . . . Lyncurie, because it issueth out of the body of a spotted beast, called Lynx." In his *Family Dictionary* in 1696, one Dr. Salmon advised, "For the falling sickness, take half a drachm of choice amber, powder it very fine, and take it once a day in a quarter pint of white wine, for seven or eight days successively." For a "falling fundament," Dr. Salmon prescribed one to, "Take bits of amber, and in a close-stool put them upon a chafing-dish of live charcoal, over which let the patient sit, and receive the fumes." Even into the early twentieth century, amber was thought to aid those suffering from asthma, dropsy and toothache. Amber has long been believed to be resistant to the transmission of disease and has therefore been used as the stem-piece in pipes and cigarette holders.

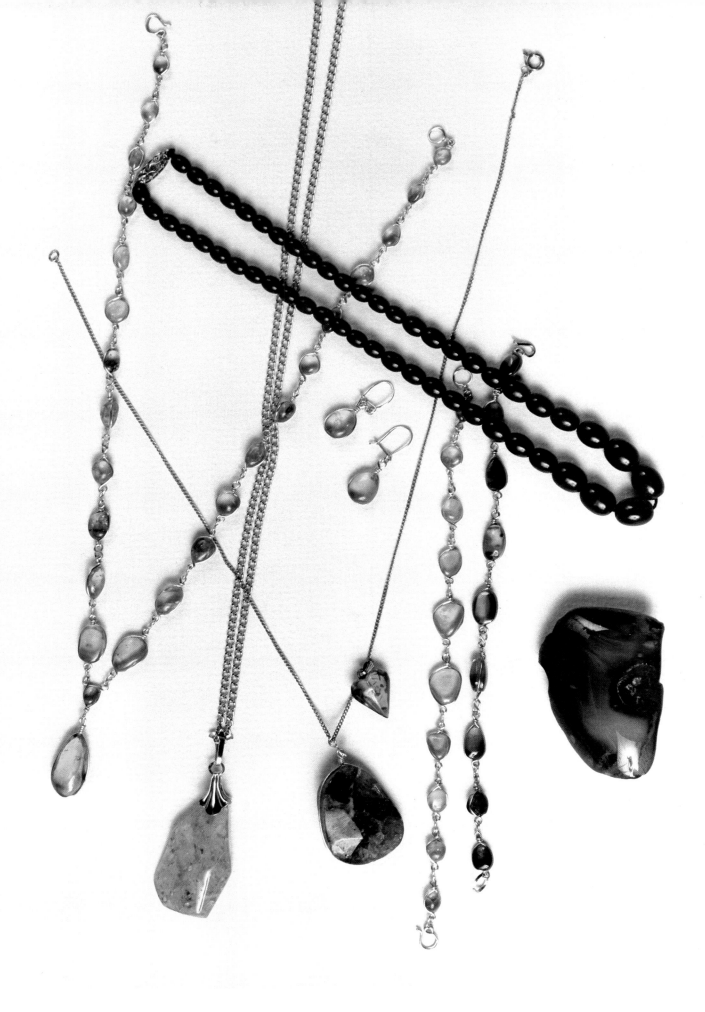

Amber of varying colors used in necklaces, bracelets, pendants, earrings and pin.

Amethyst

Amethyst is the most popular variety of quartz and is found in colors ranging from a deep purple to bluish violet. Depending on the source of the stone, the amethyst may also take on a reddish tone. A mixture of colors may appear in a single stone, but stones of a single, pure color are considered more desirable. This crystallized gem owes its beautiful and legendary color to an infusion of manganese and iron. Though the gem is found throughout the world, the finest amethysts originate from mines in Brazil, Uruguay and the Ural Mountains of Russia. Amethyst was at one time considered very rare and often was preferred over the diamond until recent discoveries in Brazil made vast quantities available and reduced their value and desirability somewhat. However, the amethyst, in all its beauty, remains one of the most popular of all gems. Amethyst is the gem of the House of the fishes—Pisces. Also, the ancients wrote of the amethyst's sympathetic Aries vibration, and it has long symbolized spirituality in the highest degree.

Egyptian soldiers believed that by wearing amethysts they would be successful in their deeds and remain calm in the face of danger. Pliny described the Magi, priests of Ancient Medes and Persia, as believing amethyst, with carvings of the sun and the moon, to be mighty charms against witchcraft. These charms were also said to be able to bring to the wearer good luck, success and the admiration of those in authority. In Peru it was held that an amethyst with engravings of the names of the sun and the moon would ward off witchcraft when worn as a necklace with baboon's hair and swallow feathers.

Perhaps the most enchanting of the legends associated with amethyst may be found by examining the source of its name. Amethyst is derived from the Greek word *amethystos* meaning "not drunken," or "without drunkenness." For it has been believed, from the time of the ancient Greeks, that drinking from a chalice lined with amethyst, or keeping an amethyst beneath the tongue would allow one to indulge to excess in wine without feeling the effects of intoxication. The source of this belief is an ancient myth whose cast of characters includes Bacchus, son of Jupiter and god of wine, Amethyst, a beautiful nymph, and the goddess Diana.

As the myth tells, the beautiful nymph called on Diana to protect her from the advances of Bacchus. Diana did so by turning the nymph into a sparkling gem. Bacchus, as a symbol of his love, poured wine upon the gem giving amethyst its color and power to protect its users from intoxication. From such a myth sprouted variations of the belief that amethyst held the power to prevent drunkenness. One prescription told that by binding an amethyst to the navel, one could restrain the vapor of the wine and retain sobriety. The amethyst is one of the twelve sacred gems of the Jewish breastplate and was symbolic of the tribe of Issachar. It is said that Saint Valentine wore amethyst, and in Christianity a religious significance of amethyst may be found. Often the rings of Bishops are comprised of amethyst as are rosary beads. As a prayer is said holding each amethyst rosary bead the believer becomes more and more at peace in his prayers.

The amethyst also signified the humility of Christians to their Saviour as in this verse composed by Marbodus in the eleventh century.

> On high the Amethyst is set
> In color like the violet,
> With flames as if of gold it glows
> And far its purple radiance throws;
> The humble heart it signifies
> Of him who in the Saviour dies.

Saint John the Divine reported the amethyst as being one of the stones in the wall of the Holy City along with sapphires, emeralds and pearls. It was believed

Pin of sterling silver with four amethysts and a central foil-backed pink paste, English, circa 1830.

Pin of sterling silver and amethyst marked Dixelle, circa 1950.

Necklace and earrings of gold and
amethyst, French, circa 1890; the earrings
have been re-worked.

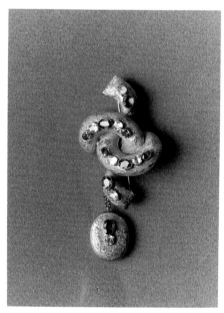

Necklace of silver links and six oval amethust stones, 56 inches long. Necklace of amethyst beads and pendant. Pin of textured silver with amethyst, 20th century. Pendant of silver with amethyst in cross shape from Jerusalem, circa 1950.

Earrings of platinum, gold, amethyst and diamond, English, circa 1900.

Pin of gold, amethyst and citrine, circa 1880.

Finger ring of silver, gold, amethyst and diamond, English, circa 1800.

during the Middle Ages that a dimmed amethyst or one that had changed color indicated the presence of poisons, personal danger or ill health. It was also believed that if bound to the left wrist, the amethyst enabled the wearer to see the future in his dreams, and that the stone itself indicated the success of the traveler, clergyman, sailor, philosopher, teacher and mystic.

For headaches and toothaches, it was advised that an amethyst be immersed in hot water for a few minutes, taken out, dried carefully and gently rubbed over the aching parts. By carving a winged horse on the surface of an amethyst, it served as an effective talisman for the protection of horses and their riders. Worn as an amulet, the amethyst may also cure a man of gout, and one may induce pleasant dreams by placing an amethyst beneath the pillow before sleep. The virtues of amethyst appear endless as they were used as a cure for false vision, bad memory and color blindness. Belief in the powers of the amethyst prompted Camillus Leonardus to write that it "represses evil thoughts and all excesses, prevents contagion, and gives good understanding of hidden things, making a man vigilant and expert in business."

Catherine the Great of Russia was quite fond of amethyst and accumulated a vast collection of the stones, many of which remain in the Soviet Treasury. Amethysts also adorn the coronation jewelry in England. An amethyst more than one inch high rests on the coronation orb and is said to signify the Christian dominance over the world. The scepter of the King and the coronet of the Prince of Wales also contain fine amethysts. One king-sized bed of amethysts discovered in Brazil early this century was contained in a geode measuring thirty-three by five feet and weighing more than thirty-five tons. Beautifully colored amethysts covered the entire inside of the formation.

Necklace of gold, amethyst and pearl,
American, circa 1900.

Necklace with large oval aquamarine set in platinum and diamond frame suspended from a double line diamond chain. Cushion shaped unmounted aquamarine of approximately 50 carats. Pair of pendants of pear shaped diamonds and platinum. Finger ring of aquamarine and diamonds set in white gold.

Aquamarine

Aquamarine is a variety of beryl that has been beautifully described as being the color of sea water parted by the bow of a sailing ship. Aquamarine is related to the emerald but is much more common and therefore not as highly valued. The color of the aquamarine may vary from greenish blue to bluish green. The finest specimens are found in Brazil, however they are also found in quantity in Madagascar, Russia and Ceylon. The aquamarine is one of the gems of the house of Scorpio, and alternates, with the bloodstone, as the birthstone for March.

Aquamarine acquired its name from the Latin word for "seawater" and has long symbolized eternal youth and happiness. It was also believed that aquamarine could induce sleep and provide for the wearer foresight and insight. The aquamarine was believed to hold power over evil. By holding one of the gems in your mouth, you were said to be able to call on the devil and ask of him any questions which you may have. Medicinal powers were also attributed to the aquamarine. To cure the hiccups, one need only to drink water in which an aquamarine had been soaked. This water was also good for eye and breathing troubles. The aquamarine was the symbol of a rise in social stature and to dream of an aquamarine symbolized loving friendships.

The ancient Greeks and Romans often used aquamarines for intaglio work. One of the most beautiful examples is a two-inch square intaglio depicting a bust of Julia Titi, daughter of Roman Emperor Titus. The piece is signed by "Euodus Epoiei", a Roman artist, and formed the knob of the Golden Reliquary in the Abbey of Saint Denys for nearly a thousand years. In 1920, a 243 pound aquamarine was discovered in Brazil. The stone sold for a mere $25,000, and many beautiful gems were cut from it. An 880-carat aquamarine rests in the British Museum of Natural History, and the American Museum of Natural History holds several large specimens including a 335-carat Ceylon stone. Mrs. Franklin D. Roosevelt was presented a 1,847-carat aquamarine by the Brazilian government in 1935. It rests now in the Hyde Park Museum in New York.

Dress clip of baguette and fancy shaped aquamarines, diamonds and platinum by Cartier, London #232, circa 1945, in rollover and arrow design.

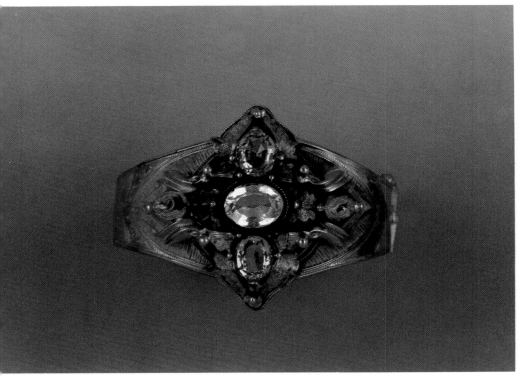

Bracelet of gold and aquamarine, circa 1855.

Necklace/tiara of aquamarine and
diamond, circa 1880. Pin/pendant of opal
and diamond, circa 1900. Pin of diamonds
designed as a narcissus, the flower head
mounted en tremblant, circa 1885. Pin of
diamonds in oval cluster design, 19th
century. Pin of diamonds in square
openwork design adapted from a bracelet,
circa 1860.

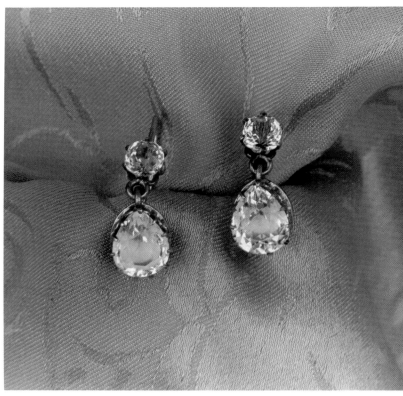

Earrings of aquamarines and gold, circa 1875.

Pendant and earrings of briolette aquamarines, diamonds and platinum, English, circa 1900.

Bracelet of gold, aquamarine and diamond, European, circa 1945.

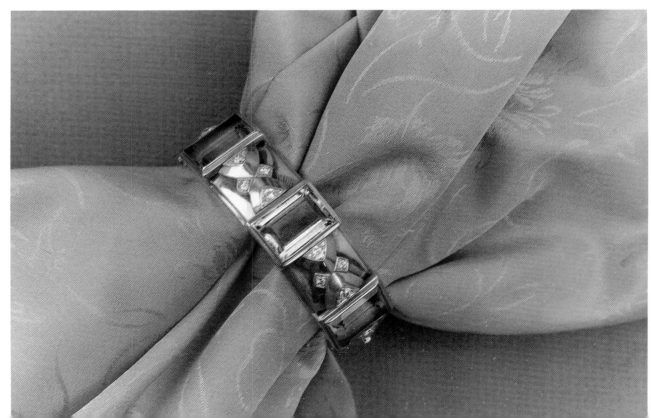

Beryl

Beryl is a classification of aluminium-glucinum silicate crystal. This classification includes several types of gemstones such as the emerald and aquamarine. While the names emerald and aquamarine apply to beryls of certain colors and properties, the term beryl may apply to these and the many other members of this classification. Beryl in its pure form is colorless, however, the pure beryls may become colored by the intrusion of various metallic oxides. Consequently, beryls may vary in color from yellowish and bluish green to the blue of certain aquamarines and deep green of emeralds. Many beryls are named for their color such as the golden beryl and pink beryl. Another popular beryl is the purple-red variety called morganite which was named for tycoon J. Pierpont Morgan in recognition of the contribution of his gem collection to the American Museum of Natural History.

Excepting the emerald, beryls are considered to be relatively tough. Beryl is most often found in giant beds of granite, called pegamites. The pure, colorless beryls are found in gas cavities within these pegamites where metallic oxides are unable to permeate the crystals. The pegamite fields which bear the highest quality beryls are found in Brazil, Argentina, Afghanistan, Africa, India, the United States and Madagascar. Beryl is one of the stones of the House of Scorpio and is also associated with Gemini.

It was believed that beryl could assist the bearer in battle or in litigation by rendering one unconquerable, yet amiable, with a quickened intellect and heightened energy. The love of unmarried people was asserted to be reawakened by beryls. In the East, the beryl was held to be sensitive to personal influence and was frequently presented to brides with the notion that the auras of the newlyweds would blend within the gem thus elevating their love.

Beryl was used by mystics because its transparency allowed the seers to gaze into them for their prophecies. It was popular for use as an oracle and was indispensable in a ceremony of witchcraft to call on Saint Helen. To perform the ceremony, the seer, at sunrise on a clear day, would first write the name of St. Helen and draw a cross with olive oil on a beryl. The seer would then turn to the east while placing the gem into the hands of an innocent child, born in wedlock. As the seer repeated prayers, whatever he wished could be seen in the stone until St. Helen herself would materialize as an angel to answer any questions.

Mystics wielded beryls in other rituals to foretell future events. In the water divination, a ritual of the Middle Ages, a beryl was suspended to barely touch the surface of water in a bowl. When asked a question, the beryl would respond by automatically striking the edge of the vessel. Beryl was also tossed into a shallow dish of water so mystics could interpret the movements of the sun's reflection in the surface of the water.

In *The Majick of Kiram* it was written: "Take a Beril Stone, and engrave a Crow upon it; and under its feet a Crab; wear it as you will; for Joy, and Exultation, and Acquisition, and Union, and Conjugal Love; and it will make the Bearer cheerful, and Rich; and it is as excellent as anything for lascivious and Conjugal Love."

Camillus Leonardus wrote of beryl, "it renders the bearer cheerful and increases and preserves married love." He continues into the medicinal virtues of beryl prescribing, "it cures distemper of the throat and jaws, and is good for indispositions of the liver and disorders of the stomach." Freeman, in the early eighteenth century, wrote that if a person held a beryl in his mouth, he may call on a spirit and receive answers for any questions he may have. The stone was also held to be beneficial to mariners and adventurers as it preserved them from danger and sickness and would assist in the discovery of hidden objects. It was also a symbol of eternal youth, and to dream of the gem signaled happy news to come.

Certain beryls may attain a weak cat's-eye effect or chatoyancy. This effect is not nearly as discernable as the chrysoberyl cat's-eye however, and is not as

desirable. The Los Angeles County Museum of Natural History holds a cat's-eye beryl weighing more than 211 carats. Also in the Los Angeles Museum is a star beryl of more than eleven carats. This type of beryl is a dark yellow to sometimes black, and a faint star may sometimes be seen on the surface of the stone.

Necklace and earrings of gold, pearl and yellow beryl by Tiffany and Company, New York; the pendant includes a yellow beryl of approximately 150 carats.

Bloodstone

Pin of silver with topaz, bloodstone, agate, and carnelian in the shape of a dirk, made in Edinburgh, Scotland, 1905.

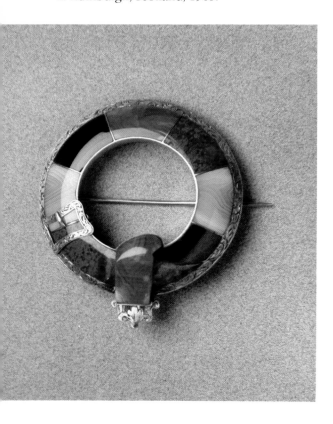

Pin of sterling silver with bloodstone, agate and granite designed in the shape of a belt and buckle, English, circa 1880.

Bloodstone is a variety of green chalcedony that has been permeated by iron oxide to form bloodred specks. The stone is also known as heliotrope from the Greek words for "sun-turning". This name arose from the belief that the stone, when immersed in water, could turn the sun's image bloodred. Bloodstone can be highly polished and is very suitable for engraving often being used for seals and cameos. The highest quality bloodstones come from India and the Ural Mountains of Russia. The bloodstone alternates with the aquamarine as the birthstone for March and is, with the diamond, the gem of the House of Aries, the Ram.

Great powers have been attributed to this stone including the ability to cause great thunder and lightening. The ancients scraped powder off of the stone and used it to stop internal and external bleeding. This bloodstone powder was also used to soothe bloodshot eyes and served as an antidote for snakebites. A scorpion carved on a bloodstone as the sun was entering the sign of Scorpio was believed by the ancients to prevent stones in the bladder. The Leyden papyrus ascribes tremendous power to the bloodstone: "The world has no greater thing; if any one have this with him he will be given whatever he asks for; it also assuages the wrath of kings and despots, and whatever the wearer says will be believed. Whoever bears this stone, which is a gem, and pronounces the name engraved upon it, will find all doors open, while bonds and stone walls will be rent asunder."

One talismanic bloodstone was worn by Nechepsos, an Egyptian king, to strengthen the digestive organs. On the stone was engraved a dragon surrounded by rays. The ancient Greeks and Romans also held beliefs in the bloodstone's powers. The stone was believed to bring for the wearer renown and the favor of the great, and to inspire constancy and endurance. One tale reveals that the bloodstone was formed during the Crucifixion when blood dripped onto a bed of jasper from the sword of a Roman soldier. Hence the belief that the bloodstone could stem bleeding and Roman soldiers wore it as a talisman for this reason.

In the same belief, Menardes wrote: "The vertue of this stone is much above any other gem, for it stops the flux of blood in any part. We have seen some that were troubled with flux of the Haemorrhoides who found remedy by wearing rings made of the bloodstone continually on their fingers." Leonardus wrote of the bloodstone, "the virtue of the heliotrope (bloodstone) is to procure safety, and a long life to the possessor of it." The Indians would dip bloodstone in cold water and place it directly upon the wound for this purpose.

During the early years of Christianity, the Gnostics wore the bloodstone in the belief that it would prolong their life and make them courageous and wealthy. The Gnostics also believed that the bloodstone would strengthen the stomach of the wearer and decrease melancholy. In the Middle Ages the bloodstone was believed to assist those who worked in the breeding of cattle. The powers of bloodstone inspired Marbodeus Gallus to write a poem describing the virtues of the stone:

> Again it is believed to be a safeguard frank and free
> To such as ware and beare the same; and if it hallowed bee,
> It makes the parties gratious and mightier too that have it
> And noysome fancies as they write who ment not to deprave it
> It doth dispel out of the mind. The force thereof is stronger
> In silver, if this stone be set, it doth endure the longer.

Also in the Middle Ages, it was believed that the bloodstone had the power to stem nosebleeds. In an essay entitled "The Origine and Virtues of Gems" by Robert Boyle, dated 1675, is told the story of a man who was susceptible to excessive nosebleeds. The man could not stem the bleeding until, as the essay relates: "an ancient gentleman presented him with a Bloodstone the size of a pigeon's egg, to be worn round the neck, and upon use of this stone he not only cured himself, but stopped hemorrhage in a neighbour." The power of the bloodstone to render the wearer invisible is referred to in a poem by William of Paris:

> To many a gift divine this Stone lays claim;
> Surpassing which the power that makes its fame
> Is,—when conjoined with herb of title quaint,
> Same as its own; whilst, spoken by a saint
> Are incantations, holy, and a spell
> Invoked,—with words the pious tongue can tell;
> Of Gem, and Plant combined, the wearer the
> Becomes invisible to the eyes of men.

Further belief in this power was ascribed to the bloodstone in 1801 by Magus, in *The Celestial Intelligencer*: "The stone heliotropium, green, like a jasper, or emerald, beset with red specks makes the wearer constant, renowned, and famous, conducing to a long life; there is likewise another wonderful property in this stone, which is, that it so dazzles the eyes of men, that it causes the bearer to be invisible."

Pin of silver with bloodstone and granite designed in the shape of a stag's leg, English, circa 1875.

Pin of sterling silver, bloodstone, carnelian, granite and agate in the design to symbolize the Prince of Wales, English, circa 1900. Pin of bloodstone, carnelian and granite designed as a fence gate, English, circa 1900.

Carnelian

Finger ring of gold with carnelian carved as a scarab beetle and mounted to spin. The carnelian is carved on the reverse with a scene depicting Cincinnatus giving up his plow to command the Roman troops.

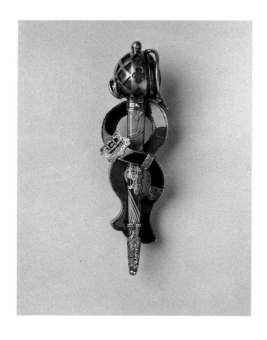

Pin of sterling silver with carnelian, bloodstone and agate designed as a daggar and belt, English, circa 1880.

Carnelian is one of the several varieties of chalcedony or cryptocrystalline quartz. What distinguishes carnelian from the rest of the chalcedony types is its distinctive translucent red to brownish orange coloration. Carnelian was originally named "cornelian", but this appellation was changed to carnelian in the fifteenth century when it was mistakenly believed that the name was derived from the Latin word for "flesh"—"carneolus". In fact, the original name, cornelian was derived from the Latin word "cornum" meaning "cornel berry," and has since become antiquated.

As a chalcedony, the carnelian is a tough gemstone and suitable for all types of fashioning. The majority of quality carnelian is mined in Brazil, India and Uruguay. Carnelian is an alternate birthstone for the month of July and is, with Jade, a gemstone of the House of Virgo.

Primitive peoples, with their beliefs in the powers of the Shaman, or witchdoctor, were said to carry carnelians under their left arms, and employed these stones to separate the astral from the physical body. The Shaman used the carnelian in his magic and believed it to be a stone of tremendous and wonderful power. The carnelian, it was thought, had the power to drive away the evil effects of sorcery, witchcraft, enchantment and fear and make the soul happy. It was also designated as the stone of victory and victors.

The carnelian was used extensively, both as a talisman and an ornament, by the Egyptians and mention of it is made in *The Book of the Dead*. The Hebrews believed the carnelian to hold the power to preserve life from the dangers of the plague. Arabs used the carnelian to stop bleeding and to protect against the evil eye and poverty. The carnelian was coveted throughout the Middle East for its talismanic powers, and it was not uncommon for Moslems to carry their gems to Christian priests whose blessings were considered to be more effective. Many such stones were found engraved with verses from the Koran.

Carnelian was referred to as the stone of the martyrs, and was believed to be a window to gaze into the astral plane. To do so, one would place a stone before a light for several minutes then stare steadily into the gem and the astral plane would appear.

The Reverend C.W. King wrote of a carnelian which Napoleon carried with him throughout his campaign in Egypt. Napoleon wore the stone on his watch chain as a seal which bore the inscription in Arabic, "The slave Abraham relying upon the merciful (God)." In the Orient, the stone was thought to protect against witchcraft and ward off the evil eye. Camillus Leonardus thought the carnelian kept the wearer safe in lightening and storms. Marcellus Empiricus designated the carnelian as an amulet for the prevention of pleurisy. In India, the carnelian was held to protect the wearer against falling walls. The Lapidario of Alfonso X recommended the carnelian to those who have a weak or timid voice, and the stone was said to be able to give the speaker courage so he may speak boldly and well.

In the eleventh century, Marbodus believed that if worn on the neck or finger, the carnelian would cool the blood and discourage angry passions and drive away evil thoughts. It was also believed that a ring of carnelian would make a man peaceful and slow to anger, but cool in argument and dignified in a dispute. A bad temper was thought to be a form of black magic, and the carnelian was able to deflect the evil light of the waning moon away from the wearer. To dream of a carnelian served as a warning that evil thoughts were being directed toward the wearer.

Schroder, in 1669, on the virtues of the carnelian wrote: "the pouder of them is good to drink against all fluxes; carried about it makes cheerful minds, expels fear, makes courage, destroys, and prevents fascinations, and defends the body against all poysons; it stops blood by a peculiar property; and, bound to the belly, keeps up the birth."

Symbolic virtues have been attributed to the carnelian giving the stone an almost human quality. The color is said to express the warm and affectionate nature of the stone. The stone is lively and denotes friendships and enjoyment. Psychologically, the carnelian denotes emotional ties, and spiritually, the stone shows a reverence for life and represents a mystical union with God and all creation. On the dark side, however, the stone signifies a certain manipulativeness, a lack of self-respect and the characteristics of overindulgence.

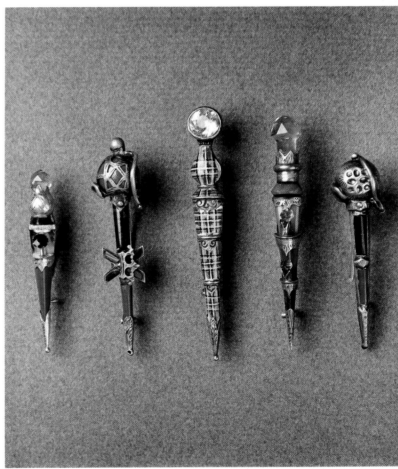

Five pins in the forms of dirks with carnelian, bloodstone, agate, amethyst, and enamels, Scottish, circa 1875.

Necklace of carnelian beads and brass spacers.

Pendant of gold, chrysoberyl, sapphire, diamonds and enamel by C. Giuliano, London, circa 1880.

Pendant of gold, cat's eye, diamonds and enamel by C. Giuliano, London, circa 1880.

Opposite page:
Pendant with cat's-eye of approximately 36 carats, diamonds and gold, nineteenth century.
Pin with two cat's-eyes of approximately 92 and 63 carats, diamond, silver and gold, circa 1890.

Cat's Eye

Cat's-eye is a variety of chrysoberyl which, when held in the proper way and light, resembles, as its name suggests, the eye of a cat. These stones are said to display chatoyancy by showing a streak of light that waves across the stone's surface as it is turned. Chatoyancy is caused by bundles of parallel, thin crystals within the stone. When cut *en cabochon*, the dome of the stone serves as a sort of lens giving the stone its peculiar characteristic. The color of the cat's-eye may range from a greenish yellow to brownish green. In a finely cut stone, the eye may appear to open and close as it is revolved.

When carried by those with Capricorn rising in the horoscope, or with the sun, Jupiter or Venus in Capricorn, the cat's-eye is credited with special value as a charm for success in speculative ventures. The stone is also associated with Cancer—the House of the Crab.

The cat's-eye was believed to be able to put color into pale faces, to relieve the soul of melancholy and to give pleasure to the mind. It was also thought to cure chronic disorders and wasting diseases and to keep the wearer free of financial distress and ruin. Cat's-eye was said to be successfully employed to relieve croup and asthma. When pressed between the eyes, it enhanced thought and encouraged foresight, and if lightly rubbed on closed lids, cat's-eye would soothe inflammations of the eyes. To dream of a cat's-eye was considered a warning of treachery. As a talisman, it was thought to have the power to make the wearer invisible to his enemies.

The cat's-eye was highly revered in India as a talisman to prevent its wearer's wealth from diminishing. It was also considered to hold power against the terrors of the night and if worn as a necklace would relieve the symptoms of asthma. The cat's-eye was said to have no equal as a charm in gambling and games of chance. In the Middle East, men who suspected infidelity, would soak a cat's-eye in milk and have their wives drink it in the belief that it would prevent pregnancy as a result of any infidelity. During the Middle Ages, the cat's-eye was set in a ring and used as protection against the evil eye. Physically, the cat's-eye denotes insight, shrewdness and vision. It gives the psychological gift of being able to understand the problems of others, and spiritually provides the willingness to forgive and the ability to understand flaws in yourself and others. The dark side of the cat's-eye may suggest a judgmental spirit, cattiness and gossip.

Several beautiful examples of the cat's-eye rest in the world's museums. The Hope Collection in the British Museum of Natural History boasts a large specimen that is carved to represent an alter and measures an inch and a half in diameter. A 47.8 carat cat's-eye lies in the American Museum of Natural History.

Chalcedony

Chalcedony is the cryptocrystalline class of quartz which usually appears light blue or grey. Chalcedony is divided into several gemstone types according to variations in its color and structure. Several of these types include agate, sardonyx, sard, carnelian, chrysophrase and onyx. Chalcedony is porous and is often stained to change or intensify the color of the stone. It is formed as water dissolves organic matter which may be present in rocks near the surface, and replaces it with particles of chalcedony until it lines or fills the cavity of a geode. Chalcedony is found throughout the world, but the highest quality deposits are in California, Iceland and Siberia. It is believed that the name chalcedony was derived from the name of a source of the stone—Chalcedon, a port in Asia Minor. Chalcedony is associated with the House of Cancer and is a symbol of enthusiasm.

Chalcedony was believed to protect the ocean voyager from storms and terrors and had the power to drive away evil spirits and reduce sadness and melancholy. Chalcedony was thought to gain public favor for the wearer and protect him in times of political revolution. It was used to ease the passage of gallstones and to lower fevers. Milky white beads of chalcedony were worn by women during the early Iron Age to aid in their nursing. Women in Italy wore chalcedony for the same reason and gave it the name *pietra lattea* or milk-stone. Gonelli, writing in 1702, believed that the alkaline quality of the stone cured evil humors in the eye thereby driving away visions of ghosts which infected eyes might create. Chalcedony was believed to protect the wearer from the evil eye, and give him a pleasant disposition.

Necklace of blue chalcedony beads of uniform size.

Necklace of chalcedony, citrine and gold links, Scottish, circa 1865. Pin in the shape of a butterfly with chalcedony, banded agate and cabochon citrine in gold, circa 1875.

Pin/pendant of gold with chalcedony, Scottish, circa 1865. Bracelet of gold, chalcedony and cairngorms, Scottish, circa 1870.

Citrine

Citrine is a crystalline variety of quartz which varies in color from its usual yellow to a reddish orange. Citrine was popular for use in jewelry during the Victorian period when it was inaccurately referred to as "topaz." Citrine is still sometimes sold on the market as "Spanish topaz" or "Saxon topaz" in its reddish or orange coloring. The word "citrine", was derived from the French word for "lemon", *citron*. Sources of the finest citrine are in Brazil and Madagascar, however it is also found in Uruguay, the Ural Mountains of Russia, Spain, Hungary and the United States. Citrine alternates with topaz as the birthstone for November and is under the zodiacal Scorpio.

Citrine was carried as a talisman against plague epidemics, eruptive skin diseases, evil thoughts and forms of indulgence such as alcoholism. It was also used as a charm to protect against the bites of snakes, venomous reptiles, and insects. Citrine was believed to guard against scandal, libel and treachery.

Cloak pin of sterling silver and citrine, Scottish, circa 1855 in its original box.

Tiara of citrine, sapphire and diamond designed as two laurel sprays, English, nineteenth century.

Pin of three citrines and gold, English, circa 1875.

Necklace, pendant and earrings of citrine and two colors of gold, English, circa 1830.

Necklace and two bracelets which can join to make a long necklace, pendant, tiara piece and two finger rings of gold and citrine, English, circa 1820.

Pin of silver and citrine, Scottish, circa 1900.

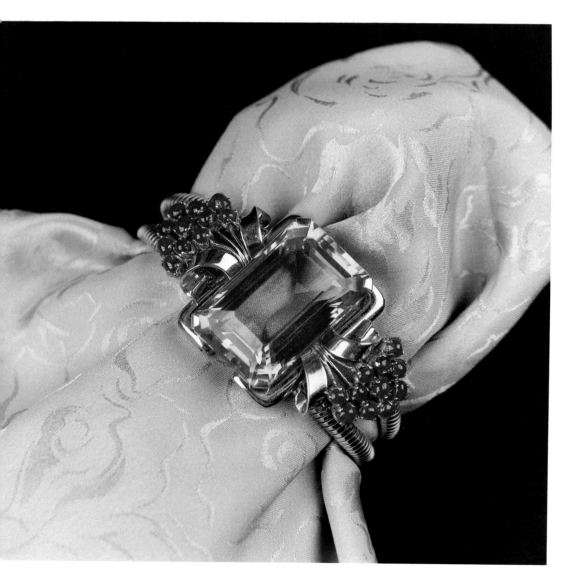

Bracelet of citrine, cabochon rubies, and two colors of gold in snake link chain, circa 1945.

Coral

Coral, though considered a gem, is actually a conglomeration of the skeletons of tiny marine invertebrates that live and grow together in colonies. The skeletons consist of calcium carbonate in the form of calcite which attach to rocks and other objects on the ocean floor. Great masses of coral may come together forming treacherous reefs. Of the several varieties of coral just one, "precious coral", has been of particular interest to jewelers, mystics and physicians. Precious coral, *corallium nobile*, varies in color from a pinkish white to bloodred and is found in most tropical and subtropical oceans such as those along the coasts of Algeria, Morocco and Corsica. Most coral is found at depths of less than fifty feet, though it has been found as deep as a thousand feet.

Since ancient times, coral has held a special significance to civilizations surrounding the Mediterranean—a source of much of the material. A great variety of medicinal and talismanic qualities have been ascribed to coral and it remains a popular and fashionable ornament today. Coral falls under the sign of Pisces and is associated with the House of Balance—Libra.

The ancient Chinese greatly valued coral which was supposed to represent a tree called *T'ieh shu* which grows on the ocean floor and flowers but once a century. This tree symbolized longevity and official promotion. The Romans hung pieces of coral around the necks of their children to protect them from childhood illnesses and danger. The Romans also powdered coral and ingested it to soothe aching stomachs. This same powder was burned and used in ointments for application to ulcers and sore eyes. Pliny relates how people of his time believed coral to have the power to quiet tempests and protect the wearer from lightening and tornadoes. Dog's collars were decorated with coral by the Romans so they would not fear the water, and many Romans used it simply as ornamentation. Women in Rome wore coral around their necks as charms against sterility.

Top: Necklace of coral beads and spacers.
Center: Necklace of coral and silver beads.
Bottom: Necklace of coral and agate beads.

The ancient Greeks believed coral to have the power to baffle witchcraft and to protect against poisons, storms and robbery. The Greeks also ground coral into a powder, mixed it with seed-corn, and spread it about their fields to guard against locusts, thunderstorms and blight. Coral, a Greek myth tells, was formed as blood dripped from the severed head of Medea which Perseus had placed up in a tree near the ocean. The blood dried as it fell, and sea nymphs picked it up and carried it to the water where it was planted.

In India, coral was coveted as having many sacred properties. Here, as well as in China and Japan, it was very popular for use in rosaries and was thought to prevent cholera and all epidemics. It was also believed, by changing color, to indicate the presence of poisons or impending sickness. Coral was thought to benefit decrepit persons and those who have aged prematurely. It was said to quicken the senses and preserve eyesight by preventing gradual loss of energy in the optic nerve. Coral was likewise believed to strengthen the mental faculties. To dream of a red or pink coral of beautiful lustre is said to indicate recovery to the ill and good health to all. But to dream of a dull, poor-conditioned coral warned of sickness and poor health.

Camillus Leonardus advised that coral be used to keep the house clear of evil spirits and prevent nightmares and mental delusions. He also thought it to be effective for intestinal trouble and diseases of the spleen. In the fourteenth century, Rabbi Benoni, a reputed alchemist of his era, believed coral, if worn at all times, to aid in digestion. In 1564, the physician Rulandus prescribed half a drachm of coral to stimulate the heart, stop bleeding and ward off contagion.

Sir John Harrington wrote, in his *School of Salerne* in 1624, that one should always wear a ring of coral on the little finger of the left hand for he thought it to be, ". . . endued with occult, and hidden vertues." Similarly, Dr. John Schroder writing in 1660, recommended coral as it: ". . . strengthens the heart chiefly, then the stomach; makes men merry; it stops all fluxes of the belly, and womb; it prevents epilepsies in children, if you give ten grains to a newborn child (before it takes anything else) in the mother's milk; it is outwardly good against ulcers, and fills them with flesh; it helps to extenuate scars, to stop weeping eyes, and to refresh the sight, put into collyria. The dose to give is from twenty grains to one drachm. The tincture of coral is of great force as against convulsions." Dr. Schroder also wrote that, "The shining coral, according to Paracelsus, makes an amulet against fear, and frights, fascinations, incantations, poysons, epilepsies, melancholy, devil's assaults, and thunder." And that, "The white coral hung about the neck to touch the breast, stops abdominal cholic, and dispels the pain thereof."

Less than forty years later, in 1696, one Dr. Salmon gave direction on the procedure to make tiny pills of coral for, ". . . strengthening the heart, in fevers, and such-like violent diseases, and to restore the decays of nature." To make the pills, he wrote: "Take such a quantity as you think convenient; make it into a fine powder, by grinding it upon a porphyry; or in an iron mortar; drop on it by degrees a little rosewater; and form it into balls for use." In the eighteenth century, the French wore a necklace of coral beads known as a *pater de sang* or blood rosary. The rosary was believed by many to stop bleeding though some suspected that if the rosary could harden the blood, it could in fact prove dangerous as it might affect the internal blood as well.

Early in the nineteenth century coral was esteemed by the Navajo Indians as one of the eighteen sacred objects and made used it for jewelry and ornamentation. Even into the late nineteenth century, a diluted powder of coral was prescribed by physicians to cure whooping-cough as M. Teste wrote on coral, "For a chronic convulsive cough, it is like water thrown upon fire." Coral has long been greatly esteemed by dancers and is especially a good luck charm of those involved with the ballet.

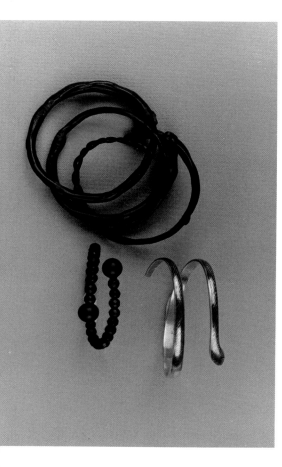

Three bracelets of black coral, bangle style, late nineteenth century. Bracelet of black beads, probably jet, late nineteenth century. Bracelet of silver niello work designed as a snake, late nineteenth century.

Opposite page: Choker necklace and pin of carved coral and diamonds in white gold and platinum, signed Cartier, Paris, circa 1940. Dress clip of carved coral, emerald, diamond and gold designed as a flower basket, signed Cartier, Paris, circa 1940.

Necklace of gold chain with a two tier
pendant of coral, enamel, diamond and
pearl, circa 1850; the lower pendant
includes an entwined snake motif.

Necklace of gold chain with pendant of
coral, enamel and diamonds, French, circa
1850; the coral is carved in relief with a
portrait.

Two bracelets of openwork silver, coral
and marcasite, circa 1930.

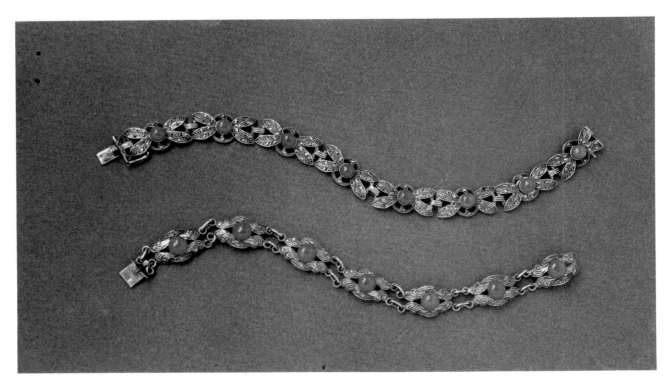

Necklace and pin of gold and coral, circa 1860.

Crystal

Quartz is composed of silicon dioxide, and is the most common mineral type in the earth's crust. Quartz exists in a variety of colors due to the infiltration of different oxides. The word crystal has been used to define a variety of different substances, but the only definition acceptable to modern gemologists is its original significance which represents quartz in its beautiful, clear and pure form. The term crystal can be traced back to the ancient Greeks who believed it to be clear water which had permanently solidified. N.F. Moore in his *Ancient Mineralogy* wrote in 1834, "As for rock crystal, it was the universal opinion of ancient naturalists, and the belief, indeed almost to our own time, that it was water congealed to that hardness, by long continued and intense cold."

As quartz exists in a variety of colors it has acquired a great number of different names. These names may designate color, such as "rainbow quartz" and "rose quartz" or they may give a hint to other characteristics of the stone such as "rutilated quartz." Quartz is present in some form in most types of rock on the earth's surface. As the stone weathers and wears with time, particles of it are washed by the rains and rivers to the oceans where it becomes the major component of gravel and beach sand. Quartz is popular for use in jewelry, but its use goes far beyond into such areas as the manufacturing of electronics, eyeglasses and porcelain. Crystal is the birthstone for the month of April, and it is said that the moon, the ruler of the zodiacal Cancer, has influences on the brain which allow persons sympathetic to this house to visualize future events by crystal-gazing.

According to Pliny in the first century A.D., the ancients used crystal as a burning glass in medicine and also to reduce swelling of the glands, heart disease, fever and intestinal pains. Mothers used crystal mixed with honey as a means to increase their milk supply while they were nursing. To the early Christians, the crystals symbolized the immaculate conception. The clans of Scotland kept crystals which they called "stones of victory" and would administer water that had washed over the stones to cure sickness in men and animals. It was also believed that if one drank from a vessel of crystal it could prevent dropsy and toothache. Certain Mexican Indian tribes held that the souls of the dead were contained in crystals. And in Australia, it was used by magicians to bring rains during drought. Crystal was considered a talisman of concentration and perseverance. It was said to enclose within its brightest forms, all the knowledge and secrets there have ever been.

Pin of gold, crystal, enamel and citrine by C. and A. Giuliano, London, circa 1900.

Bracelet of crystal, platinum, ruby, sapphire and diamond designed as links and gem-set panels: circa 1930.

In sleep, crystal would banish evil dreams and spells and could guard the wearer against sorcery and witchcraft, secret enemies and evil thoughts. If crystal broke or became cloudy, it indicated the presence of poisons, and was therefore used in ancient times to line wine goblets. Crystal was thought to be effective as a preventative medicine for wasting and infectious diseases, tumorous complaints, blood impurities and heart troubles. Crystal was also esteemed as an instrument for heightening the imagination and to bring out the gazing power of the "third eye." Crystal has been said to be for the pure in heart and those who think of a better life. The Chinese believed crystal, if held in the mouth, could satisfy thirst. To some, the crystal represents clarity of outlook, emotional harmony and peace. It has the power to influence good relationships with others based on self-respect and allows clear views of spiritual truth. On the dark side, crystals may initiate arrogance and the fear of change. A crystal which is only half-clear may represent confusion and hasty or prejudice thinking, and may prevent you from seeing the whole situation. With a cloudy crystal, you may hide the truth from yourself, and therefore refuse to trust yourself.

Jasper

Jasper is another type of quartz which contains grains of impurities which provide a variety of different colors from black and white to blue, green, red and orange. The jasper in ancient times was thought to be able to bring rains and was held in the fourth century to have the power to drive away evil spirits and protect the wearer from the bites of venomous animals. In the eleventh century, an anonymous German author prescribed jasper as a cure for snakebites if placed directly on the wound. Jasper was supposed to draw the venom from the wound and into itself. Green jasper worn at the neck and touching the gastric region, was thought to be a cure for all types of stomach diseases.

Jaspers in the shape of a pear were more highly valued for use as amulets. Italians used red jaspers to represent drops of blood for use in the curing of excessive bleeding of wounds. Such amulets were hung by a red ribbon on the bedposts of the wounded. Jasper represents joy, happiness and relief from pain. It was also thought to bring victory to the wearer not by bringing strength but by making him timid for "the timid usually conquer, since they avoid a doubtful contest if possible." In the Orient, the emerald jasper, combined with silver, was used to quell any illness.

Pin of sterling silver with cairngorm, clear crystal, amethyst, and topaz designed as a royal badge, English.

Two sets of gentlemen's shirt studs and cuff links. Right: carved crystal, gold, platinum and diamonds, circa 1920. Left: platinum and diamonds, circa 1900.

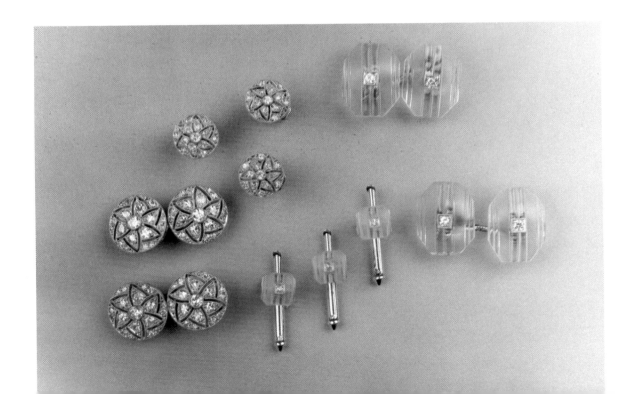

Finger ring with seven brilliant cut aqua crystal stones, early nineteenth century.

Four necklaces of silver with carved clear crystal pendants, circa 1900.

Two pins of gold set with central cairngorms and chalcedony, circa 1870.

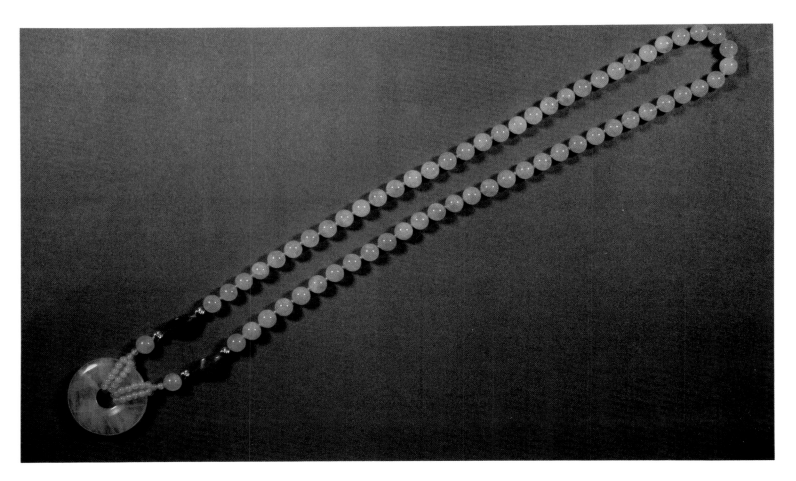

Necklace of rose quartz and nephrite beads, circa 1980.

Necklace and earrings of silver and aqua crystal gems, circa 1890.

Necklace and pendant of white gold, carved crystal and diamonds, English, circa 1900.

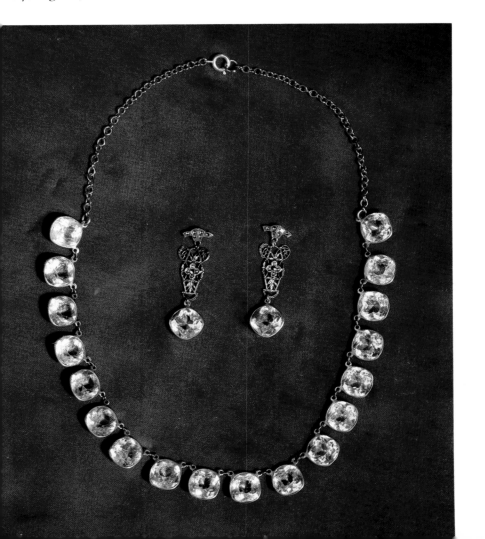

Diamond

Eight unmounted fancy blue diamonds.

The diamond is pure, crystallized carbon making it the simplest of all gems in terms of its chemistry. It is the hardest natural substance known and is desirable not only as a gem, but is used in industry for all types of cutting, grinding and boring. The diamond is one of the most brilliant and precious of all the gems and just mention of its name implies riches, beauty and mystery. Diamonds have been found, though rarely, in colors such as blue, red, green and yellow, but are most desirable and valuable in their characteristic pure white.

Diamonds are believed to be formed when carbon is subjected to intense heat and pressure deep in the earth and then driven through "pipes" toward the surface. These pipes, through which volcanic magma once flowed, are now filled with what is called "blue rock". Diamonds are found both deep in this blue rock and in the upper fifty to sixty feet of the layer which consists of a loose mass of lighter stone called "yellow ground". The diamond is one of the rarest and most vaiuable of all gemstones because as others occur as the gem variety of common types of minerals, there are no common mineral diamonds; all are rare and potential gemstones.

More than 95 percent of all diamonds are mined today in Africa. Among the most prolific areas are the Kimberly diamond fields in South Africa. These fields were "discovered" in 1867 when the young son of a Boer farmer picked from the Vaal River what he thought was a pretty pebble. The boy gave the pebble to his mother who then turned it over to a neighbor. The pebble turned out to be a diamond worth twenty-five hundred dollars. Word spread and miners descended on South Africa seeking fortune. During the thirty years following this discovery, the Kimberly fields relinquished more than seven and a half tons of diamonds.

Central India is believed to be the site of the first discovery of diamonds when Hindus mined them from the sand at the bottom of streams more than three thousand years ago. At first, before the perfection of gem cutting, diamonds were simply rubbed against one another until they were acceptably polished. Diamonds were discovered in Brazil in 1725 in such vast quantities that the Portuguese government imposed heavy taxes upon diamond miners lest the value of diamonds greatly depreciate. The diamond fields of Brazil remained the most prolific in the world until the young Boer boy made his discovery more than 150 years later. Other patches of diamonds have been worked in Australia, Borneo, British Guiana and the United States at Murfreesboro, Arkansas. The diamond is the gemstone of the House of Aries—the Ram. Ancient astrologers believed the diamond to be powerful for people under the planet Mars. They held that it could provide fortitude, strength of mind, and continued love in marriage as well as ward off witchcraft, poisons and nightmares.

The Romans believed that if they wore a diamond against the flesh of their left arm, it would help them remain brave and daring in battle and give them strength over their enemies. One ancient passage relates: "He who carries a diamond on the left side shall be hardy and manly; it will guard him from accidents to the limbs; but nevertheless a good diamond will lose its power and virtue if worn by one who is incontinent, or drunken." The Romans also set diamonds in fine steel as a charm against insanity. Pliny, in his *Historia Naturalis*, wrote in the year 77 A.D.: "The greatest value among the objects of human property, not merely among precious stones, is due to the adamas (diamond), for a long time known only to kings and even to very few of these."

Jewish High Priests were said to have worn diamonds in their ephods or vestments to determine the guilt or innocence of the accused. If the diamond was held before a guilty person, it would lose its brilliance and become dull, but if the person were innocent the brilliance of the stone would increase tenfold. Diamonds, therefore represented innocence, justice, faith and strength. The diamond was a symbol of the Lord to the early Christians who also held it to be an antidote against both moral and physical evil. In India it was believed that

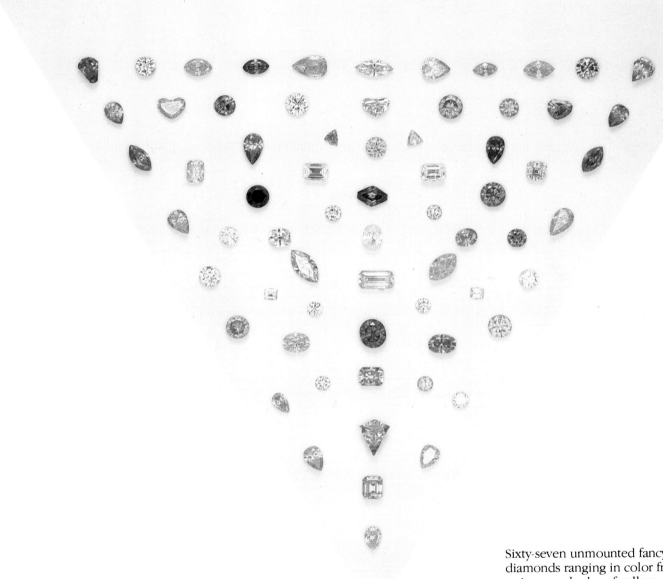

Sixty-seven unmounted fancy colored diamonds ranging in color from very light to intense shades of yellow, orange, pink, blue, greenish yellow, purplish pink, brown and black.

diamonds had the power to prevent harm from lightening, but also that they could cause your teeth to fall out if held in your mouth.

The diamond was also considered to be an antidote for all poisons when worn on a ring. However to the contrary, during the Middle Ages it was considered to be a powerful poison although it was commonly known that diamond mine workers swallowed the stones as a means to steal them. The medieval Italians called it *pietra della reconciliazione* or "stone of reconciliation" and believed the diamond possessed the power to maintain harmony between the husband and wife.

In India, the wealthy natives would sprinkle tiny diamonds from a white cloth over the heads of infants during a ritual in which the child was named in the belief that it would keep them pure and virtuous. It was often believed that the diamond held more power if worn on the left side of the body. Marbodus called

Unmounted circular-cut fancy light bluish-gray diamond of approximately 2.5 carats. Unmounted pear-shaped fancy pink diamond of approximately 1.4 carats. Unmounted marquis-cut fancy blue diamond of approximately 3.5 carats. Bracelet of platinum and diamonds of graduated marquise, pear, and circular shapes by Harry Winston, New York, circa 1955.

Ten unmounted diamonds of pear and circular shapes weighing approximately three and a half carats each.

the diamond a potent magical charm for protecting the sleeper against evil dreams and the child from the dreaded goblin. To dream of diamonds was considered symbolical of success, wealth, happiness and victory. The people of the Middle Ages used the diamond to protect themselves from the dreaded plague. Queen Elizabeth I was said to have worn a diamond about her neck for this reason.

In the fourteenth century, Rabbi Benoni wrote that the diamond was capable of producing somnambulism and spiritual ecstasy. In the *Mani Mali* it is stated that; an ill-shaped diamond carries danger; a dirty diamond carries grief; a rough diamond carries unhappiness; a black diamond carries trouble; a three-cornered diamond carries quarrels; a four-cornered diamond carries fear; a five-cornered diamond carries death and that a six-cornered diamond carries fortune. However, the three, four and five-cornered diamond, if flawless and of good color, would not foster evil.

Necklace of platinum and diamonds of baguette, pear, marquise, and circular shapes.
Earrings of silver and diamonds, English, circa 1870.

Necklace of platinum and baguette
diamonds supporting a pendant with a
pear-shaped diamond of approximately 49
carats and two trapese shaped diamonds,
by Alexandre Reza, Paris.

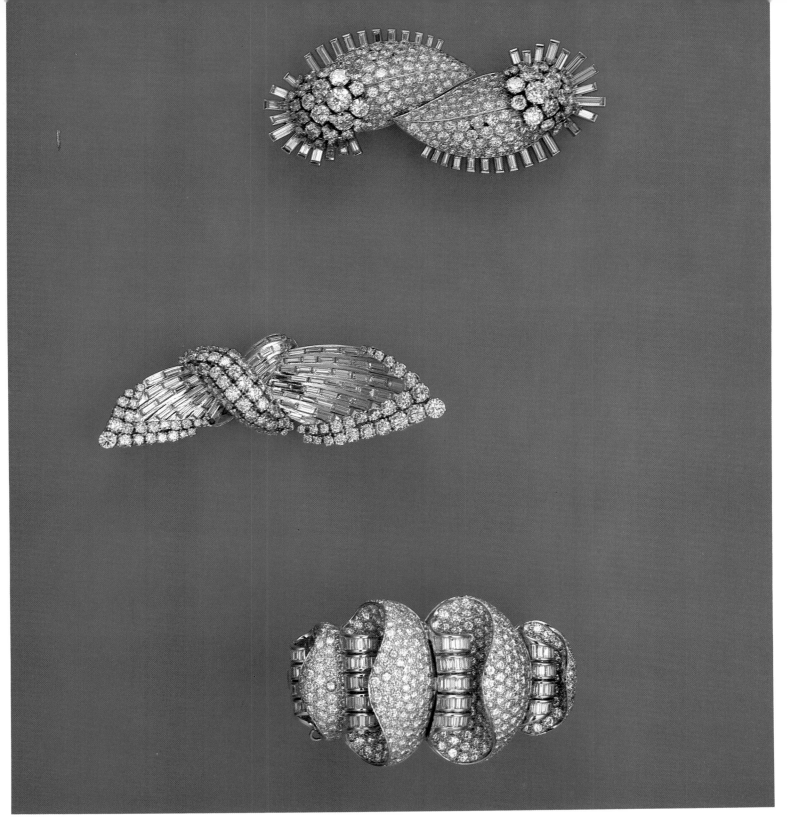

In 1473, Serapion attributed many powers to the diamond for he believed it to drive away ghosts, nightmares and calamities and also make men courageous and magnanimous. And, if placed with a loadstone, the diamond's powers will greatly increase.

Camillus Leonardus, likewise wrote: "It is a help to lunaticks, and such as are possessed with the devil; being bound to the left arm it gives victory over enemies; it tames wild beasts; it helps those who are troubled with phantasms, and the night-mare, making him that wears it bold, and daring in his transactions." Reflections as to the source of diamonds fostered many fanciful stories. It was commonly thought that diamonds could reproduce, as one story from the mid-sixteenth century relates that a women had hidden two inherited diamonds with her other jewelry only to find several years later that the original diamonds had spawned a few similar stones. Ancient philosophers told that

Double clip of white gold, platinum and diamonds designed as two leaves, circa 1940. Double clip of white gold, platinum and diamonds designed as a stylized bow (one baguette section missing), by Sterlé, Paris, circa 1950. Bracelet of white gold and diamonds designed as four shells.

diamonds and other gems could be obtained by throwing beefsteaks into dangerous crevices. Eagles would then fly into the crevices to retrieve a steak covered with gems.

The word "diamond" is believed to have been derived from the Latin word *adamas* meaning hard or impenetrable and it was thought that the diamond could transfer its impenetrability to the wearer and protect from all types of poisons and dangers, as this anonymous verse tells:

> The evil eye shall have no power to harm
> Him that wears the diamond as a charm.
> No king shall thwart his will
> And even the gods shall his wishes fill.

While it was thought that diamonds were an effective antidote for poisons, it was also believed that they were a powerful poison. This belief stemmed from the notion that beds of diamonds were guarded by venomous creatures who were cut as they crawled over the points of the diamonds and dripped venom onto them. Many other medicinal virtues have been attributed to the stone. For example the diamond was thought to protect against plague and pestilence, jaundice and leprosy. For all its powers, the diamond is said to be most effective only if it is given freely—never sold, lent or stolen.

The true stories that surround some of the more famous stones are just as interesting as the legends associated with them. Napoleon believed greatly in the powers of diamonds, and wore the Regent diamond on his sword. The stone was discovered by a slave in the Parteal Mine in India in 1701 and weighed 410 carats in the rough. It was purchased in 1702 by a Thomas Pitt when it was cut (a process which took two years) to 140.5 carats. The diamond was sold to the Regent of France in 1717 and was there named the Regent Diamond. It was worn by several French kings and queens including Marie Antoinette. In 1802 Napoleon had the Regent set in the hilt of his sword, but following his exile to Saint Helena, it was returned to the French Government where it remains on display at the Galerie d'Apollon in the Louvre, Paris. In the mid-nineteenth century, a diamond was credited with saving the life of Queen Donna Isabel II. As the tale goes, an assassin's knifepoint was thwarted by a diamond which the Queen apparently wore in her girdle.

The Koh-i-Noor ("Mountain of Light" in Persian) Diamond boasts an interesting history as well. Indian legend traces the stone back some five

Pendant/pin of platinum and diamonds designed as a stylized bell with openwork and articulation.

Pin of silver and diamonds with a detachable pear-shaped diamond drop, English, circa 1875.

Pendant of platinum and diamonds designed with moveable concentric ovals, American, circa 1900.

thousand years. The diamond changed hands several times and at one point was even bequeathed to the Shrine of Juggernaut by Runjeet Singh King of Lahore, in hopes that it would gain him favors in his death. However following his death, the diamond was rather presented to Queen Victoria as a personal gift when India was annexed in 1850. Since the diamond was not considered a Crown Jewel, legend grew that it should never be worn by a male in the belief that the crown would lose India if it were. Subsequently, the Koh-i-Noor has been passed down through the female heirs of the throne and has been worn by Queen Mary and Queen Elizabeth (the present Queen Mother). The Koh-i-Noor rests now in the Cross Formee, the crown made for the Queen Mother.

The Orloff is another famous diamond with an intriguing history. A French soldier saw the diamond as the eye of the statue of Brahma in the temple at Trichinopoli in southern India. The soldier dressed as a native and stole the stone whereupon he escaped to Madras and sold it to a sea captain for ten thousand dollars. Eventually it landed in the hands of Catherine II of the Crown of Russia and remains there, in all of its original 195-carat splendor as a treasure of the Soviet Union.

The 279-carat Great Mogul leaves as evidence to its existence only sketches as it was lost from sight shortly after being observed by the French traveler Jean Baptiste Tavernier in 1665. The legendary, however small, 53-carat Sancy diamond rests now in the Louvre in Paris where it was placed in 1976 following a long history of owners. This pear-shaped stone was at varying times the property of the British, French and Spanish royalty.

One of the most famous of all diamonds is the Hope Diamond. Marie Antoinette wore this stone and she lent it to her friend Princesse de Lamballe. As both were beheaded in the revolution, the Hope was considered for some time to be a bad luck charm. The light-blue Hope Diamond was donated to the Smithsonian Institution by its owner diamond merchant Harry Winston in 1958 where it sits today in a necklace of fourty-eight other diamonds.

In January of 1905, a diamond weighing 3106 carats was discovered in the Transvaal, a province in South Africa. This giant stone, named the Cullinan after the President of the mining company, was cut in 1908 into nine major stones and ninety-six small brilliants. Six of the major stones are now the property of the British royal family. The whereabouts of the brilliants is not positively known, but it is believed that two of them are owned by the family of General Louis Botha, first Prime Minister of the Union of South Africa.

Pendant of white gold, platinum and diamonds with dangling fringe motif, circa 1910.

Necklace of yellow and white diamonds of cushion, marquise, lozenge and hexagonal shapes, circa 1910.

Necklace of platinum and diamonds of colorless, light yellow, faint pink, brown, greenish yellow and grey hues designed as five graduated strands with a single strand backchain. Finger ring of platinum and marquise diamonds, the central one of fancy blue color and six colorless stones. Finger ring of yellow gold and platinum with marquise and pear-shaped diamonds of orange-yellow and colorless hues. Finger ring of platinum set with a single cushion shaped diamond of approximately 11.3 carats. Finger ring of platinum and marquise and round diamonds of fancy yellow, light brown-pink, very light pink and colorless diamonds, designed as a flower. Finger ring of platinum with a pear-shaped fancy light brown diamond of approximately 30 carats and pavé diamond swirl mounting.

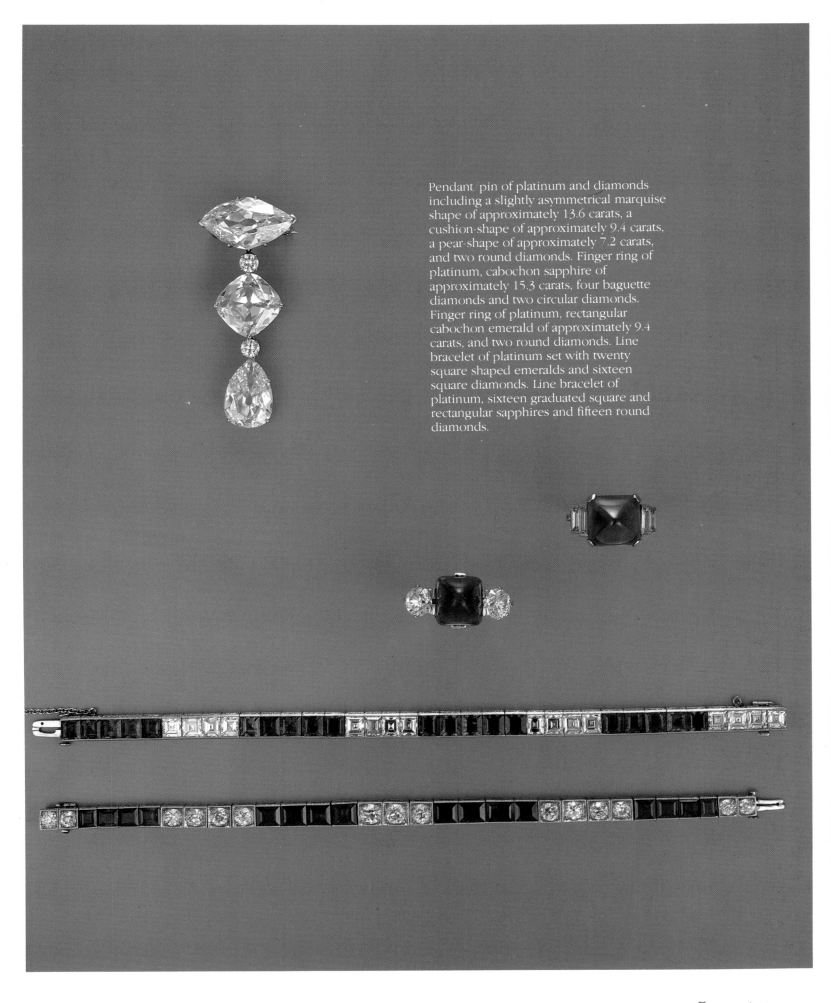

Pendant/pin of platinum and diamonds including a slightly asymmetrical marquise shape of approximately 13.6 carats, a cushion-shape of approximately 9.4 carats, a pear-shape of approximately 7.2 carats, and two round diamonds. Finger ring of platinum, cabochon sapphire of approximately 15.3 carats, four baguette diamonds and two circular diamonds. Finger ring of platinum, rectangular cabochon emerald of approximately 9.4 carats, and two round diamonds. Line bracelet of platinum set with twenty square shaped emeralds and sixteen square diamonds. Line bracelet of platinum, sixteen graduated square and rectangular sapphires and fifteen round diamonds.

Tiara/necklace of ribbon and floral design set throughout with round diamonds, circa 1905. Tiara of intertwined ribbon design including circular-, cushion- and pear-shaped diamonds, circa 1905.

Necklace of graduated diamonds and silver with detachable diamond string festoons and pendants of round, pear-shaped and briolette diamonds and a clasp of four diamonds as a pendant, early 19th century.

Necklace of diamonds designed as a floral garland, circa 1900. Pin of diamonds designed as a crescent, late 19th century. Pin of diamonds and sapphires designed as a crescent, late 19th century. Pin/corsage ornament of diamonds designed as entwined flowers and leaves, circa 1855. Pin of circular diamonds and graduated step-cut emeralds, designed as a ribbon bow. Tiara/necklace of diamonds designed as a graduated fringe, late 19th century.

Necklace of platinum and graduated circular and baguette diamonds designed in fringe style by Van Cleef and Arpels. Earrings of platinum with baguette and circular diamonds, modified from originals designed by Van Cleef and Arpels. Finger ring of platinum set with a rectangular diamond of approximately ten carats and two baguette diamonds, by Cartier.

Lapel watch of platinum, diamond, onyx, sapphire, emerald, grey, brown and white pearls and a square clock, by Boucheron, Paris, circa 1925. Bracelet of platinum with carved emerald and sapphire, and diamond by Charlton, New York, circa 1938.

Pin of white gold and diamonds designed as a ribbon bow. Pin of platinum with baguette and round diamonds designed as a scroll, circa 1935. Pin of platinum, rock crystal, pearl and diamond in octagonal form, circa 1930.

Pin of platinum and diamonds in rectangular shape with radiating design by Dreicer & Co., New York, circa 1920. The pin was designed to adapt as the center of a seed pearl dog-collar style necklace.

Necklace of platinum and diamonds with link chain and detachable tassel pendant/pin of graduated diamonds. Finger ring of white gold, platinum, diamonds and cabochon emerald. Finger ring of platinum, marquis diamonds and rectangular emerald of approximately 8.8 carats.

Bracelet of platinum and diamonds in triple line style with elaborate buckle and link closing. Bracelet of platinum with baguette and round diamonds designed as scroll links. Line bracelet of platinum with baguette and round diamonds.

Necklace of platinum and diamonds with a detachable pendant of a single, pear-shaped, treated yellow diamond of approximately 4.2 carats. Pair of pins of yellow gold, platinum and diamonds including marquise and round shapes and several shades of yellow and colorless stones, designed as flower heads. Bracelet of platinum and six rows of baguette and round diamonds.

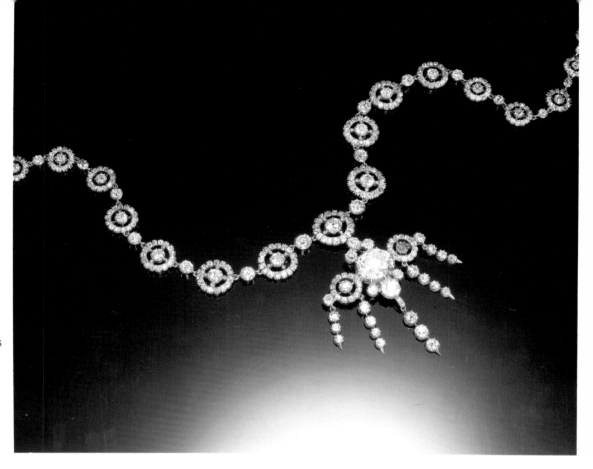

Necklace of diamond-set links from the eighteenth century supporting a nineteenth century pendant with central cushion-shaped lilac pink diamond and five graduated diamond drops.

Pin of diamonds designed as an open rectangle, circa 1930. Line bracelet with two rows of diamonds and a row of sapphires. Bracelet of square and oval links set with diamonds. Double clip of diamond, sapphire and synthetic ruby in buckle design. Line bracelet of diamonds and rubies with central buckle motif. Bracelet of diamonds and sapphires in repeating pattern. Double clip of diamonds entwined in a concentric ring design.

Bracelet of diamonds and emeralds with graduated links and central cluster. Bracelet of three rows of cushioh-shaped diamonds with central buckle motif including baguette, triangular and cushion-shaped stones, by Cartier, France, 1927. Sureté pin of diamonds, emerald and seed pearl tassel by LaCloche-Freres, Paris, circa 1925. Pin of diamonds in stylized floral scroll design by Cartier, London, circa 1943.

Pin of platinum and diamond ribbon lace intertwined as a flower. Necklace of platinum chain with pendant of two diamonds.

Choker necklace of platinum and
graduated marquise, round and pear-
shaped diamonds by Harry Winston, New
York. Finger ring of platinum and marquis
diamonds of fancy brown-pink and near
colorless hue.

Choker necklace of platinum and
graduated baguette and circular diamonds,
the clasp representing a ribbon bow.
Bracelet of platinum and baguette, circular
and marquise diamonds designed as an
entwined and pinched ribbon with floral
group.

Pin of platinum and rectangular, baguette
and round diamonds designed as a
geometric composition with flexible
tapering tassel, circa 1930. Finger ring of
platinum with a square diamond of
approximately 9.3 carats and small
diamonds, circa 1930. Hair comb of
tortoise shell ornamented with platinum
and circular, baguette and square
diamonds, by Cartier.

Earrings of platinum and diamonds of baguette, pear and marquise shape. Dress clip of aquamarine and diamond designed as an arrow by Cartier, London, circa 1930. Necklace of platinum chain with pendant of a square emerald of approximately 3.6 carats and circular diamonds. Pin of platinum with baguette and marquise diamonds designed as a floral cascade and ribbon loops. Earrings of platinum, white gold and diamonds of marquis, pear and circular shapes designed as a floral spray. Bracelet of platinum, onyx, and circular and marquise diamonds, circa 1930.

Choker necklace of platinum, yellow gold, and diamonds of circular and baguette shape designed as seven large graduated links, a back chain and matching clasp.

Pin of platinum and diamonds with marquise, pear, round and baguette shapes and fancy colors including brownish-yellow, orange brown and colorless, designed as a floral arrangement with blossoms mounted en tremblant, probably made by Bulgari.

Pair of pins of platinum, white gold, diamonds and cushion-cut sapphire designed as openwork scrolls by Petochi, Rome, circa 1935.

Pin of platinum, diamond and calibre emerald designed as a ribbon bow, circa 1910. Pin of platinum, white gold and diamonds, designed as a ribbon bow, circa 1910. Pin of platinum, diamond and calibre sapphires designed as a ribbon bow, circa 1910.

Opposite page:

Earrings of round diamonds designed as tassels by Ruser. Necklace of platinum link chain and pendant of platinum, diamonds, and a ruby of approximately 2.5 carats. Bar pin of platinum, 12 round diamonds, and two sapphires and five rubies cut in unusual shapes. Bracelet of platinum with three lines of baguette and round diamonds and invisibly set sapphires. Ear clips and pin of platinum and pave' daimonds by Van Cleef and Arpels, Paris. Earrings of white gold with square and round diamonds and oval rubies.

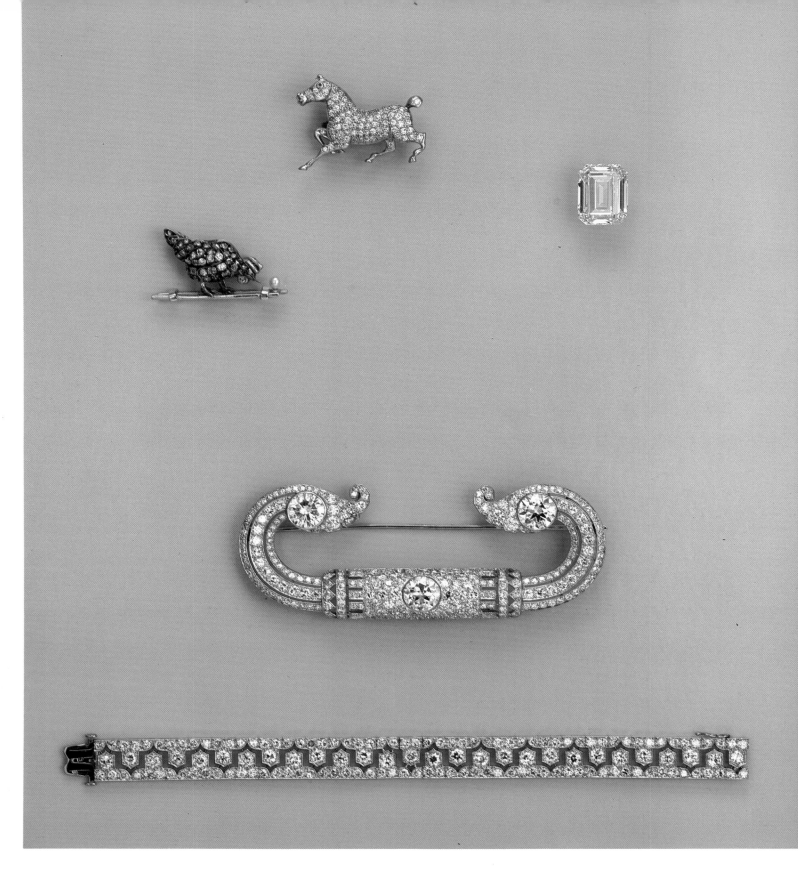

Pin of gold and silver, diamonds, ruby and
pearl designed as a pecking rooster. Pin of
platinum, yellow gold, diamond and ruby
designed as a trotting horse. Unmounted
rectangular fancy light yellow diamond of
approximately 14.2 carats. Pin of platinum
and diamonds designed as an Egyptian-
inspired curve, by Cartier, circa 1933.
Bracelet of platinum, white gold and
diamonds designed in moroccan style
with pierced geometric motifs, circa 1925.

Pin of platinum, diamonds and sapphire in openwork badge and garland design with pendant pear-shaped diamond.

Pin of platinum and diamonds in rectangular form, circa 1900.

Pendant/pin of platinum and diamonds in pierced shield design, circa 1875.
Pendant/pin of silver, gold and diamonds designed as a sunburst, circa 1920.

Pendant/pin of silver, gold and diamonds designed as a *fleur de lis,* circa 1890, English.

Finger ring of diamond and ruby clusters, circa 1885. Pin of diamonds and rubies designed as a spray of holly, circa 1885. Three pins of diamonds designed as sprays of flowers with flowerheads mounted en tremblant, circa 1880. Two diamond clusters, circa 1790, later mounted as pins. Pendant of diamonds with central glass compartment for a keepsake, circa 1830.

Pendant of platinum and diamonds in shades of yellow, brown and colorless hues, circa 1905. Pin of gold, diamond and blue enamel, circa 1800. Finger ring of gold, diamond and blue enamel, circa 1800. Pendant of gold, silver, diamond and pink topaz of Sevigné design, late 18th century. Aigrette/pin of diamonds designed as a spray of flowers, circa 1880. Pin of diamonds designed as a peacock's feather, circa 1870. Pair of pins of diamonds designed as flowerheads mounted en tremblant, circa 1885.

Opposite page:

Pin of platinum and diamonds designed as an open flower. Ear pendants of white gold, circular and baguette diamonds and champagne colored cultured Baroque pearls. Ear pendants of gold and diamonds designed as three interlocking loops by Wander, France. Bracelet of platinum and circular, hexagonal, triangular and baguette diamonds designed as three matching openwork panels. Wristwatch with platinum case and band set with circular diamonds and calibre rubies, by Patek Philippe, Geneva.

Necklace of circular and step-cut diamonds in a flexible bombé band by Cartier, London, 1939; which can be divided into two bracelets and an extension. Dress clip of diamond, carved emerald and pear-shaped amethyst designed as a bunch of violets by Cartier, 1955. Finger ring with a step-cut diamond of approximately 6.2 carats and baguette diamonds. Pair of dress clips of diamond and ruby designed as porcupines in mirror images.

Emerald

Emerald is a beryllium-aluminum silicate with traces of chromium or vanadium oxides which give it its rich and legendary assortment of green tones. As a beryl, the emerald is somewhat softer than rubies and sapphires making it difficult, at times, to set them in rings without risk of bringing damage to the edges of the stone. The emerald is regarded as one of the most valuable gemstones and at varying times has been more desirable than even diamonds and rubies. Emeralds were first discovered more than three thousand years ago in southeastern Egypt. The mines there produced beautiful emeralds for several centuries, and were worked in the past by the great civilizations of the Egyptians, Greeks, Romans and Turks. These mines have since been abandoned for more profitable ventures in other parts of the world. The finest emeralds in the world today are found in Columbia in mines such as the Muzo, Chivo and Cosquez. Russia's Ural Mountains also provide beautiful emeralds as do mines in Brazil, Zimbabwe, Tanzania and Zambia. The emerald is designated as the birthstone for May and symbolizes the coming of a beautiful, and hopeful Spring. It is also one of the gemstones of Cancer—the House of the Crab.

Pliny the Roman scholar of the first century A.D. noted the beauty of the emerald in his writings. "Indeed," wrote Pliny, "no stone is more delightful to the eye, for whereas the sight fixes itself with avidity upon the green grass and the foliage of the trees, we have all the more pleasure of looking upon the emerald." Pliny told of one legend describing a sculptured marble lion with eyes of emeralds placed on the tomb of King Hermias on the island of Cyprus. The emeralds were said to have been so bright that the fish around the island were scared away. Disgruntled fishermen replaced the emeralds with common stones and the fish returned. The Romans believed that by gazing upon the emerald, one could restore weary or dimmed eyesight. The Emperor Nero is reported to have watched gladiator combat through an emerald for this reason. The Emperor Claudius was convinced of the powers and virtues of emeralds and clothed himself in garments decorated with the gems.

It has been believed that the virtues of the emerald are for those who aspire to wisdom and seek enlightenment. The emerald is the symbol of life, agriculture and abundant nature. It was also known as a love stone and was identified closely with Venus. It was regarded as particulary fortunate for women, bringing happiness in love, comfort in domestic affairs and safety in childbirth. In India, the natives ground up emeralds for use as a laxative, and as a remedy for heartburn and the pain of childbirth. There it was also thought that the emerald could give the gift of knowledge of secrets and future events. They also used emeralds essentially as a vitamin. The Peruvian Indians held the belief that demons and evil spirits guarded emerald mines.

The medieval people used emeralds as a cure for eye disease and to guard against the evil eye and epilepsy. To predict future events, one need only place an emerald under the tongue and by wearing an emerald ring, one could ensure purity of thought and conduct. Emeralds were suspended from the necks of children to preserve them from epileptic convulsions and the falling sickness. It was thought that birth could be hastened by binding an emerald to the thigh of the woman giving birth. Some believed the emerald to hold the power to preserve man from every type of accident. One fable tells how the emerald could strike such fear into vipers and cobras that their eyes would leap out of their heads.

In the Orient, emeralds represented hope in immortality, courage and exalted faith and protection from pestilence. One ancient Oriental fable related in the *Oriental Memoirs* of Forbes tells how an observer of a swarm of fireflies watched as one fly, brighter than all the rest, landed on the ground. This particular fly remained in the grass for such a period of time that the observer walked to it only to find that it had been replaced by a shining emerald which he picked up and

Finger ring with step-cut emerald of approximately 2.3 carats and two round diamonds of approximately 2.2 carats each. Pendant with a step cut emerald, a polished emerald drop, and circular diamonds, circa 1870.

Opposite page:
Necklace of thirty-one graduated fluted emerald beads of between 10.9 and 21.9 mm, and a clasp of platinum, yellow gold, marquise fancy light yellow diamond and twelve circular diamonds, by Alexandre Reza, Paris.

set into a ring. The people of the Orient also believed that if one should carve a verse of the Koran upon an emerald, its powers greatly increase.

The emerald was also said to protect sailors from dangers at sea. The emerald was held to give eloquence and sharpen the mind. The change in color of an emerald was believed to be able to tell of infidelity as Miss Landon, an English poetess wrote of the emerald:

> It is a gem which hath the power to show
> If plighted lovers keep their faith or no.
> If faithful, it is like the leaves of Spring
> If faithless, like those leaves when withering.

In 1669, Dr. W. Rowland wrote of the emerald that it is: "a clear transparent gem; very beautiful and most brittle of all gems. It stops (being drunk) all Fluxes whatsoever, chiefly the Dysentary, whether they come from a sharp humor, or venome; and it cures venomous bitings. For a dose, six, eight or ten grains are given. Among Amulets it is chiefly commended against the Epilepsie; it stops bleeding if held in the mouth; it cures all bleedings, and dysentaries; it expels fears, and the Tertian Ague, if hung about the neck." It was said that some engravers, while working on minute objects, would set an emerald in front of them on which to rest their eyes.

Alfred, Lord Tennyson wrote in his epic *Idylls of the King* depicting the legend of King Arthur, that the Holy Grail, the cup from which Christ drank at the Last Supper, was carved from a single emerald. This chalice was endowed by heaven and had the power to preserve chastity and prolong life. The Holy Grail was told to have been brought by angels from the hands of God. Tennyson wrote that if a man:

> Could touch, or see it, he was healed at once,
> By faith, of all his ills.-But then the times
> Grew to such evil that the holy Cup
> Was caught away to Heaven, and disappear'd.

And so began King Arthur's legendary quest for the Holy Grail.

Earrings with pear-shaped emeralds and diamond frame suspended from clusters of simulated emeralds and diamonds in white gold, silver and non-prcious metal. Pin of gold, silver, emeralds, diamonds, black enamel and pendant baroque pearls.

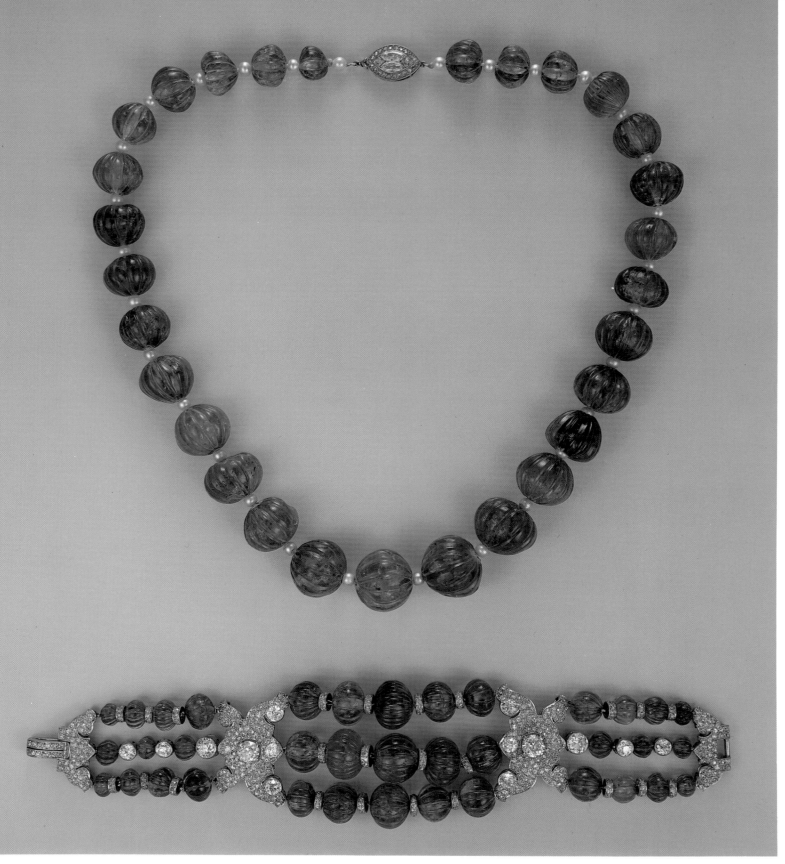

Several large and fascinating emeralds are recognized, though, unlike diamonds, they are rarely given names. The Devonshire Emerald was taken from the Muzo mines in Columbia, and in 1831 was given to the sixth Duke of Devonshire by the abdicated emperor of Brazil, Dom Pedro I. The 1398-carat emerald is now part of the Devonshire Collection. The Patricia emerald was discovered in the Chivor mine in Columbia and weighs 632 carats. It rests now in the American Museum of Natural History in New York City. Several emeralds of more than one thousand carats lie in vaults of the Bank of the Republic of Columbia and a 1,965-carat stone is on display in the Los Angeles County Museum of Natural History.

Necklace of twenty-nine graduated fluted emerald beads of between 9 and 17 mm, alternating with seed pearls, and a clasp of marquise, square and rose-cut diamonds, by Cartier. Bracelet of graduated emerald fluted beads and diamonds in three strings with a platinum clasp set with diamonds, by Cartier.

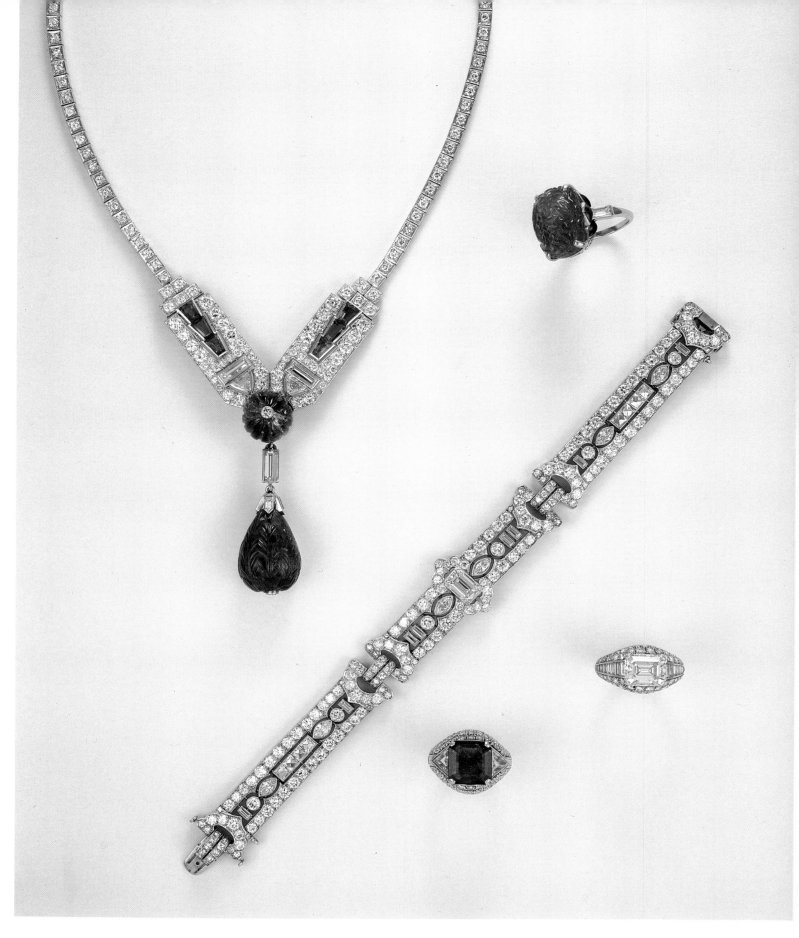

Necklace of platinum with a flexible line of circular diamonds and pendant support of triangular, baguette and circular diamonds and emeralds of keystone, carved bead and carved pear-shaped pendant shapes, by Cartier, circa 1930.

Finger ring of platinum with oval carved emerald, four cabochon sapphires, two cabochon rubies, round and baguette diamonds. Bracelet of platinum with panels of circular, marquise and rectangular diamonds, circa 1930. Finger

ring of platinum with square emerald and triangular, circular and baguette diamonds. Finger ring of platinum with rectangular diamond of approximately 3.2 carats and baguette diamonds.

Sautoir and earrings of ruby and emerald
beads, diamonds and pearl tassels.
Earrings of yellow gold, emerald, ruby and
sapphire beads and circular and baguette
diamonds designed as flower blossoms.

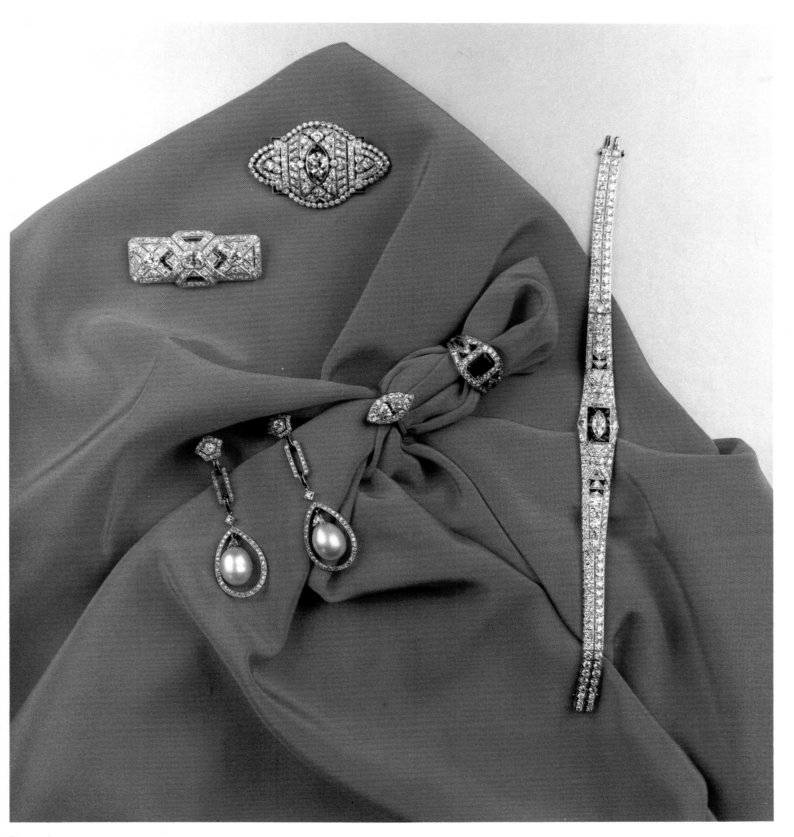

Opposite page:

Necklace and earrings of platinum with rectangular and pear-shaped emeralds and circular and marquise diamonds by Van Cleef and Arpels, Paris.

Finger ring of platinum with an oval emerald of approximately 22.2 carats and marquis and baguette diamonds. Bracelet of platinum with five rectangular emeralds and baguette diamonds, by Van Cleef and Arpels, Paris.

Pendant/pin of platinum, diamonds and emeralds in pierced panel design, circa 1920. Pendant/pin of platinum, diamond and calibre sapphire in rectangular panel, circa 1910. Ear pendants of diamonds, calibre emeralds and pearl drops, circa 1925. Finger ring of platinum and diamonds, circa 1920. Finger ring of platinum, emeralds and diamonds, circa 1920. Bracelet of platinum, diamonds and emeralds dated 1916.

Opposite page:

Necklace of platinum with circular, baguette, square and marquise diamonds suspending a fluted emerald bead. Finger ring and ear pendants of platinum with rectangular emeralds and circular and baguette diamonds. Finger ring of gold with rectangular emerald of approximately 1.6 carats, rectangular diamond of approximately 1.1 carats, and small baguette emeralds and diamonds. Finger ring of gold and platinum with rectangular emerald of approximately 9.9 carats and trapeze and triangular diamonds. Finger ring of platinum with an oval cabochon emerald and circular diamonds. Finger ring of platinum with a swirl pattern of alternating circular emeralds and baguette diamonds around a rectangular diamond. Bracelet of platinum links set with circular diamonds.

Choker necklace of platinum with emeralds of fluted carved bead, buff top, and cabochon types and diamonds of round, baguette, and square shapes, by Mauboussin, Paris, circa 1930.

Necklace of gold, emerald, mother of pearl, and uncut, unidentified yellow stones by Castellani, mid-19th century.

Pin of gold and rectangular emeralds with a glass enclosed space for a keepsake, English, mid-19th century.

Pin of gold, rectangular emeralds, pearls, diamonds and enamel in the style of A. W. N. Pugin, English, mid-19th century.

Necklace of emerald and ruby beads with a pendant of circular diamonds framing emerald carved as a parrot, and small ruby beads. Cuff links of yellow gold, pink and green carved tourmaline, and diamond. Pin of platinum, emerald, ruby, sapphire, citrine, chalcedony and diamond in fancy mosaic setting of oval shape. Pin of platinum and yellow gold, emerald, ruby and diamond. Bracelet of platinum, square emeralds, circular and pear-shaped diamonds designed as five repeating panels.

Necklace and ear clips of gold, graduated cabochon emeralds and circular diamonds. Pin of gold with cabochon emeralds and rubies, and circular diamonds, French.

Bracelet of gold, oval cabochon sapphire and emerald and circular diamonds, French.

Necklace and earrings of gold with step-
cut and pear-shaped emeralds and circular
diamonds, English, circa 1870, in its
original case.

Earrings of platinum and white gold with shield-shaped emeralds of approximately five carats each, and marquis and baguette diamonds, by Cartier. Watch pendant of platinum, carved and cabochon emerald, circular diamonds, seed pearls and black enamel, by Cartier, circa 1925.

Bracelet of platinum, nine graduated rectangular emeralds and circular and baguette diamonds.

Choker necklace which converts to two bracelets of platinum, sixteen pear-shaped emeralds, and baguette, bullet and round diamonds. Finger ring of platinum and yellow gold with an oval green jade cabochon and circular diamonds. Double clip of platinum, carved emeralds, rubies and sapphires, and baguette, circular, bullet and trapeze diamonds, by Yard. Bracelet of platinum, triangular and square emeralds and marquise and circular diamonds designed as six repeating rectangular panels, by Udall & Ballou, New York, circa 1930.

Garnet

The term garnet applies to a group of minerals which consists of six main varieties. These varieties are grossular, pyrope, almandine, andradite, spessartite and uyarovite and they differ as to their chemical composition and color. The name garnet was derived from the Latin word *granatum* meaning "seed-like", as the garnet resembled, to some, the seed of a pomegranate. Depending on the type of garnet, the chemical composition will vary but contain at least two of the following: calcium, magnesium, ferrous iron, manganese, aluminum, ferric iron and chromium. The garnet, though commonly thought to exist only in red, actually appears in almost all colors of the spectrum.

The different garnets are found throughout the world in Brazil, India, and Africa as well as The United States, Canada, Germany and Russia. Garnets are particularly susceptible to fracture with changes in the temperature but with care will remain durable and tough. This stone is under the celestial Aquarius.

The red garnet has been held as the stone of inspiration and a remedy for diabolical influences. *Pietra della vedovanza* or the "stone of widowhood," was the name given to the garnet by the Italians because it was commonly worn by widows in necklaces.

Carbuncle

The carbuncle is an almandine garnet that has been cut *en cabochon* and in Christianity is significant of blood and suffering because of its deep red coloring and is symbolic of Christ's passion and martyrdom. Five carbuncles set on a cross represent the five wounds which Christ received during the Crucifixion. Camillus Leonardus prescribed carbuncle to protect against poisons and infectious illnesses. He also believed that it had the power to repress extravagance and increase the popularity of its wearer. The carbuncle is said to physically strengthen and vivify the vital and generative forces in human nature. It sharpens business propensities and gives energy to the dull and lethargic and may aid those who suffer from anemia.

The ancient Hebrews called the stone *baraketh* or "flashing stone." During the Middle Ages, the carbuncle was used as protection against the plague, to eliminate sadness and prevent evil thoughts. And if hung around the neck, it was believed to cure indigestion and a sore throat. In India and Africa, some tribes used carbuncles to protect themselves from being wounded. Epiphaneus wrote that it is impossible to hide this stone when it is worn, "for, notwithstanding with whatever clothes it may be covered, its lustre shows itself outside its envelope." Another Greek name for the carbuncle was *nuktalopos* which means "lamp-stone" and represents the belief that a carbuncle, worn around the neck, will give the power to see in the dark. One biblical legend tells that Noah used a large carbuncle as a lamp on the Ark.

Demantoid garnet

A demantoid is a green andradite garnet which may even show a gleam of yellow. It was believed that the demantoid had the power to drive away pestilential airs and banish unworthy thoughts. It was considered a binding charm for friends and protected the wearer from epidemics and lightening.

In the thirteenth century, deep red, transparent garnets were considered excellent insect repellents. In fact, to test the authenticity of a garnet, the owner would remove his clothing and smear himself with honey. If he was not then swarmed by insects, the garnet was considered genuine. Garnets in general represent energy, devotion and loyalty and are held to promote sincerity. A garnet amulet was believed to protect one from nightmares and was worn on the body to prevent skin diseases. Garnets were also held to warn of danger by losing their brilliance.

Pendant of gold with garnet, pearl and cloisonne enamel in Holbeinesque style, English, circa 1865. Front and back views.

Earring and necklace of gold and oval, round and pear-shaped garnet designed as flowerheads, English, circa 1820. Necklace and bracelet of gold with oval and pear-shaped garnet, amethyst and topaz, English, circa 1800. Bracelet of gold with oval and circular foil-backed crystal, 18th century.

Two pendants of gold with cabochon garnets, diamonds and enamel in Holbeinesque style, English, circa 1890.

Corsage ornament pin of carbuncle, enamel and diamonds with drop pendant, circa 1850. Pendant of gold, carbuncle carved as two hearts, and diamonds, circa 1880. Pendant of carbuncle and diamonds in a bow design, circa 1860.
Two similar pendants of carbuncle and diamonds, each with drop pendants, circa 1865. Pin of pear-shaped and circular diamonds designed to depict a peacock's feather, 19th century.

Pendant pin of gold with cabochon and faceted garnets, mid-19th century.

Pin of gold, polished garnets and diamonds with locket back, English, circa 1845. Necklace of gold, ruby, pearl and blue enamel designed as a serpent with heart drop, English, circa 1845. Necklace of gold with pendant of cabochon garnets, pearls, and diamond in trefoil shape, English, circa 1845. Necklace of gold, garnet, emerald and diamonds designed as a serpent with heart drop, English, circa 1845.

Necklace of gold with pendant of almandine garnets and pearls, circa 1850.

Necklace of gold, demantoid garnet, and pearl, English, circa 1870.

Necklace, earrings and pin of gold with oval and pear-shaped garnet, late 18th century.

Necklace, bracelet and earrings of gold, garnet and pearl, English, circa 1825.

Pendant of gold, platinum, demantoid garnet, pearl and diamond, English, circa 1905.

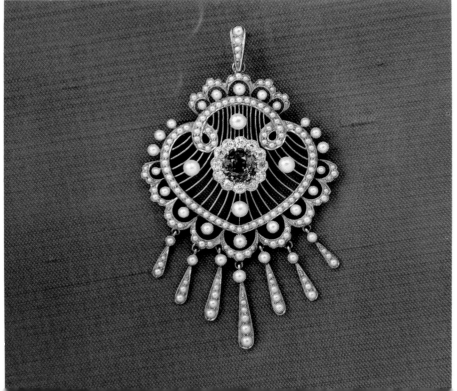

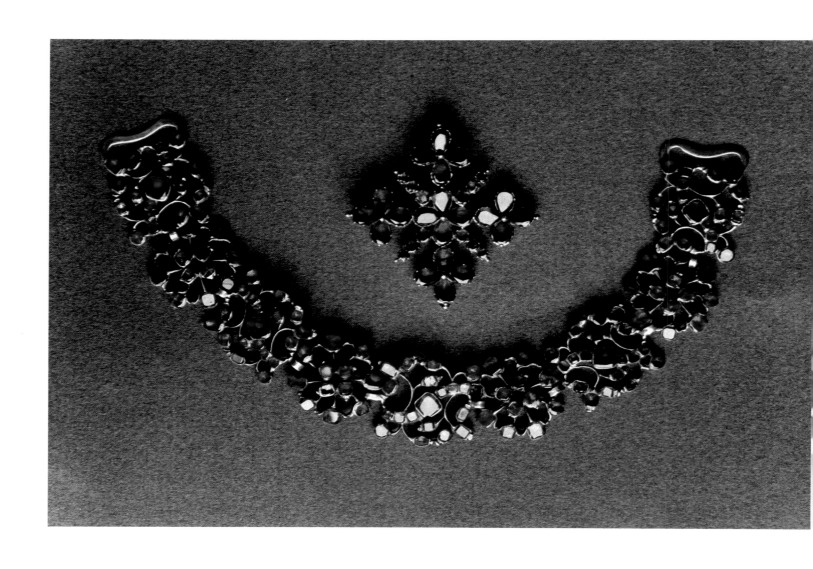

Choker necklace and pin of silver and garnet, the necklace to be tied with a ribbon, circa 1800.

Pin of pinchbeck and garnet, the domed surface decorated with raised star pattern, circa 1840.

Pendant, earrings, three bracelets and two
finger rings of gold with garnet, circa 1860.

Jade is the name given to two mineral types that resemble each other in hardness and color, but differ in chemical composition. In past centuries, jade often referred to any stone of greenish color that took a fine polish. However, today it most commonly refers to either one of two stones of the pyroxene mineral family. Nephrite, one of the two, is a silicate of lime and magnesia and is a hard, translucent stone light green to bluish in color. Jadeite, the other, is a silicate of sodium and aluminum, and may appear in color from pink, white, blue and orange to the highly prized bright green. The brightest greens are the result of an infiltration of chromic oxide which is the same oxide that gives the emerald its beautiful green color. Both jadeite and nephrite are crystalline aggregates making them exceptionally tough. Jadeite is slightly harder than nephrite, but it is often quite difficult to distinguish the two without the use of laboratory tests.

Nephrite was the main working material of the Chinese until jadeite was discovered in mines in Upper Burma in the mid-eighteenth century. These same mines, near the town of Mogaung, continue to produce jadeite today in much the same way they had centuries ago; relying more on the miners' instinct than on technological devices. Jadeite mines are also worked presently in California, Guatemala and Japan. Nephrite is found in great quantity China, Russia and New Zealand. It is also mined in Wyoming and Alaska in the United States.

The toughness of jade made it particularly suitable for shaping into functional tools such as axe heads and weapons. Jade artifacts have been found by archaeologists in Egypt that date back to 5000 B.C. As metals evolved, the use of jade in tools began to diminish, and its significance as an aesthetic and talismanic object began to flourish. The Spanish Conquistadors called the stone *piedra de ijada* or "colic stone" when they observed natives using the stone to heal stomach pains. It is from this name that the English, "jade", was derived. "Nephrite" was derived from the Greek word for kidney in the belief that the stone had the power to relieve pain in the kidneys.

Finger ring of gold with oval shaded lavender jade.

Jade has, for centuries, been highly regarded by the Chinese not only for its many talismanic virtues, but also for its spiritual symbolism. The Chinese philosopher Confucius in the fifth century B.C. wrote beautifully of the virtues of jade. "In ancient times, men found the likeness of all excellent qualities in jade. Soft, smooth, and glossy, it appeared to them like benevolence; fine compact and strong—like intelligence; angular, but not sharp and cutting—like righteousness; hanging down (in beads) as if it would fall to the ground—like (the humility of) propriety; when struck, yielding a note, clear and prolonged, yet terminating abruptly—like music; its flaws not concealing its beauty; nor its beauty concealing its flaws—like loyalty; with an internal radiance issuing from it on every side—like good faith; bright as a brilliant rainbow—like heaven; exquisite and mysterious, appearing in the hills and streams—like the earth; standing out conspicuously in the symbols of rank—like virtue; esteemed by all under the sky—like the path of truth and duty."

The ancient Chinese used perforated disks of jade to represent heaven, and it was thought that these tokens embodied the qualities of solar brilliance and that their magical power could connect them with the powers of the heavens. The Emperor, as the sun of heaven, was believed to be able to communicate with heaven through one of these jade disks. Jade gave physical strength to the Chinese and protected them from all types of ills. It was also ingested to relieve asthma and heartburn and was taken regularly as a health tonic. Businessmen in China often held jade in their hand for consul as they undertook a big transaction. As the color of jade represented green and fertile fields, it was believed that it had the power to bring fertility to women.

Jade was often powdered and drunk before death in the belief that it would prevent decomposition of the body. Chinese wiseman Ko Kei wrote of one man

Pin of gold and onyx, the square frame with gold beads and relief work around a circular placque of black and white onyx carved in deep relief as a child's head and scrolled vines, probably by John Brogden, London, circa 1870.

Bracelet of onyx, gold and diamonds designed as two intertwined rows embracing the diamonds, English, circa 1890.

Necklace of graduated onyx beads in two strands, the beads alternating solid black and striped black, brown and white.

Earrings of gold with black and white onyx pendant drops, nineteenth century.

Opposite page:

Seven finger rings of silver, onyx and marcasite from the late nineteenth century.

Bracelet of platinum, onyx and diamonds, French, circa 1910. Pin of platinum, onyx and diamond designed as a checkerboard ribbon bow, by Cartier, London, circa 1920. Pin of platinum, onyx and diamond designed as a striped ribbon bow, by Cartier, Paris, circa 1920.

Pin of sterling silver, onyx and coral by Theodore Fahrner, France, circa 1930.

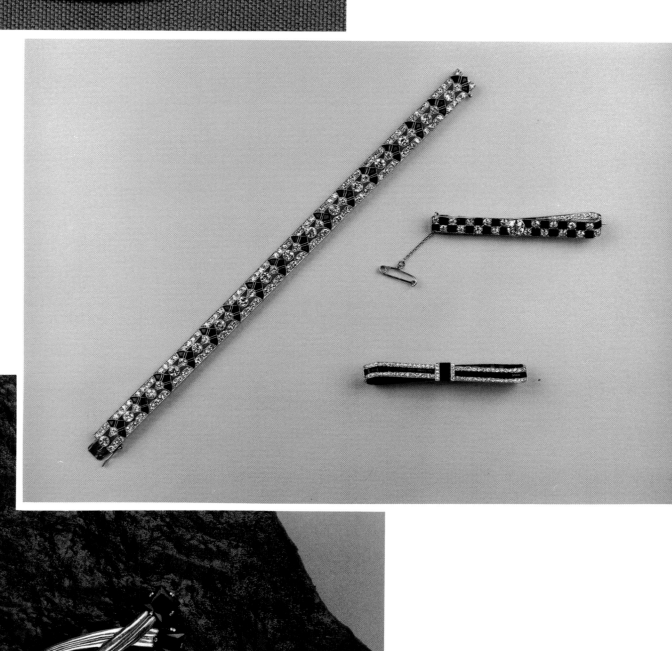

Unmounted oval black opal of approximately 3 carats. Unmounted black opal of approximately 15.5 carats. Unmounted black opal of approximately 19 carats. Pin of opal, pink sapphire and diamonds designed as a butterfly, circa 1900. Unmounted black opal of approximately 13 carats. Pin of opal, ruby and diamonds designed as a moth, circa 1900. Unmounted oval black opal of approximately 9.4 carats. Unmounted oval black opal of approximately 4.8 carats. Unmounted oval black opal of approximately 2.4 carats.

Opal

Opal is a quartz variety composed of silica particles and water in regular arrangement which defracts light into the spectral colors. The visual result is a unique play of mingled colors. Many color variations occur among opals with backgrounds ranging from black and dark blue, green, brown and red through white and transparent. The ranges of polychrome flashes are equally varied. Fire opals from Mexico usually is nearly transparent and solid red without colorful flashes. Harlequin opals from Hungary and Czechoslovakia have flakes of color evenlydistributed creating patches of color.

The Roman scholar Pliny the Elder, from the first century A.D., wrote that, "in the opal you shall see the burning fire of the Carbuncle or Ruby, the glorious purple of the Amethyst, the green sea of the Emerald, and all glittering together."

In 1846, Ruskin wrote in *Modern Painters*, "everyone knows how capriciously the colours of a fine opal vary from day to day, and how rare the lights are which bring them fully out."

There is a wide variety of color and pattern effects among opal deposits and a broad group of combinations of opal with other materials including wood, bone, shell and minerals. Common and less valuable specimens lack the play of color characteristics except for opal, and are found in translucent to opaque varieties of every possible color. One variety, called a Magic Stone, appears white or opaque yellow until it is left inwater or oil to absorb moisture, after which it takes on a brilliant color range.

The opal's structure with natural particles in an aqueous medium cause its very fragile nature. Sudden changes of temperature have been known to shatter the stones. This nature is probably the root of opal's reputation for bad luck; however, under normal conditions and with reasonable care, opals will remain stable.

Opals are known to vary in brilliance with temperature changes, so that coloring is best when worn and kept dry and warm.

Besides Hungary, Czechoslovakia, and Mexico, there are severalimportant opal fields in Australia. White opals have been found in the Stuart Range of South Australia and the White Cliffs area of New South Wales. They have yielded large stones not unlike harlequins, but with wide flashes of color, and also fascinating fossilized remains of shells, wood and bones replaced by gem opal. Other opal fields in Australia at the Barcoo River in Queensland and the Lightning Ridge area of New South Wales have yielded dark opals known collectively as black opals. These are the most prized variety of the group and are believed particularly to bring good fortune to their owners. The color flashes of black opals are quite brilliant against their dark grounds.

Opal is a Libra gem, not lucky for anyone with Venus afflicted in their horoscope. It is a lucky stone for persons who entered life with the sun in Leo, Libra or Aquarius, and has been traditionally been a token of the pledge of friendship.

Collar necklace of gold, platinum, opal, diamond and pearl in flexibly linked lattice design which can be separated into two bracelets, circa 1900.

Pendant of oval fire opal, silver and diamonds.

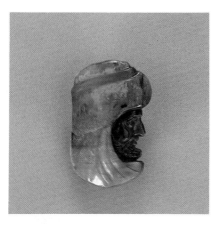

Unmounted opal of approximately 36.6 carats, carved as the head of a turbaned Arabian chieftain.

Pin of gold, opal and diamond in starburst design, circa 1870.

Pin of platinum, blue opal, and diamond, English, circa 1910.

When light strikes an opal and creates a brilliant color display, the traditional mystic explanation has been that the colors signify a favorable response, success and good fortune. When the light creates a dull reflection of color on an opal, interpreters have usually taken that for an unfavorable response, failure and disappointment.

The ancient Greeks believed opals gave foresight and prophecy to its owners if the stone were not used selfishly. Opals were considered a good stone for love relationships except that if one lover were false to the other, the opal's good influence is reversed upon the false lover. Therefore, they interpreted its misuse as bringing bad luck in love, and opals became known as unlucky as an engagement ring.

Other long-held beliefs grew up around opals. If held between the eyes, it direct thoughts. If held in the left hand and gazed upon, it favors personal desires. In the Middle Ages, changes in the brilliance of an opal (attributed to atmospheric and temperature changes) were associated with the ravaging plague and earthquakes which killed three-quarters of the population of Europe. It was thought at that time that opals worn by people stricken with the plague would show brilliantly, then dull at their death. Also in the Middle Ages, opals were credited with all the virtues of the stones whose colors it resembled.

In the fourteenth century, opals were believed to strengthen eye sight. In India, a belief grew up that one could pass an opal across the brow to clear the brain and strengthen the memory. Opals were credited with such powers as protecting the wearer from cholera, kidney problems and lightening. It could also soothe the heart, the eyes and the nerves.

Ben Jonson, in *New Inn*, 1630, wrote, "I had no medicine, sir, to go invisible, nor an opal wrapped in a bay leaf, in my left fist, to charm their eyes." The belief in opal's ability to confer invisibility made it the favored stone of thieves. Over a century later Marbodus (1740) says opal would render its wearer invisible.

Sir Walter Scott gave his heroine the Baroness Hermione in *Anne of Gierstein* an opal to wear, upon which a drop of holy water fell and caused a brilliant light to be given off, after which the stone fell dull and colored as a common pebble. The story is an unhappy tale, and its great popularity helped to confirm the unlucky associations connected with opals. Despite this, England's Queen Victoria gave an exceptional opal to each of her five daughters, and thereby helped to dispel the bad luck symbolism they had acquired.

The popular French actress Sara Bernhardt frequently wore opal jewelry as it was her birthstone. Even recently in Russia opals were thought to embody the evil eye, so that upon seeing an opal among goods for purchase, nothing more would be bought that day.

Famous opals include: the oval Devonshire opal, a black specimen from Australia of one hundred carats and more measuring one by two inches; the Roebling opal from Virgin Valley, Nevada, U.S.A. of 2,610 carats; the Roebling Black Opal, also from Nevada, of 355.19 carats; the Dark Jubilee opal of 318.4 carats. The last three can be seen publicly at the Museum of Natural History of the Smithsonian Institution, Washington, D.C.

The Andamooka opal from the Andamooka mines in South Australia is an oval green specimen with brilliant color of 205 carats. In 1954 it was mounted in a necklace and given to the Queen of England.

The Flame Queen opal of 233 carats from Australia is a black opal with a red center.

Another dramatic Australian specimen is the Light of the World opal of 273 carats found in the Lightning Ridge area of New South Wales.

Pendant of gold, a round, brown wood opal, a pear-shaped blue opal, and a diamond, probably French.

Pendant of opal and diamond in a cascading, flexible design. Bracelet of thirteen graduated opals and round diamonds as repeating links, circa 1905. Bracelet of gold and silver with a detachable circular medallion and tapering band set with opals and diamonds, circa 1870. Pin in the form of a dragonfly with diamonds and rubies, circa 1890.

Pin of platinum, gold, black opal and diamond designed as a rectangular panel, circa 1910.

Pendant of gold and opal
designed as a star.

Pendant of gold, opal and
diamonds in a ribbon and
garland design.

Pendant/pin of gold with opal and
demantoid garnets in a symmetrical,
openwork design.

Necklace of graduated opal beads, clear crystal beads and a gold clasp set with diamonds.

Finger ring of gold and platinum, Australian opal and diamonds.

Pendant of gold, Australian opal and diamonds.

Necklace with seven strands of pearls and
a pendant and clasp of enamel, gold and
diamonds, by C. Giuliano, London, circa
1880.

Pearl

Pearl is a gem material composed entirely of calcium carbonate particles arranged in overlapping layers and bound together with organic material by oysters, members of the mollusk family of sea creatures. When an irritating foreign particle, which could be a piece of sand, parasite, worm of small fish, enters the oyster, the creature responds by covering the irritant with smooth layers of body material and an iridescent layer, called nacre, which build up to become a pearl. A variety of saltwater, non-edible oysters and a variety of freshwater oysters produce gem quality pearls.

Several types of pearls are differentiated by their origins. Completely oyster-made pearls are called "natural." "Oriental" pearls are natural, saltwater pearls from the Persian Gulf. For many centuries, up to the last hundred years, the Persian gulf was the source for the majority of pearls in the world. The term "French pearl" has been used in recent times to identify irregular pieces of oyster shell with some of the characteristics of natural pearls. "Freshwater" pearls come from oysters living in rivers, and "cultured" pearls are made with the help of mankind, including the introduction of a carefully placed and precisely designed foreign particle to sea-living oysters. Cultured pearls have become an important commercial industry throughout the world, but primarily in Japan, over just the last fifty years.

Natural Pearls

Blister pearls remain attached to the shell of their host oyster and must be cut out along with part of the shell. Therefore, the sizes and shapes of blister pearls varies. Seed pearls are very small pearls of irregular shape which have usually been used massed together in close fitting settings or strung together in multiple rows.

Pearls are measured by weight in a unit called a grain such that there are four grains in a carat and twenty grains in a gram. By size, pearls are measured in millimeters. Seed pearls are two millimeters in diameter or less.

The colors of pearls vary from light to dark in a wide range of body colors and a variety of overtones. Light pearls have soft shades of pink, white, or cream bodies and overtones of blue, green, red, pink and grey. Dark pearls are called black. This term refers to pearls silver grey, dark blue, purple, blue-green, green and bronze with and without metallic overtones. Besides these are colored pearls, not light or black, but light to medium shades of yellow, green, blue, violet, purple or grey. Color is more common in freshwater than saltwater pearls. It is common to find in a group of natural pearls a significant number of examples with irregular, nonuniform coloring. Commercially, two-color pearls are not valuable for jewelry, so they may be cut or mounted to minimize the odd coloring, or separated for eventual use in powdered form as medicines in Asia.

There are many shapes of pearls. Round, perfectly regular pearls are commercially the most valuable but are just one of the many natural shapes which include also pear, egg, tear-drop, button (flat on one side), and baroque (un-even in surface texture regardless of shape). In fact, perfectly round and regular shapes do not occur in nature so that the variations make future identification of particular pearls possible.

Because pearls are organic, they are affected by conditions in their environment. Excessive heat or an open flame causes pearl to turn brown, split, crack and burn. Even dry air will cause pearls to dehydrate and the nacre to crack. Acids will corrode pearls as well as harmful gasses. When worn on the body regularly, pearls are lubricated by natural body oils which help them to retain their reflective qualities. When left stored too long, they loose their moisture and turn dull, as though responding to neglect. The many mystical properties that have been credited to pearls over time may have their origins at least in part to the changes caused by these natural conditions of their environment.

Necklace of silver with a pendant of silver set with diamonds and pearls ranging in color from white through grey to black.

Pendant of gold, enamel, twenty-six pearls and thirteen rubies in an openwork square panel with pearl drop, by C. Giuliano, circa 1880.

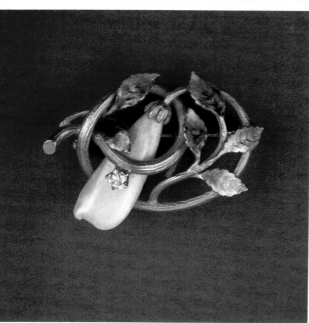

Natural pearls are found in many parts of the world besides the Persian Gulf, their primary origin in the ancient world. The coastal area of the Island of Bahrain has provided pearls for generations. As these waters became depleted, sources were found in the tropical waters of the South Seas including Tahiti, Burma, the Gulf of Manaar near Sri Lanka, Madras, the north coast of Australia, and the Pacific shores of Venezuela, Panama, Mexico and Southern California.

Freshwater pearls can be found in any large river of the temperate zones. Abundant quantities have come from the Mississippi River and its tributaries, and rivers in Scotland and China.

Perhaps because of their round and glowing form, pearls have traditionally been considered the sacred stone of the moon, and Cancer, the celestial sign of the ocean, is its designated sign of the Zodiac. Therefore, pearls are favorable to persons with their planets in Cancer and in whose nativities the lunar aspects were favorable. In modern times, pearl, moonstone, and Alexandrite share the position as birthstone of June. Monday is the pearl's special day of the week.

According the Sanskrit books of the Brahmans of India and other Oriental literature of ancient times, the Ancients believed pearls were formed from drops of dew or rain by oysters rising to the surface of the water. The oysters were said to open in the morning to imbibe the dew drops which were transformed through air and sunlight into pearls. If the air and light are not right, the pearls will be faulty.

In Roman times in Europe, Clodius, the son of Aesopus, discovered that dissolved pearls have a most exquisite flavor, so he gave a pearl to each of his guests to swallow. Cleopatra is reputed to have swallowed a pearl of fabulous price.

In these times powdered pearls were credited with correcting complaints of the stomach in China. As a cure for irritability, it was ground to a powder and a small amount taken in new milk. As a charm against pestilence, pearl powder mixed with sugar was recommended. Through Arab influence, ground pearl was used for nearly every ill imaginable. In 1669, the famous chemist Dr. Schroder wrote (in Latin) that pearls, "are an excellent cordial, that strengthens the balsam of life, resists poison, pestilence, and putrefication, and clears the spirits; and they are so famous that men in the greatest agonies are refreshed thereby."

The author Pomet wrote in 1712: "As to pearls, all the Eastern countries are much of our minds in choosing them white. For I have always made it my observation that they love the whitest pearl, the whitest diamonds, the whitest bread, and the fairest women . . . All pearl is esteemed cordial, proper against infection, recruiting and restoring lost spirits; but their chief virtue is to destroy, and kill the acids, as other alcalies do, and likewise to correct the acrimony of the stomach . . . Pearl is also good against a canine appetite, a flux of the belly, and the hemorrhage. The dose is from six to ten grains to a dram . . . Ladies of quality use the fine-ground powder of seed pearls to give a lustre and beauty to the face. They make use thereof likewise with acids, etc., in a magistery, and a salt, to which they attribute large virtues; besides other imaginary preparations, as "the arcanum of pearl," the flowers, spirits, essences, tinctures, and the like; to pick fools' pockets; but the best and only useful preparation of it is the powder, well levigated."

The colors of pearl also took on meaning in the Middle Ages when so much explanation of life was ascribed to natural phenomena:

> gold pearl was an emblem of wealth
> white was an emblem of idealism
> black was an emblem of philosophy
> pink was an emblem of beauty
> red was an emblem of health and energy
> grey was an emblem of thought

When worn at the neck, pearl was an emblem of chastity, and generally denoted purity, innocence and peace. Among Bengal virgins, the pearl was an amulet for purity.

In Renaissance Europe, pearls became a symbol of tears because the oyster was trying to correct an irritation (seen as pain) in order to produce the pearl. Therefore, the pearl was considered unfortunate for those in love, signifying tears to the married, so it was rarely used in engagement rings.

Pendant/pin of gold with pearls, heart shaped Alexandrite, and diamonds, circa 1880. Necklace of seven strands of pearls with gold and enamel clasp and pendant, including trapeze zircon, and diamonds, by C. & A. Giuliano, London, circa 1890. Pin of gold and cabochon sapphires designed as a wheel and cross with enameled accents and granulation, by Castellani, circa 1860.

Necklace of gold with pendant of rubies, enamel and pearls in Holbeinesque style, English, circa 1870. Pendant cross of gold, enamel and sapphire, by C. & A. Giuliano, 1906.

Necklace of gold, enamel and both freshwater and saltwater pearls in floral design with drops, English, circa 1920.

Opposite page:

Pendant of gold and freshwater pearl, French, circa 1910.

Pin of gold, freshwater pearl and diamond in floral design, French, circa 1910.

Pendant earrings of gold, diamonds and pearls designed as grape bunches.

Necklace and earrings of yellow gold, thirty-one graduated cultured pearls, and circular and marquise diamonds.

By the sixteenth century, pearl was considered a gem for the exclusive use of royalty. Both Queen Elizabeth I and Catherine deMedici were painted overlaid with pearls. The officials of Augsburg, in 1530, permitted noble women to have four silk dresses but no pearls. The Duke of Saxony legislated in 1612 that: "the nobility are not allowed to wear any dresses of gold or silver or those garnished with pearls; neither shall the professors and doctors of the universities nor their wives wear any gold, silver or pearls for fringes, or any chains of pearls, or caps, neck ornaments, shoes, slippers, shawls, pins, etc., embellished with gold or silver or pearls."

In the Americas, freshwater pearl ornaments have been found in ancient burial mounds. Elsewhere, it is recorded that if pearls are buried at the time of a difficult birth, good will come to the child until the pearls are unearthed. Swedenborg wrote that pearls represent truth.

Among noteworthy pearls in the world are the incredible Miracle of the Sea, a teardrop shaped gem of 1,191 grains which was formerly among the Crown Jewels of the Emperor of China, and now is owned by the Imperial Pearl Syndicate. The Museum of Zozima in Moscow has a round Oriental pearl of 111 grains known as *La Pellegrina*. The Queen Pearl, found in 1857 near Paterson, New Jersey, is a freshwater, round and translucent specimen of ninety-three grains which was owned by the Empress Eugenie. Marvelous pearls are included in the Pahlavi crown and the Kiami crown of the Crown Jewels of Iran. The famous La Reine Pearl weighs 111 grains.

Cultured Pearls

Cultured pearls were developed commercially in Japan in the early years of the twentieth century. According to research by Dr. A.R. Cahn of the U.S. Bureau of Fisheries, Japanese carpenter Tatsuhei Mise discovered the techniques that would produce cultured pearls before 1904, but his patent application of 1907 was refused. At nearly the same time, Japanese zoologist Tokichi Nishikawa applied for a similar patent in 1907 which was granted finally in 1916, two years after Nishikawa had died. This patent was shared by Mise, giving an indication of credit to both men. Thereafter, Nishikawa's father-in-law Kokichi Mikimoto commercially developed and extended the techniques to create a worldwide business in cultured pearls.

Pin of white gold, circular and baguette diamonds designed as four ribbon loops. Pin of silver and gold, baroque pearl and circular diamonds in two rows. Finger ring of silver and gold with pearl and round diamonds. Circle pin of platinum, five round diamonds and purple pearls. Pin of silver and gold, baroque black pearl and round diamonds in two rows. Finger ring of white gold with a black pearl and baguette diamonds in a looped frame.

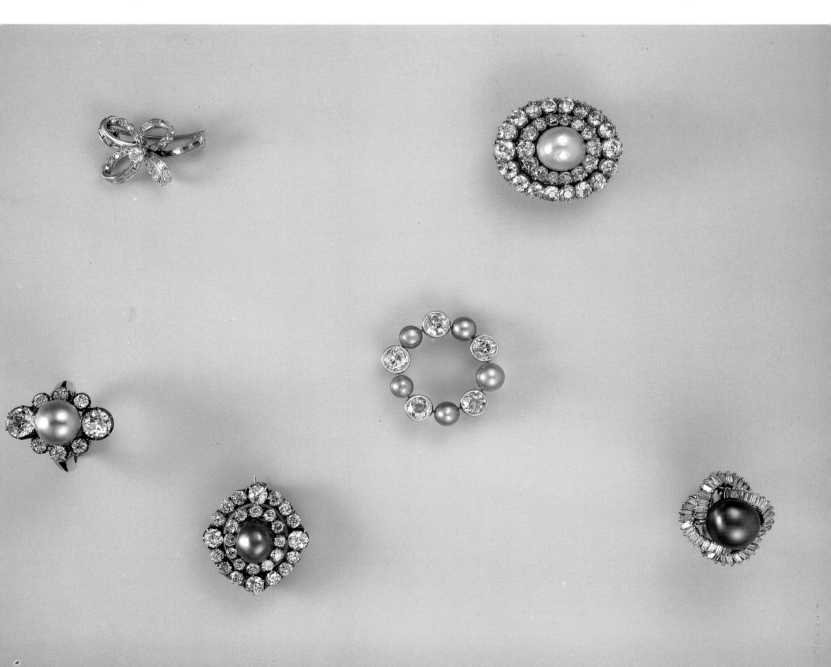

Necklace of platinum, seventeen pear-shaped cultured pearls, circular, marquise, pear, and baguette diamonds designed as a floral garland, by Alexandre Réza, Paris.

Because of overfishing of the sources of natural pearls and international unrest in the major producing and consuming regions of the world, as well as changing economic structures in the operation of farming for natural pearls, the market for natural pearls is all but gone except at the highest levels of the world market. Yet the demand and breadth of the consumer market for pearls is at an all-time high. Into this void, cultured pearls have taken the place of natural pearls. Besides Japan, which continues to supply the largest share, producers of cultured pearls today include Australia, Burma and Tahiti.

Cultured pearls are primarily found on the market as pink or white bodies with a rose overtone. The colored and black varieties are quite rare. There is considerable variety, however in the available shapes of cultured pearls, for they are readily found as round, button, oval, pear, egg and many baroque shapes.

Pin of platinum and white gold with four black button pearls, three black pear-shaped pearls, and circular and baguette diamonds designed as a flexible floral spray.

Pendant earrings of black and white pear-shaped pearls and marquise and round diamonds.

Earrings of platinum, circular and baguette diamonds, a baroque cultured pearl and a black baroque natural pearl. Finger ring of platinum, a button pearl, and baguette and triangular diamonds making a stepped frame, by Cartier. Dress clip of platinum, oval black and white pearls, and baguette and circular diamonds, designed as a shield-shaped openwork panel. Pin of platinum, pink pearls, and circular and oval diamonds. Bracelet of three strands of pearls with a central panel and clasp of platinum set with cushion and round diamonds.

Sautoir of five strands of pearls and panels of circular diamonds in round and square settings, by Cartier, late nineteenth century. Ear pendants of platinum, circular diamonds, cabochon, calibre and square emeralds, and onyx designed as hoops and fringe, by Van Cleef and Arpels, Paris.

Necklace of thirty-seven cultured pearls, ruby beads, sapphire beads, and yellow gold. Necklace of thirty-eight graduated peach colored cultured pearls, faceted sapphire beads, diamond rondelles, and white gold.

Bracelet of gold bangle hoop set with half pearls and round diamonds.

Opposite page:

Sautoir of thirty-five graduated cultured pearls and gold and diamond rondelles leading into a gold rope with yellow gold and diamond terminals and strands of graduated cultured pearls to form tassels, by René Boivin, Paris, circa 1930.

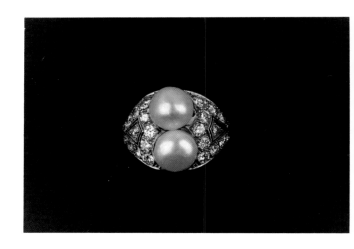

Finger ring of platinum, two pearls, and diamonds, circa 1900.

Pendant earrings of silver, graduated diamonds, oriental pearls, and in each twenty strands of graduated pearls to form tassels.

Pin of graduated pearls strung and woven to a mother of pearl backing in a symmetrical floral and ribbon design, English, circa 1830.

Necklace of many strands of seed pearls twisted into a rope and terminating in a gold clasp, circa 1820.

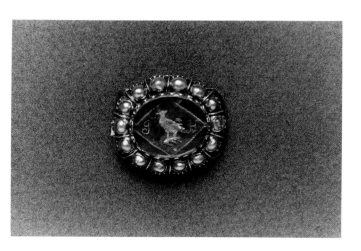

Finger ring of gold, pearls, and crystal engraved and set-in with gold, eighteenth century.

Pendant/pin of platinum, pearls, emeralds and diamonds designed as a tassel, with black silk rope, circa 1925.

Necklace with platinum and pearl chain and pendant of platinum, diamonds, and twelve strings of pearls forming a tassel.

Pin of platinum, diamonds and colored pearls, circa 1900.

Necklace with five strands of pearls and platinum and diamond panel, circa 1915.

Pendant earrings of platinum, square, baguette and circular diamonds and pear-shaped colored pearl drops.

Opposite page:

Necklace of thirty-nine graduated Tahitian black cultured pearls and white gold clasp with diamonds. Ear pendants of platinum, circular and pear-shaped diamonds, and detachable cultured pearl drops. Finger ring of platinum, an octagonal diamond of approximately 18.6 carats, and baguette diamonds.

Peridot

Pendant of gold with peridot, amethyst and pearls, English, circa 1880.

Pendant of silver and gold openwork with peridot, pearls and diamonds designed as a ribbon bow and garland, English, circa 1880.

A gem variety of the mineral chrysolite, peridot is a silicate of magnesium and iron found in basaltic igneous rock. Its occurrence is common, but there is only a small supply of gem quality available in the world. Peridot has a characteristic double refraction in cut stones, especially in large examples, which enables the unaided eye to see a double image through the table. This feature is helpful in identifying peridot.

Depending on the amount of iron in its composition, peridot can be a fine, rich olive green which tends toward green-brown when more iron is present, or shaded to a yellow-green if there is less iron and more magnesium. The finest stones are a rich green and have been called the "evening emerald."

Peridot is a soft stone not well suited to mountings as fingerrings because of the possibility of receiving a sharp blow. Also, the stone is easily damaged by direct or excessive heat, and manyhave been ruined under the careless hand of a would-be repairer or careless mounter whose torch seared the stone during an attempt to tighten the setting. It can be used very effectively in hanging settings, especially of modern design where its fantastic color is shown to advantage.

Since about 1500 B.C., peridot has been found principally on the island of Zabargad in the western region of the Red Sea, opposite the Egyptian port city of Berenice. Deeply colored peridots have been found here. Also, a few deep colored peridots have been found in Burma at the Mogok area of the Bernardino Valley. Very small pebbles of light color and numerous quantity come from Arizona and New Mexico in the United States. In Arizona, on the San Carlos Apache Indian Reservation stones known as Job's Tears are found near deposits of pyrope garnets, but these are not fine quality and are small, usually less than five carats in weight. Other sources of small stones are Queensland, Australia; Sondmore, Norway; Minas Gerais, Brazil; Czechoslovakia; Hawaii; Russia; and Kenya. None of these, however, has been an important source or produced large or first quality stones.

The Ancients called peridot the "gem of the sun" and believed in its powers to dissolve enchantments and banish evil spirits. To exert its full powers, peridot had to be set in gold, and as such chased away the terrors of the night. Peridot was considered effective as a protection against evil spirits when it was pierced, strung on a donkey's hair, and worn on the left arm.

In powdered form, peridot was considered a remedy for asthma. Because of its yellow tones, it was considered a relief for liver diseases. Also, peridot was credited with relieving the mind from envious thoughts. If held under the tongue, peridot was believed to relieve thirst in a person afflicted with fever. In modern times, peridot alternates with sardonyx as the birthstone for August.

Crusaders brought many peridots back to Europe in the Middle Ages and presented them to local cathedrals as emeralds. The cathedral in Cologne has a wonderful peridot in the shrine of thethree kings—Caspar, Melchior and Balthazar.

Today, noteworthy peridots can be seen in some of the world's great gem museums. A nearly flawless, cut, yellow-green peridot of over 192 carats and belonged to Russia's Czars is now in the Diamond Treasury in Moscow. In the United States, an enormous 310 carat cut peridot from Zabargad and a 289 carat stone from Burma can be seen in the Smithsonian Institution in Washington. A spectacular peridot is in the Morgan Collection at the American Museum of Natural History in New York City. Fine examples are also displayed at the Chicago Museum of Natural History and the Los Angeles County Museum of Natural History. At the British Museum in London can be seen a stone of 136 carats from Burma, and the Topkapi Museum in Istanbul has many unmounted, tumbled pebbles on view. In modern times, in Sri Lanka, water worn fragments of bottle glass have deceptively been sold as peridot.

Necklace of gold with graduated, heart-shaped peridots, cabochon rubies and round diamonds.

Necklace of white gold, oval and pear-shaped peridot, topaz and diamonds in a garland design, English, circa 1890.

Choker necklace of oval cabochon rubies, diamonds and yellow gold with a pear-shaped cabochon ruby of approximately 6.5 carats, designed as a star. Pin of obsidian carved as the head of an African chieftain with turban of carved emerald, ruby, and fancy colored and colorless diamonds, by Cartier.

Ruby

The transparent red variety of corundum is called ruby after the Latin adjective meaning "red". It is composed of about 75 percent oxide of aluminum (alumina crystal), 17 percent magnesia, 4 percent iron, and trace quantities of silica and minor elements. These minor elements and the amount of iron help to give ruby a variety of shades from light rose to deep carmine. The optimal color is a deep shade of clear red generally called "pigeon's blood". The light pink varieties are commonly called pink sapphires. Blue varieties of corundum are called sapphires.

In times past, ruby was sometimes set with a blue section of apeacock's feather under it to give an iridescent brilliance in much the same way foil was used to enhance other stones. Over theyears and up to the present, rubies have been more valuable than diamonds of the same size because they are much rarer. The value of rubies increases dramatically with the increase in size, and stones over ten carats are extremely scarce. Therefore, they are among the most valuable of all gems.

Rubies that are cut *en cabochon* and with apparent asterism are called star rubies. These gems are also quite rare, so that a broader range of colors is allowed for them than for star gems of other stones. Star rubies may also be less transparent, as the asterism adds a grey tone to rubies.

In many parts of the world rubies have been found in small sizes and in areas where the other colors of corundum are found, but their most famous source is Burma. In the Mogok area of this high mountain country, the largest rubies with the best colors and minimal flaws have originated. Some fine stones have also been found in Thailand, and border areas with Cambodia, but generally these stones have been dark red shaded to brown which do not bring the best prices. From the Tsavo West National Park and other small areas of Kenya good stones have come, primarily small stones up to five or seven carats. Mines in Tanzania have produced small stones, also. From Sri Lanka, fancy colored rubies including light and medium light red or purple toned stones have originated. Scattered sources on India, Pakistan, Afghanistan, and Australia have unearthed medium quality rubies for the most part. In Macon County, North Carolina and Fergus County, Montana in the United States, small rubies have come.

Ruby is the birthstone for people born in July according to ages old traditions originating in Poland and Russia, and it is the special gem of the zodiac sign Cancer which governs events between June 22 and July 22. An anonymous rhyme about the ruby has come down to present usage:

> The gleaming ruby should adorn
> All those who in July are born,
> For thus they'll be exempt and free
> From lover's doubts and anxiety.

The superstition alluded to in the poem is one of the many that have grown up through the years in different parts of the world. Rubies are specially endowed with different attributes by different peoples. To the Greeks, rubies were thought to be living coal, as though red hot coals were made into stone. According to Hebrew legend, rubies became symbolic of the boy Reuben whose conduct to his father made him blush. Also, ruby wasone of the twelve gems which made up the sacred Ephod of the Hebrews. To the ancient Burmese and other early peoples, rubies were believed to ripen in color gradually while maturing in the earth, as fruit ripens on a tree over time. The Burmese also had the belief that a ruby could provide invulnerability if it were inserted in the owner's flesh voluntarily through an intentional wound. A warrior so inflicted was believed to be immune from harmof spear, sword, gun or other skin-piercing implements.

In ancient Ethiopia, rubies were treated with a vinegar bath for fourteen days to increase their brilliance, but this treatment only made them soft and more brittle.

Pin of platinum with cushion-shaped rubies and diamonds of colorless and fancy brown, pale yellow and rose hues, designed as an orchid blossom with the flowerhead mounted *en tremblant.*

To the early Roman people, any red stone was called "carbuncle" (a term used today for a variety of garnet), so it is difficult to be precise today in interpreting the significance they placed on rubies specifically. Nevertheless, Pliny, the first century A.D. Roman author related that red stones were enhanced by placing, "a red foil beneath them to make them brilliant and glitter like fire." He also described glass imitations of rubies which could be detected easily by their difference in weight, "for glass imitations are the lighter of the two" (which we know today to be accurate). Romans also believed rubies to be male or female, and to this idea Pliny explains that, "the males were more vigorous and acrid, the females more languishing."

Rubies have many purported uses as medicines. In general they were made into amulets by ancient peoples to guard against poisons, plague, evil thoughts and wicked spirits. For example, a long held belief has persisted that rubies warn of the presence of poison by growing dark and cloudy, and then resume their brilliance when the danger is past. Some writers have extended this ability to warn to any danger that threatens the ruby wearer. Relative to this notion, the Italian poet Francesco Petrarch in the fourteenth century related that the French king, John II was not protected by a ruby ring when he was captured by the English in 1356 at the Battle of Poitiers. Years later, when the king was reunited with this ring, Petrarch tells that he was pleased, "to see an object of infinite value and beauty but of nouse whatever."

Other writers stress the ruby's power to keep its wearer in health and his mind cheerful. In 1669, Dr. J. Schroder wrote: "You may try the goodness of the Rubine by the mouth, and tongue; for the coldest, and hardest are the best . . . it resists poison, . . . sadness, . . . frightful dreams, clears the mind, keeps the body safe, and, if a mischance be at hand, it signifies this by turning of a darker colour."

The attributes of a ruby are many as the following demonstrate:

The wearer of a ruby was blessed with health, wealth, wisdom, and outstanding success in affairs of the heart.

Rubies provide a remedy for biliousness and flatulence.

Some say rubies could draw blood, but others know it prevents bleeding.

It was formerly believed that rubies bruised in water relieved eye problems and helped sick livers.

Ruby dispersed infectious airs.

If the four corners of a house, garden, or vineyard were touched with ruby, they would be preserved from lightning, tempest and worms.

Rubies banished sadness and forms of sin and vice.

The wearer of a ruby acquired the magic ability to live in peace with his enemies, provided a ruby ring was worn on the left hand or a ruby brooch on the left side.

A ruby cannot be concealed when it is worn. Its lustre shows beneath the thickest clothing.

Ruby, because of the magnesia in its composition, is regarded as a skin healer—based on the experience of sea-bathers whose skin problems are aided by their contact with the magnesia in sea water.

Several rubies have become noted historically. One huge ruby was casually handed to England's King William III in 1697 by young Peter the Great of Russia while he was learning ship building in England. Another ruby, the size of a small chicken egg, was presented to the Empress of Russia in St Petersberg by Gustavus the Third of Sweden (1746-1792). In the coronation ring of English kings is a large ruby engraved with the figure of St. George's Cross. The English consort's ring, too, includes a central ruby with sixteen smaller rubies surrounding it.

Public museums display several important rubies including the Edwardes Ruby of 167 carats at the Natural History Museum in London. At the American Museum of Natural History in New York is the Edith Haggin deLong Star Ruby which is magnificent at one hundred carats. Also in the United States is the magnificent 137 carat Rasser Reeves Ruby at the Smithsonian Institution in Washington, D.C.

Necklace of gold and un-cut rubies in Renaissance-revival style by Marcus & Co.

Choker necklace of four strands of
cultured pearls with platinum and white
gold, diamonds and a floral panel with an
elongated ruby of approximately 19 carats.
Bracelet of platinum links set with calibre
rubies and round and baguette diamonds.

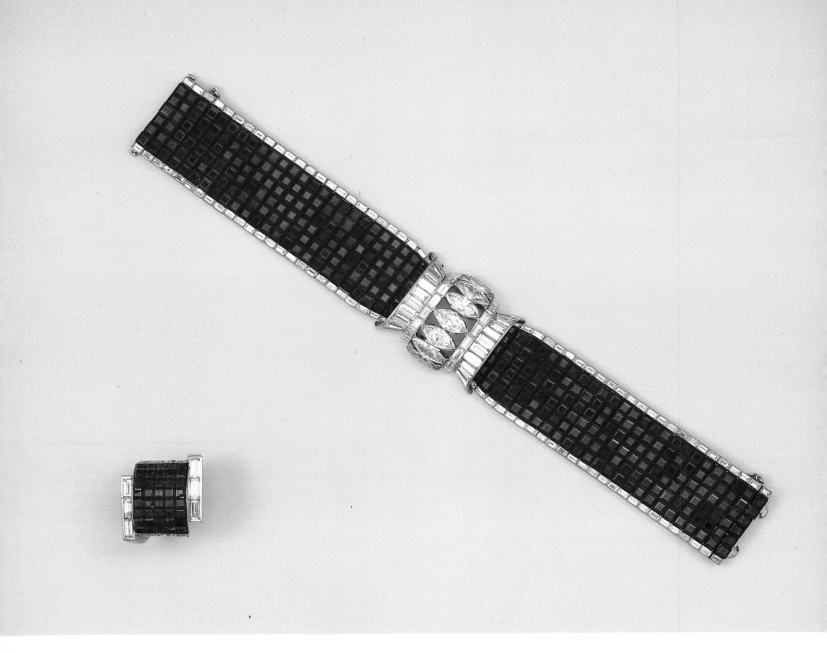

Bracelet of platinum, calibre rubies, and marquise and baguette diamonds by Cartier. London, circa 1940. Finger ring of platinum, calibre rubies and baguette and round diamonds, by Van Cleef and Arpels, Paris, circa 1940.

Double dress clip of platinum, sapphire and diamond designed as mirror images, circa 1920. Double dress clip of platinum, calibre rubies and diamonds designed as mirror images, circa 1940.

Two finger rings of rubies and diamonds, English, circa 1870 (left) and 1895 (right).

Finger ring of platinum and white gold, circular ruby of approximately 6.5 carats and two rubies of approximately 1.5 carats each, and circular and baguette diamonds. Bracelet of platinum and white gold, five oval rubies, and diamonds of kite, rectangular, baguette, and circular shapes. Earrings of platinum and white gold, calibre rubies, and circular diamonds by Van Cleef and Arpels, Paris, circa 1940.

Choker necklace and earrings of rose toned gold, silver, rectangular rubies, and circular and baguette diamonds designed as two ribbons and floral clusters, circa 1940.

Pair of pins and earrings of platinum, oval and round rubies, and round and baguette diamonds designed as floral sprays. Finger ring of platinum with oval ruby of approximately 2.5 carats and triangular cluster of round and tapered baguette diamonds. Pin of platinum, oval rubies, and round and baguette diamonds, by Van Cleef and Arpels, Paris.

Pin of platinum with rubies, colorless diamonds, and graduated yellow heat-treated diamonds designed as a floral spray, circa 1925.

Pin of platinum and yellow gold with oval rubies and graduated circular diamonds, designed as a floral cluster, by Van Cleef and Arpels, Paris. Bracelet of yellow gold, round and oval rubies, and circular diamonds designed as repeating raised clusters, by Van Cleef and Arpels, Paris.

Earrings of platinum and yellow gold with circular rubies and diamonds designed as ribbon bows by Tiffany-Schlumberger, New York. Bracelet of platinum, rubies, and baguette diamonds designed as a twisted rope. Bracelet of platinum, round and calibre rubies, and marquise, round, and baguette diamonds designed as a floral and ribbon group. The ruby lines detach to convert the bracelet into two pins. Cuff links of platinum in triangular shape with a tapering line of rubies on one side and a tapering line of diamonds on another side.

Choker necklace of platinum, graduated
pear-shaped rubies, and circular diamonds
designed to separate into two bracelets
and an extension. Pendant earrings of
platinum with pear, hexagonal and round
diamonds.

Necklace of graduated ruby beads with a cluster of cushion and round diamonds in platinum, by Bulgari, Rome. Finger ring of platinum, a light yellow cushion diamond of approximately 14 carats, and baguette and round diamonds set pavé in a bombé mount. Earrings of platinum and white gold, oval rubies of approximately 2.5 carats, and round and baguette diamonds set *pavé* in a floral design. Link bracelet of white gold with calibré rubies and diamonds, by Bulgari, Rome.

Necklace of three strands and four strands of graduated ruby beads and diamonds set in white gold. Ear pendants of platinum, pear-shaped spinel cabochons, and circular, pear and baguette diamonds. Earrings of platinum oval rubies and round diamonds designed as tassels.

Opposite page:

Sautoir of graduated ruby beads with yellow gold links and panels set with diamonds and a cabochon oval ruby of approximately 16 carats, and a pendant tassel, by M. Gérard, Paris, circa 1970.

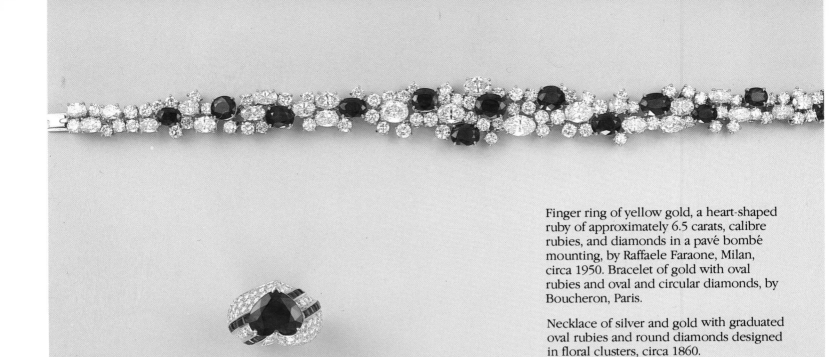

Finger ring of yellow gold, a heart-shaped ruby of approximately 6.5 carats, calibre rubies, and diamonds in a pavé bombé mounting, by Raffaele Faraone, Milan, circa 1950. Bracelet of gold with oval rubies and oval and circular diamonds, by Boucheron, Paris.

Necklace of silver and gold with graduated oval rubies and round diamonds designed in floral clusters, circa 1860.

Ear pendants of platinum with pear-shaped and circular diamonds. Finger ring of platinum and a rectangular diamond of approximately 3.7 carats, by Ayre and Taylor. Necklace of white and yellow gold with round and oval rubies and circular diamonds.

Finger ring of platinum with an oval ruby of approximately five carats and diamonds set pavé in the mount. Pin of silver and yellow gold with an oval ruby and round diamonds in an openwork, floral design.

Bracelet of yellow gold and six cushion rubies intaglio carved to depict wild animals and a palm tree, and circular diamonds. Stick pin of platinum and yellow gold with round and baguette diamonds, and octagonal, pear-shaped and trilliant rubies in openwork design. Earrings of platinum, square rubies and circular diamonds designed as bird wings, circa 1940. Earrings of platinum with oval rubies and circular diamonds. Finger ring of platinum, a cushion ruby of approximately 4.2 carats, a diamond of approximately 3.3 carats, and baguette diamonds.

Opposite page:
Earrings of gold with cabochon rubies and emeralds, and diamonds designed as leaf clusters. Earrings of gold and rubies designed as an orb with radiating rays, circa 1940.

Earrings of gold and rubies designed as an orb and radiating loops, circa 1940.

Earrings of pink gold and rubies designed as an orb, circa 1940. Wristwatch of yellow gold with rubies and diamonds marked Movado and Tiffany & Co., New York, circa 1940.

Pin of gold and platinum with cabochon rubies and diamonds designed as a flower by Rabert & Hoeffer, Mauboussin, circa 1940.

Finger ring of gold with pearl, rubies and sapphires, circa 1940.

Necklace of platinum with two rows of
baguette sapphires, three oval sapphires of
approximately 24, 41 and 27 carats,
circular diamonds, and a pendant of an
oval sapphire of approximately 114 carats
known as "The Blue Princess."

Sapphire

The Sapphire is a precious stone and is blue in color most like to heaven in fair weather and clear, and is best among precious stones and most apt and able to fingers of kings.
 Bartholomew Angelicus, thirteenth century

Transparent corundum of any color except red is known commonly as sapphire; the red variety is called ruby. Sapphire is most popularly thought of in its medium to dark blue variety, and this is the most costly and famous variety historically. Colors other than blue are considered fancy varieties and less valuable. These appear in a wide array of shades including clear, pink, yellow, violet, green, brown, bluish grey and black. The yellow has erroneously been called Oriental topaz, the violet Oriental amethyst and the green Oriental emerald, but these terms are discouraged because they are misleading. "Yellow sapphire," for example, is the correct terminology.

All sapphires are composed for the most part of Alumina (98.5 percent) with lime (.5 percent), oxide of iron (1 percent) and trace oxides. Oxide of cobalt, for example, determines the blue color. The stones are very hard and will darken when exposed to intense heat. A graphic example is the sapphire worn as a ring by the Russian Grand Duke Sergius when he was assassinated by a bomb and resulting fire. The stone became black. Today, the intensity of color of many commercial stones is increased by a heating process. To the touch, sapphire is cold because it is so dense. Its coolness contributed to the ancient writer Epiphanius' belief that the sapphire had the power to extinguish fires.

In the early days of history, many dark stones were called sapphires. Therefore, ancient descriptions must be carefully judged—the terminology may be confusing. The Bible records, for example, that the ten commandments were written on tablets of stone. This stone was long thought to be sapphire, however, as no sapphires even close to the required size are known, it is now believed that the tablets were of Lapis Lazuli.

Sapphires have been found in riverbeds in Ceylon for many generations and the best have traditionally been found in Burma and India. The Zanskar range of the Himalayas in Kashmir have produced magnificent specimens, and the famous Hill of Precious Stones has more than earned its auspicious name in Thailand. In more recent ages the Helena area of Montana in the United States has been the source of light blue sapphires, and the Anakie region of Queensland, Australia has been an impressive source, perhaps with future finds to come.

The legendary first person to wear a ring set with a sapphire was Prometheus whose stone came from the Caucasus, where he stole fire from heaven for man.

In Ancient Persia, the earth was believed to rest on a huge sapphire which reflected its color as the blue sky.

To the Jews, King Solomon's seal stone was said to be made with sapphire, and in Exodus XXIV:10, a description of the manifestation of Jehovah describes, "There was under his feet as it were a paved work of sapphire stone, and as it were the body of heaven in his clearness." This clearness can be taken to mean transparency, as such describes the sapphire stone we think of today. Sapphire was also one of the stones of the Breastplate of Aaron.

Pendant of gold, an oval sapphire, pearls, diamonds and enamel in Holbeinesque style, French, circa 1880.

Pin of gold with five round black star sapphires, probably Italian, circa 1880.

Necklace of platinum with link chain including pearls, and a pendant of openwork set with diamonds and an oval light blue star sapphire by J. E. Caldwell & Co., Philadelphia, circa 1920. Finger ring of platinum, diamonds, and an oval light blue star sapphire.

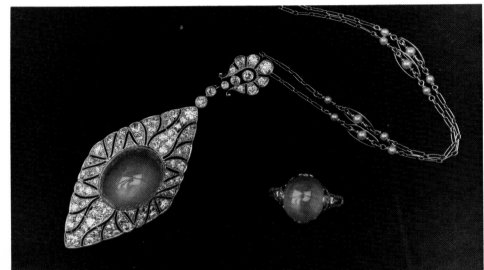

Necklace, pin and earrings all of pendant style with cushion, oval and round large sapphires and circular diamonds, early nineteenth century. Earrings of large pear-shaped diamonds and circular diamonds with ribbon bow design. Finger ring of gold and circular diamonds in cross-over ribbon bow design.

The Greeks regarded sapphire as sacred to the god Apollo, and the stone was traditionally worn when inquiring at the oracle of Apollo's shrine. The Greek wisemen understood what seafarers had known for long ages, that sapphires protected one on journeys across water. Ever since, sapphire is credited with good luck on the sea.

Learned men understood the sapphire's power to protect the wearer at night because it held the night in the mystery of its soul.

Among Buddhists, sapphire is believed to produce a desire for prayer, to give spiritual light and bring peace and happiness as long as its wearer leads a moral life. Buddhists say a sapphire symbolically opens a closed door and sounds the sweet bells of peace.

In the Bible, it is said (Isaiah, XXX) that the sapphire procures favor with princes, pacifies enemies and gives freedom from enchantment and captivity. St. Jerome, writing in the fourth and fifth centuries, also said that sapphire saved its wearers from captivity and pacified his enemies.

Dress clip of platinum and white gold, an oval and two calibre synthetic sapphires, and round and baguette diamonds, by Cartier, circa 1930. Pin of platinum, a circular sapphire of approximately 11.8 carats, rectangular and square sapphires, and circular diamonds, designed as a Maltese cross by David Webb, New York. Bracelet of platinum links set with calibré sapphires and circular and baguette diamonds. Bracelet of platinum links set with circular and calibre sapphires and baguette and circular diamonds, by Tiffany & Co., New York.

Necklace of platinum with tapering
cushion, oval and circular sapphires, and
marquis and circular diamonds in a
symmetrical garland design. Finger ring of
platinum and a rectangular diamond of
approximately 10.4 carats. Finger ring of
platinum, an oval sapphire of

approximately 13.5 carats, and graduated
tapered baguette diamonds in a swirled
design. Bracelet of platinum with two
lines of square sapphires and three panels
of interlocking design set with circular and
baguette diamonds.

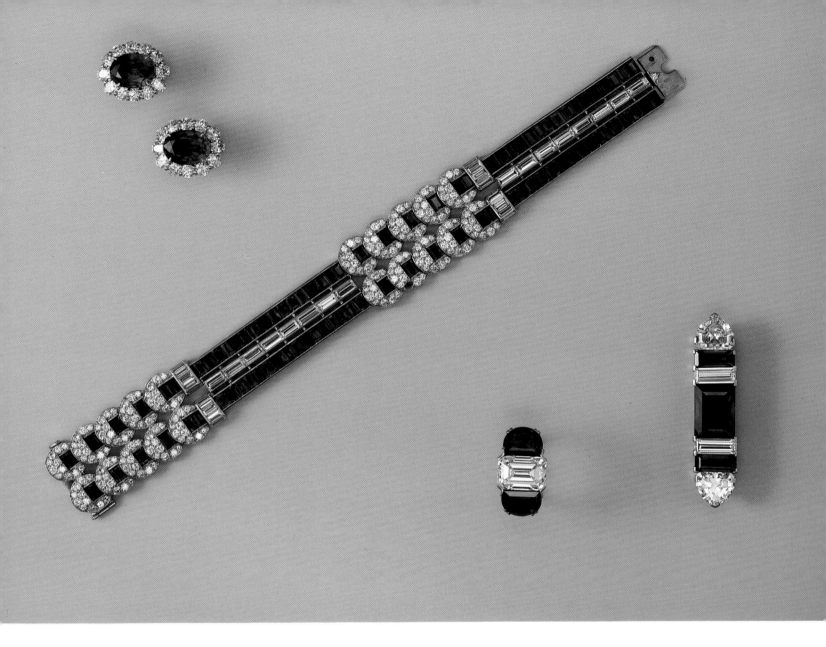

In many sources sapphire is credited with acknowledging the fidelity of a spouse, as it was believed to change color if the female (!) marriage partner cheated. Many sources agree that the sapphire refuses to shine for the unchaste or impure.

According to W. Pavitt, in his book, *Talismans, Amulets and Zodiacal Gems*, the wife of Emperor Charlemagne (742-814) possessed a powerful talisman composed of two rough sapphires and a piece of the True Cross, made to keep Charlemagne's affections constant to her. It was so effective that his love for her endured after her death. He refused to have her body interred, even after decomposition set in. Burial was permitted only after Charlemagne's confessor removed the talisman from the body. The confessor, who kept the talisman, was made Archbishop of Mains and Chancellor of the Empire. As Charlemagne suffered in his deathbed, the talisman was given to him and he was able to pass peacefully away.

In the Middle Ages, the sapphire continued to be credited with attributes of preserving chastity, discovering fraud and treachery (by turning dark) and protecting its wearer from poison, plague, fever, and skin disease, and it had great power to resist black magic and evil thoughts.

Because of its reputation to preserve chastity, sapphire was formerly worn by priests. In the twelfth century, Pope Innocent III tried to make Bishop's rings more uniform and magnificent so he declared that gold and unengraved sapphires should be used to symbolize pontifical rank. As the collection of ecclesiastical rings at the Victoria and Albert Museum in London displays, most Cardinals' rings were made of any base metal and set with a wide variety of stones, including mock sapphires of blue paste (glass). Later, by a decree of the

Earrings of white gold and platinum, oval sapphires of approximately 4.4 carats, and oval diamonds. Bracelet of platinum with calibré sapphires, and circular and baguette diamonds designed as rows interwoven with discs. Finger ring of platinum with a rectangular diamond of approximately 5.7 carats, two kite-shaped diamonds, and two half-moon shaped sapphires, by Hotz. Bar pin of platinum with a rectangular sapphire of approximately 11 carats, two baguette sapphires, two heart-shaped diamonds and two baguette diamonds.

Bull of Gregory XV in the seventeenth century, new Cardinals of the Roman Catholic Church received from the Pope, "finger rings for the right hand in gold with a sapphire to show that the Church is now his spouse, and that he must never abandon her."

A widely held belief that sapphire was the enemy of all poisons gave rise to many practices. To drink a solution made from powdered sapphire was believed to be helpful for those bitten by a scorpion. Hindus say as a medicine, sapphire is bitter to the taste and lukewarm. By the force of its own pure rays, sapphire was credited with killing all noxious and venomous creatures. Bartholomew Anglicus, writing in 1250, said: "Its virtue is contrary to venom, and quencheth it at every deal. And if thow put an addercop (viper) in a box, and hold a very Sapphire of Ind at the mouth of the box, any while, by virtue thereof the addercop is overcome, and dieth as it were suddenly." Sapphire was likewise considered powerful as a destroyer of poisonous insects which were killed when a the gem was placed at the mouth of a vessel in which they were held. Porta in his book *Natural Magic* (1561), related that sapphire, in magical and religious ceremonies, protected the wearer from the larvae of the lower spiritual world, snakes and poisonous reptiles.

In Medieval Europe, a widely held belief persisted that sapphires were particularly beneficial to the eyes. One proclaimed that when set in a ring, sapphire was useful to remove foreign bodies from eyes. Also, sapphires, if put in the eye were believed to oust any dust or gnats that may have fallen in. The virtue of sapphires gave the eye the strength necessary for the ejection of the troublesome foreign body. Further, sapphires were credited in some circles with restoring impaired sight. Sapphire was believed to preserve eyes of smallpox patients when it was rubbed on them. It was credited with drying up rhumes, and taking away inflammation. In 1391, a sapphire was given to St. Paul's Church in London by Richard de Preston, a grocer, for the shrine there of St. Erkinwald to cure eye diseases. Later, an inventory of England's King Charles V included "an oval Oriental sapphire for touching the eyes."

Other medicinal uses for sapphire are widely documented. A sapphire held against the temples stopped bleeding in the nose according to one author, while another wrote that a whole stone laid to the forehead stopped bleeding in the nose.

Pendant of gold and silver with an oval sapphire of approximately 15 carats, two round sapphires, and circular diamonds in a rococo symmetrical design.

Finger ring of gold and platinum with a rectangular light blue sapphire of approximately 10 carats and circular diamonds.

Bracelet of platinum, Burma sapphires and baguette diamonds designed as alternating links, circa 1930. Finger ring of platinum with an oval Burma sapphire and six baguette diamonds, circa 1930. Finger ring of platinum with a central rectangular sapphire and baguette diamonds, circa 1920.

Earrings of yellow gold, oval sapphires of approximately 4.3 carats each, and circular diamonds. Necklace of yellow gold with graduated cushion yellow sapphires, round blue sapphires, emeralds and diamonds, and a pendant of similar stones around an oval yellow sapphire of approximately 22.7 carats, by Van Cleef and Arpels, Paris. The necklace can separate into a brooch and two bracelets; the bracelets can be joined to form a choker.

Bracelet of four twisted strands of sapphire beads with a clasp of platinum and circular and baguette diamonds. Pin of platinum with tapered baguette sapphires and diamonds radiating from a central *fleur-de-lis* set with circular and baguette diamonds. Pin of platinum with fancy-cut and cabochon sapphires and circular and baguette diamonds designed as a flower.

Finger ring of platinum with an oval cabochon star sapphire and two keystone diamonds. Pin of platinum, calibré sapphires and circular diamonds designed as a ribbon bow. Bracelet of three platinum panels set with graduated rectangular sapphires and baguette diamonds linked to three rectangular clear crystal links.

Necklace of two strands of graduated sapphire beads, pearls, and diamond and enamel beads joined with platinum, diamond, and sapphire links to a single strand backchain of sapphire beads, by Cartier. Finger ring of platinum, a circular sapphire of approximately 16.88 carats, and two half-moon shaped diamonds. Earrings of platinum with circular sapphires of approximately 2.6 carats each, and marquise diamonds, by Cartier. Finger ring of platinum openwork with a cushion sapphire of approximately 19.2 carats and small round diamonds, by Tiffany & Co., New York. Bracelet of sapphire beads and platinum panels set with two cabochon sapphires and circular and baguette diamonds, by Cartier, circa 1930.

Pin of gold, sapphires and diamonds designed as a French straw hat with lace trim, circa 1880.

Pin of gold filigree and granulation with rectangular sapphire, diamonds and pearls, circa 1835.

Bracelet of gold and circular sapphires designed in Etruscan revival style, circa 1880.

Queen Elizabeth I of England both loved articles of personal adornment and feared superstitions. Her belief in the effects of special gemstones is noteworthy and representative of the age, and sapphires figured markedly in her life. A few examples will illustrate this. Elizabeth gave her suitor, the Earl of Essex, a sapphire ring as a token of affection, and with the pledge that if he ever needed her aid, he should send her the ring, and upon seeing it, she would do all in her power to protect and aid him. Therefore, years later when the Earl lay imprisoned and sentenced to death, he exercised his last effort to save himself and sent the ring to Elizabeth for forgiveness. Realizing that the people around him were bent on his destruction, he bribed an unknown boy to take the ring to his friendly cousin Lady Scrope who would convey it to the queen. By mistake, the boy delivered the ring to Lady Scrope's unfriendly sister who gave it to her husband, an Admiral and enemy of the Earl. The Admiral kept the ring hidden. When the Queen waited in vain for the ring from Essex, she assumed he was too proud to ask for her aid, so after once revoking his order for execution, she at last let it be carried out.

Was this the same ring that acted as a signal when Elizabeth died? Agness Strickland, in her book *Lives of the Queens of England*, 1851, relates that on March 24, 1602, (the same) Lady Scrope, as a pre-arranged signal of Elizabeth's death, dropped a sapphire ring to her brother Robert who waited beneath the royal bedchamber window at Richmond Castle, thereby circumventing the Royal Attendants who now were unfriendly to their Queen. Sir Robert caught the ring and sped away to Scotland to relate the news of Elizabeth's death to those who were making their own plans for the future of England. His strategy helped shape the history of their empire.

The many medicinal uses of sapphire over the ages make one aware of the lengths people went to find a cure for disease, prevention for harm, and antidotes for poisons. A few of these may sound strange today, but were conscientiously believed in their days of popularity. Powdered sapphire mixed with milk was used as a wash to heal sores and boils. Some reported dissolving sapphire dust in vinegar and lemon juice to make medicine. The alchemist Paracelsus of Basel in about 1520 invented a solution with gem powders called "The Great Secret." In pharmacies of old, sapphire was used as a charm against swellings, boils, ruptures, profuse perspiration, poisons, melancholy, and flatulence.

Sapphire solutions were used in all fluxes of the belly, dysentery, hemorrhoids, and other bleedings. They were used to cure ulcers and wounds, and to heal ruptured membranes. In the belief it would strengthen the heart, sapphire was placed near it on the body or hung as a pendant. Sapphire was considered a general remedy for fevers, and in specific the seventeenth century German

Necklace of gold ribbon bowknots with diamonds, and pendant graduated oval sapphires and emerald beads. Finger ring of gold with a sugarloaf cabochon yellow sapphire and circular diamonds. Finger ring of filigree platinum, octagonal sapphire, and pearshaped and circular diamonds, by Lambert Brothers. Finger ring of platinum with an oval yellow sapphire and two trilliant diamonds.

Finger ring of platinum with a circular sapphire and two circular diamonds.

Necklace of platinum with oval sapphires and circular diamonds designed in shield-and twin leaf-shaped panels. Pendant of silver and gold set with a pear-shaped sapphire of approximately 20.5 carats and graduated circular diamonds.

author J.B. Von Helmont wrote of the properties of sapphires to cure boils caused by the plague. Leonardus, in 1750, extended this view that, "the sapphire heals sores; and is found to discharge a carbuncle with a single touch." According to Francis Barrett early in the nineteenth century, if a blue sapphire was rubbed on a new tumor of the plague, and then removed, the jewel attracts the poison of the disease. In India and the Middle East, sapphire was believed to protect the wearer against the evil eye, bring peace of mind, and relief from headaches.

Star sapphire

The star sapphire, of a lovely cabochon style with three intersecting rays which move within the stone as the light source changes, is a valued charm for procuring the love of friends, for constancy and harmony. The intersecting bands have been called representations of faith, hope and charity. The ancients thought of them as love charms. In the Orient, star sapphires are regarded as good luck

bearers which ward off evil even after an owner parts with the stone. One believer of this omen was Sir Richard Burton, the explorer and translator of *Arabian Nights* who used a large star sapphire as a talisman. It brought him good horses and prompt service, and as a reward for good service, he allowed the bearers to see the wonderful stone, which they believed to then bring them the good luck.

Sapphires not of the gem grade are used in the works of watches as a hard, durable pivot upon which some of the wheels rotate.

There are many famous sapphires in the world, and quite a few large ones on public display to amaze and dazzle modern enthusiasts. The Star of India is a 563 carat star sapphire at the American Museum of Natural History in New York City. It is particularly free of flaws enabling the star effect to be quite apparent. The Midnight Star of 116.75 carats is a blue-violet stone of great beauty. In England, the St. Edward's Sapphire and the Stuart Sapphire are exciting gems. The oval Black Star of Queensland was found in 1948 in Australia. It weighed 1156 carats when found and 733 carats after cutting. It is owned by a gem firm in Los Angeles.

Earrings of white and yellow gold designed as orchid flowers with fancy yellow diamonds and circular and baguette colorless diamonds. Pin of white gold set with two pear shaped fancy-cut sapphires, circular fancy yellow diamonds, and round ruby. Finger ring of platinum set with a cushion pink sapphire of approximately 15.4 carats, marquise and baguette diamonds. Bracelet of yellow gold double snake chain and a panel of square sapphires of the fancy colors blue, pink, yellow and purple, and round diamonds, by Spaulding-Gorham, Inc., Chicago, Illinois and Providence, Rhode Island.

Double clip of platinum, white gold, graduated calibré sapphires, and circular and baguette diamonds designed as scrolled leaves.

Bar pin of platinum openwork, sugarloaf cabochon sapphires and circular diamonds. Bracelet of platinum tapered panels with square sapphires and graduated circular diamonds. Bracelet of platinum tapered panels with calibré sapphires and graduated circular diamonds in a belt and buckle design.

Wristwatch of platinum and white gold with octagonal white and black enamel face below a faceted sapphire crystal in a case and band set with calibre sapphires and circular diamonds, clock movement by Audemars Piguet, Geneva.

Necklace of graduated oval sapphires and round diamonds mounted in silver. Earrings of oval sapphires and circular diamonds mounted in white gold. Pair of pins of platinum and white gold, oval sapphires, and baguette and round diamonds designed as mirror image sprays of flowers. Scrolled pin of flexible platinum with oval sapphires and baguette diamonds.

Shell

The hard, calcareous outer covering of crustaceans, mollusks and other invertebrates is commonly called shell and is used in various forms in jewelry. In the Neolithic age, about 5000 B.C., cowrie shell from the Indian Ocean was used in necklaces, examples of which are on public view in the British Museum and other collections of ancient jewelry. In dynastic Egypt, cowrie shell was used as an amulet against sterility, and much later in africa and southern Asia as a form of money. One of the most frequent uses is carvings known as cameos which use the shells of mollusks from the western Indian Ocean and waters off the coast of Madagascar. More than ten varieties of mollusk shells are used to make cameos from the light and contrasting dark layers. Cameo subjects usually include portrait busts, architectural ruins, and Classical and mythological figures.

Since about 1500 A.D., cameos have been made in France and Italy as brooches, earrings, finger rings and pendants. Early in the nineteenth century, cameos became popular in England with the revival of the Classical style. This popularity was revived again in the mid-nineteenth century and has continued to the present. The leading cameo carving centers are in Florence and Naples and on Sicily.

Symbolically, the cockleshell, or scallop shell, is used to signify pilgrimage. Specifically, the scallop shell is an emblem for the Christian Patron Saint of Spain, Saint James the Great whose common name became Santiago. On a pilgrimage to Compostella, Spain, Saint James established the Christian religion there, yet he was beheaded when he returned to Judea. He is portrayed in Italy with a pilgrim's staff and a scallop shell or gourd, symbolic of his time in Spain.

The shell of the pearl oyster is lined with nacre, from which the material called mother of pearl is cut. Mother of pearl ornaments many decorative articles including furniture, boxes and jewelry in such diverse regions of the world as India, Asia and among the American Indians.

Wampum is highly polished black (dark purple) or white beads made from quahog shell and strung on thongs by the Indians of the northeastern United States. Wampum was formerly used to decorate woven belts and sashes, bracelets, necklaces and as currency between North Americans Indians and early settlers.

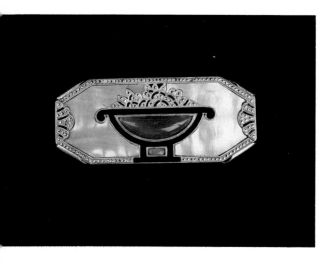

Pin of sterling silver, mother of pearl, chrisophrase, marcasite and enamel, circa 1925.

Pin of shell carved to depict Roman soldiers in confrontation set in a gold frame, circa 1820.

Pin of shell carved to depict Pan with a flute and children dancing set in a gold frame with six chrysolites, circa 1820.

Five pins of gold and shell carved as cameos including portrait heads and dancing girls in Classical style, Italian, nineteenth century.

Necklace of gold and fluted sea shells signed F. B. & R. and cased by John Brogden, English, circa 1880. Pendant/pin of cushion diamonds designed as a ribbon bow and heart, circa 1890. Pin/hair ornament of graduated diamonds set in a crescent, circa 1890. Pin of cushion diamonds designed as a twelve-pointed star, circa 1890.

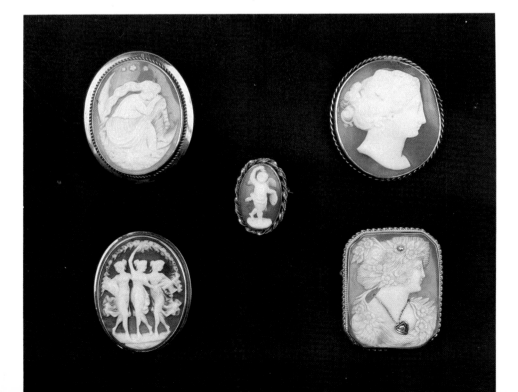

Necklace, two bracelets, pendant and
earrings of gold with gold-backed pink
topaz, chrysolite, and turquoise by Garrard
& Co. Ltd, London, circa 1820.

Topaz

*The topaz is a jewel rare and therefore
must be bought full dear;
Made up of hues, golden and light
here see the man in study bent,
a life in contemplation spent.*

Marbodus

Once, all yellow stones were carelessly called topaz, but gradually, as the differences in structure, refraction, weight and composition were identified, a more precise nomenclature has developed. True topaz is a hard gem of many colors composed of the orthorhombic fluosilicate of aluminum with double refraction properties. The many color variations have no specific names to identify them so the color tone and "topaz" are linked when speaking about this fascinating gem.

Yellow topaz is most frequently found in natural deposits and topaz the color of sherry wine, a rich golden brown with red overtones, called sherry topaz is the most valuable. Pink topaz can vary in color from light red to violet-red, and green topaz is light green with a yellow cast. Blue topaz is an alluring and clear shade of light to medium blue. Other than the sherry tone, brown topaz can be a dark red-orange. True red topaz is a warm shade and white topaz is colorless, sometimes cut to resemble diamond in ages past. A gentle heating process called "pinking" has commonly been applied to sherry topaz to create pink topaz in the laboratory. While this process is not strictly natural, neither is it counterfeit. Enhancement of color is a well established practice in the gem trade.

Originally found on the island Topazios in the Red Sea, today topaz is gathered from all over the world. From Brazil have come some of the most intense blue topazes at sites near the origins for aquamarine and other gem stones. Brazil is also a source for yellow, dark sherry, pink and pale green topaz. Light colored topaz of several shades has been found in Sri Lanka and the Mogok area of Burma when excavators have searched for the more valuable ruby and sapphire. Deposits are also known in the Ural mountains of Russia, Siberia, Thailand, India, Japan, Australia, Africa, Scotland and Ireland. In the United States, topaz has been discovered in Pala and Riverside, California, as well as Colorado, Utah and New Hampshire.

The birthstone most widely recognized for November is topaz, with citrine and topaz-quartz as the alternate choices. An old and anonymous rhyme captures the spirit of this gem.

Who first comes to this world below
With drear November's fog and snow
Should prize the topaz's amber hue
Emblem of friends and lovers true.

Red topaz is the stone for the zodiac sign of Scorpio, yet people whose birthday falls under the influence of Taurus or Scorpio should not wear yellow topaz. The yellow variety is under the influence of the sun who rules the House of the Lion. The power to guard against scalds, as will be brought out below, and the ability to quench boiling water which are ascribed to topaz are symbolic of its affinity to the fiery Mars, the planet of power in the watery Scorpio.

Topaz has been so popular through the ages, that many powers have become associated with it. Greeks of the ancient civilization considered yellow topaz a guardian against all calamity because they associated this color with the sun— itself the giver of life. Strung with the hair of an ass and worn on the left arm, topaz quickly put wicked spirits to flight. The Romans wore topaz as a preservative from bad air and to protect the wearer from danger in travel, injuries from burns and scalds, and complaints of the chest and bowels. Emperor Hadrian in the first century, ruled a peaceful Roman Empire with an antique ring set with a topaz as a talisman on which was engraved: *Natura Deficit Fortuna*

Pin of openwork silver and gold with rectangular and circular pink topaz and graduated cushion and circular diamonds, English, circa 1830.

Pin and pendant earrings with two colors of gold wire and openwork set with oval, rectangular and pear-shaped Brazilian topaz, English, circa 1830.

Pendant of gold openwork, Brazilian topaz, diamonds, pearl and enamel, circa 1860.

Mutator Deus Omnia Cervit. Later, Albertus Magnus recommended topaz as a cure for gout and Camillus Leonardus suggested topaz as a charm against hemorrhages, lunacy and sudden death and asthma.

In the Middle Ages, topaz was credited variously with preserving one from sensuality, calming anger and frenzy, strengthening the intellect, brightening wit, giving joy, and driving away broodings and apprehensions. A cure for eye diseases was found in rubbing the eyes with a topaz which had been marinated in wine for three days and nights. Old masters say it guarded against drowning, and Rabbi Benoni called topaz an emblem of strength. According to Charubel, topaz gives hope to the hopeless and strengthens the soul against evil people.

The thirteenth century Hindu physician Naharari, wrote that topaz tastes sour and is cold, yet it is a good appetizer. Any man who wears topaz, he writes, is assured of long life, beauty and intelligence.

All the abilities of topaz are believed to increase and decrease according to the phases of the moon, with stronger powers near the full moon.

Powdered topaz mixed in wine has long been regarded as a cure for asthma, insomnia, burns and hemorrhage.

As an amulet, topaz is said to drive away sadness, strengthen the intellect, and bestow courage. Mounted in gold and hung from the neck or bound on the left arm, topaz would dispel enchantment.

Topaz is included in the Nan-Ratan, a sacred nine-stone jewel in Burmese dress. In India, topaz is worn as a talisman for good health, caution, sagacity and the prevention of sudden death. In many areas topaz is believed to become colorless when it is in contact with poison.

Authors lost by tradition have credited topaz with:
fruitfulness
faithfulness
cheerfulness
calming passions
preventing bad dreams
correcting sexual disorders
banishing night terrors
protection during epidemics
soothing wild passions
giving a glimpse of the beyond
banishing the fear of death
securing a painless passing from this life into the next
giving strength to the intellect
enabling the wearer to receive impressions from astral sources

The Morganthau Topaz is a famous, deep blue stone from Brazil that weighs 1463 carats and is on display at the American Museum of Natural History in New York. Other exotic stones there include two pale blue examples of 308 and 120 carats. Another deep blue topaz of 258 carats from Brazil, a 241 carat pale orange-brown stone from Burma, a seventy carat red topaz and a crystal of nearly six hundred pounds with yellow and pink tones. In the collection at the British Museum are the 614 carat step-cut blue topaz from Brazil, a thirteen hundred carat clear stone, and a 137 pound clear gem from Norway.

Opposite page:

Necklace and earrings of gold cannetille, filigree and granulation, emerald and diamond, circa 1830. Pin of gold cannetille, oval and pear-shaped pink topaz and diamond, circa 1830. Necklace of gold and graduated oval pink topaz, circa 1830.

Five pins designed as dirks with silver, smoky topaz, crystal, amethyst, agate, bloodstone, granite, carnelian, and foil-backed paste, Scottish, early nineteenth century.

Pin of gold and topaz designed in the Etruscan revival style, circa 1830.

Pin of gold and topaz, Scottish, circa 1850.

Tourmaline

Color variety is a particular feature of tourmaline, which is a chemically complex silicate of boron and aluminum. From solid colored crystals or crystals with combinations of tones come the cut and polished gems that have delighted mankind for centuries. When seen from different angles, tourmaline stones can look lighter or darker, so that the position of the stone in a mounting is an important factor in jewelry. Fibrous inclusions are common in tourmaline, and certain of them create the cat's-eye effect cherished by many. The gem cutter can sometimes bring out the cat's-eye feature by positioning the axis of the gem to advantage. Tourmaline is a medium hard stone, not particularly suited for ring mountings unless it is well protected in the setting.

Red tourmaline is the most valuable variety, followed by green, pink and green combination known as watermelon tourmaline, pink, and then the other colors which are quite rare including blue, colorless, yellow, orange, brown and black. The shades of each of these tones can range from light to dark, and the variations within each crystal can be very interesting. As the supply of tourmaline on the world market is plentiful, the cost for most stones is not great and closely matching stones in size and color usually can be found.

Tourmaline has been found in mines with other precious stones since the geological conditions necessary for its formation are similar. Particularly fine and large tourmalines have come from the Minas Geraes area of Brazil, especially blue, pink and green varieties. From Brazil they have been exported to Europe since the seventeenth century, when they were erroneously called Brazilian emeralds. Fine stones have also been found in Sri Lanka, Burma, the Ural Mountains of Russia, Siberia, India, Madagascar, the Island of Elba, and in the United States at locations in California, Connecticut and Maine.

All colors of tourmaline are associated with the sign for Gemini in the Zodiac, and therefore tourmaline is the primary birthstone for the month of October, alternating with opal.

Tourmaline carvings have been cherished in China since ancient times. In the early eighteenth century, as the tradition goes, children in Amsterdam playing with tourmalines their fathers had brought home from sea voyages found that stones, heated in the sun, magnetically attracted bits of straw and dust. This phenomenon has since been borne out through scientific investigation. Eighteenth century scholars called it the "electric stone", and determined that its power of repulsion was greater than its power of attraction. The electrical powers were apparently known by the ancients, because the Roman first century author Pliny described tourmaline as having the power to disperse fears and melancholic passions, but says it was worn to procure inspiration, attract favors and secure friends. Tourmaline has come to be regarded as the symbol of wisdom, strength of mind, eloquence and learning. As possessing the power of knowledge, it is the favored stone for authors, poets, teachers and editors.

Finger ring of gold with a cushion tourmaline of approximately 4.2 carats and diamonds.

Pendant/pin of white and yellow gold, pear-shaped pink tourmaline, and graduated diamonds designed as concentric, free-swinging loops and ribbon bow, English, circa 1900.

Pin of gold with pear and marquise tourmalines, pear-shaped garnets, and circular diamonds designed as a flowerhead. Necklace of gold snake link chain and twenty-five pink and green cabochon tourmalines.

Turquoise

The heavenly blue-green color associated with turquoise is directly relative to the chemical composition of this hydrous copper aluminum phosphate. Its water and copper content render the blue tone, and iron, as an impurity nearly always present in some measure, governs the intensity of green. Aluminum and phosphorous are the primary ingredients. The various shades of this opaque stone range from an intense, medium blue considered the most valuable, to pale blue and greenish, with yellowish green the least desirable. Because turquoise is a semi-porous stone, it absorbs oil and external chemicals such as perspiration which cause its color to alter. Some deeply colored stones become pale when exposed to too much direct sunlight. These can sometimes be temporarily restored to close to their original color by immersing the stone in damp earth or ammonia.

Unlike so many other gems, turquoise does not form as a crystal, but is found naturally as veins and nodules in the mother rock. Stones marked with a fishnet or more pervasive matrix of mother rock are considered less valuable than clear stones, yet markings are quite common in turquoise. The dark imperfections on the face of some old stones were masked with engraving and gold in the forms of inscriptions and portraits or designs. The name turquoise dates only from the thirteenth century in Europe and comes from a French word meaning "Turkish," probably because some of these stones reached Europe through Turkey from mines in northern Persia.

Because it is a soft stone, turquoise can be easily ground. It should be kept cool, for excessive heat will make turquoise explode. It can deteriorate when exposed to water and air, and for reasons explained above, it should be kept away from acids. Its opacity and waxy surface make it suitable for cabochon cuts and for beads. It is usually formed with a smooth surface, not faceted, and sometimes is tumbled for polishing.

Turquoise is generally found near the surface of the earth in arid regions of the world. The oldest mines are on the Sinai Peninsula at a valley called Wadi Maghara which has been a source since ancient times. Beads from here have been found in graves dating from 5500 B.C. Long forgotten over time, these mines were rediscovered in 1845 by an Englishman who worked them between 1854 and 1866 with good production. In the early part of the twentieth century they were worked again by a Frenchman, but his success was minimal. They have since apparently been exhausted. Less important, but current sources are in Tibet, China, Australia, Mexico, Peru, Chile, Turkestan, Russia and Afghanistan. Today, most turquoise is found in the United States in Arizona, Nevada, northern New Mexico, Colorado, southwest Texas and southern California. An old pendant of wood with turquoise decoration was found in an ancient site in Death Canyon, Arizona.

The current popular birthstone for December is turquoise, with the alternate being zircon. Since turquoise is the favored stone of Sagittarius in the zodiac, it governs the calendar between November 22 and December 21. It also governs the hip area of humans ruled by Sagittarius. As such, it was a practice among ancient peoples to make a paste with powdered turquoise and apply it in a flat binding to an afflicted hip while whole turquoise was bound above and below the hip. Improvement in the physical condition was credited to this practice.

Many beliefs about turquoise have survived in legends and superstitions in such diverse civilizations as the ancient Egyptians, Persians, Aztecs, Incas, southwest American Indians and Tibetans. Many Orientals carry turquoise, and other blue stones, to ward off the evil Eye. Some Orientals also connect turquoise with weather changes.

In Germany, turquoise is considered a love token whose color will remain constant as long as the affections last. An Eastern proverb relates that a turquoise given by the hand of love carries good fortune and happiness. In the Middle

Bracelet of openwork gilt metal and turquoise, English, circa 1840.

Choker necklace of gold, eight round turquoise cabochons, fluted chalcedony, circular diamonds and enamel probably designed and made by Madame Suzanne Belperron, Paris, circa 1935.

Ages, young girls wore turquoise as a religious jewel for the protection of their virtue.

Old Arabian writers record a ceremony in which turquoise was held in the right hand while wishes of greater wealth were spoken to the stone and the speaker gazed steadily at the turquoise. The wishes are said to have come true.

Hindu mystics in India believed it was lucky to have a turquoise on hand during a new moon for, by gazing at the moon and then at a turquoise, one could achieve great wealth.

Originally, turquoise may have been used as a horse amulet to protect the animal against illness. By the Middle Ages, Camillus Leonardus has written that there was: "an opinion that it is useful to horsemen; and that so long as the rider has it with him, his horse will never tire him, and will preserve him unhurt from any accident. It is further said to defend him that carries it from outward and evil casualties." The writer Van Helmont recorded in 1620 that persons who wear a turquoise next to the skin may sustain a fall without injury because the turquoise absorbs the force of the fall and cracks. For these reasons, even today, turquoise is believed to protect hikers, mountain climbers, and horsemen from falls.

In the seventeenth century in Europe, turquoise suspended by a thread within a glass vessel was said to tell the hour by the number of strikes it made against the sides of the glass.

In the American southwest, turquoise has been used as a medium of exchange among the Indians as well as for personal and domestic adornment. Its color was believed to embody the sea and blue sky. The possession of turquoise was mandatory for a medicine man, for without it he would not receive proper recognition. The tribes believed that after a rain storm, a man could go to the end of the rainbow, dig in the wet earth, and find turquoise. Pueblo and Apache Indians of America employ turquoise as a rainstone which is always found concealed at the foot of the rainbow. They use turquoise on bows and firearms as a charm for good aim. Its power was thought to bring rewards to their warriors, animals to the hunters, and happiness to all. They too believe in the power of turquoise to protect man from a falling horse because it made the horse sure footed.

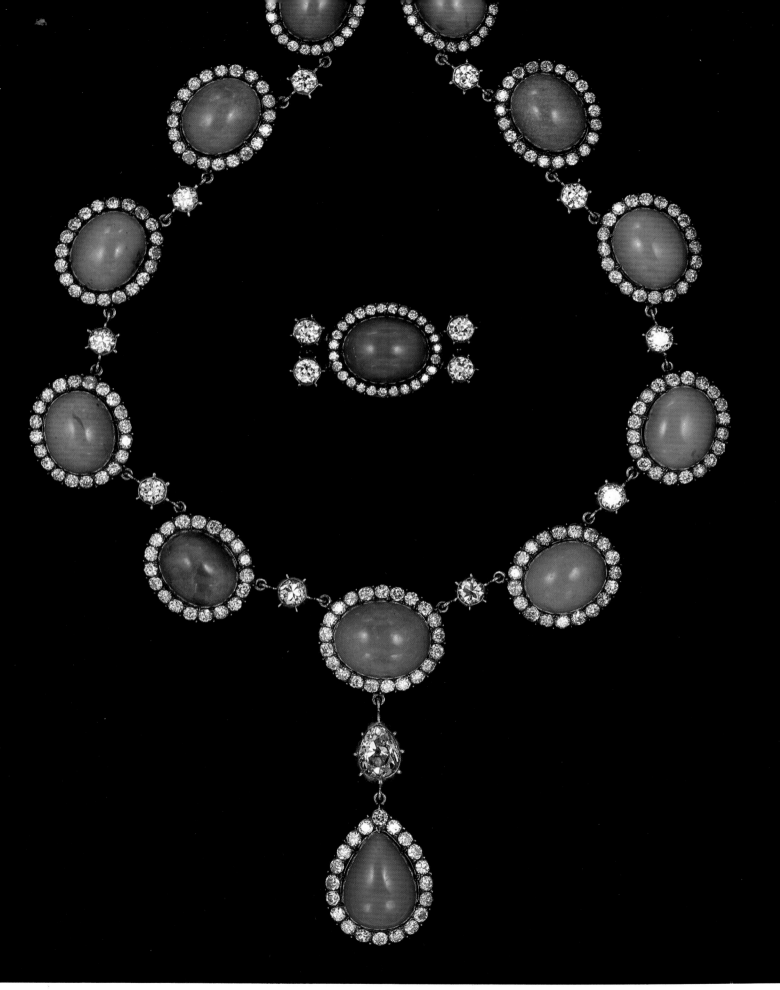

Necklace and pin of oval and pear-shaped
turquoise and circular and pear-shaped
diamond, circa 1840.

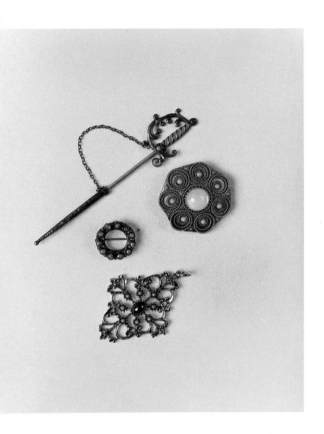

Pin of sterling silver and turquoise in the form of a sword and scabbard. Pin of silver rope design set with turquoise and moonstone. Circle pin of silver set with turquoise. Pendant of silver openwork and turquoise, by Avon.

In many societies turquoise is thought to have the power to draw to itself the evil that threatens its wearer. Fenton, writing *Secret Wonders of Nature* in 1569, described, "the turkeys [turquoise] doth move when there is any peril prepared to him that weareth it." Some traditions claim turquoise warns of poison by becoming moist and changing color. Boetius DeBoot, writing in the seventeenth century, reported that it grew paler as the wearer sickened, and lost its color altogether when he died, but regained its color when it became the possession of another, healthier person.

> Observe him, as his watch observes his clock,
>   And true as Turquoise in the dear lord's ring,
>   Look well, or ill with him.
> Ben Johnson

As a compassionate Turquoise, that doth tell
By looking pale, the wearer is not well.
John Donne

The Arabs believe turquoise as an amulet protects the wearer from poison, bites of reptiles, diseases of eyes, and warns of approaching death by changing color. Turquoise was a medicine for lung diseases, but was not to be taken internally. It was recommended for diseases of the throat and heart, as phosphoric acid is today in homeopathy (turquoise contains a large amount of phosphoric acid). In the Sudan, water in which turquoise has been dipped or washed is used as a curative for people suffering from the retention of urine. Elsewhere it is credited with relieving and preventing headaches.

Turquoise's power to strengthen the eyes was recorded by DeBoot in 1636, and is common knowledge in the German states. In modern Egypt, turquoise engraved with the name of Allah is applied to the eye as a remedy for cataracts and other ophthalmic troubles.

In 1900, four bracelets of turquoise and gold over five thousand years old were found on the arm of the mummy of Egyptian Queen Zer during excavations. The bracelets may be the oldest pieces of wrought jewelry known in the world.

The Spanish Crown Jewels include turquoise brought from New Mexico over two hundred years ago.

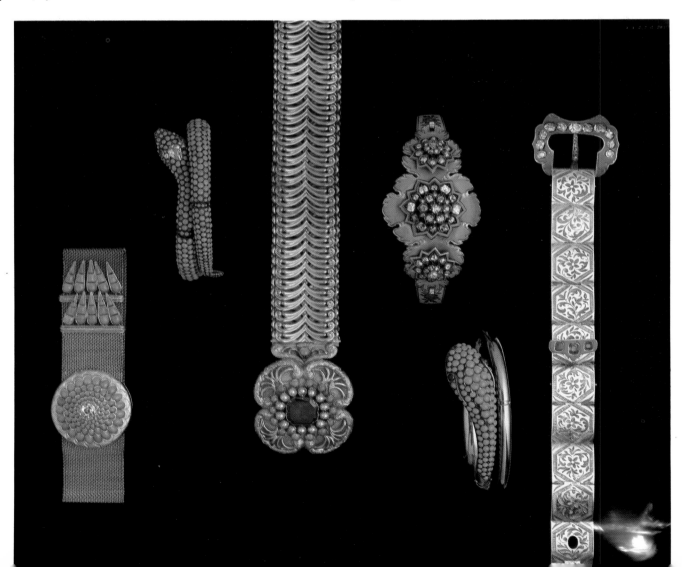

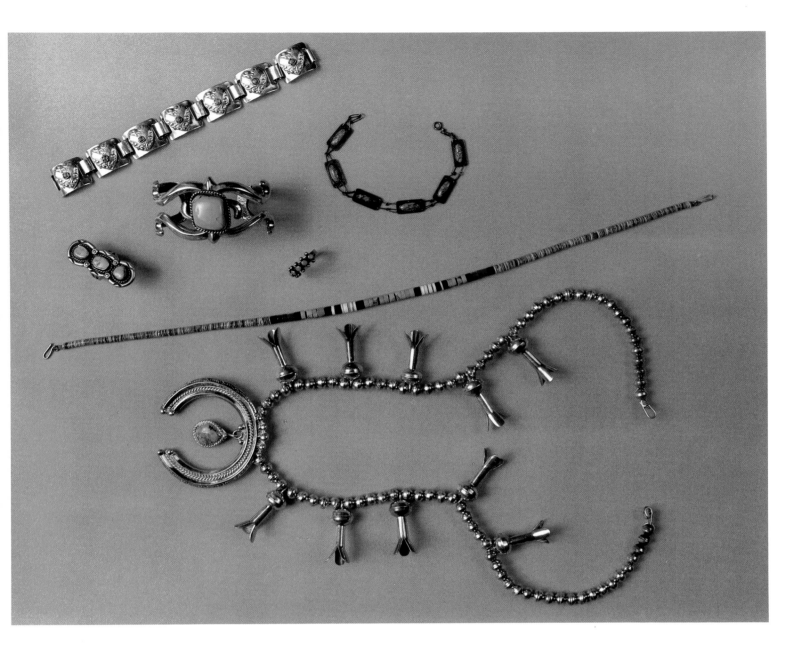

Link bracelet of silver with turquoise, Mexican, circa 1950. Link bracelet of six turquoise stones, Southwest American Indian, circa 1950. Bracelet of silver with rectangular turquoise, Navajo Indian. Finger ring of silver and three turquoise stones, Navajo Indian. Finger ring of silver with five small turquoise stones, Navajo Indian, circa 1970. Necklace of rolled turquoise and shell heishi beads, Santo Domingo Pueblo. Necklace of silver beads and squash blossoms, the central Naja set with turquoise, Navajo Indian, circa 1950.

Opposite page:
Bracelet of gold mesh, a circular clasp set with graduated turquoise and a circular diamond, and two rows of drops set with graduated turquoise, circa 1865. Bracelet of gold pavé set with turquoise, pear-shaped and circular diamonds, and rubies, designed as a serpent, circa 1845. Bracelet of gold links and a clasp set with turquoise, pearl and a cushion garnet, circa 1825.
Bracelet of gold, blue enamel and diamond, designed as a floral group with detachable clusters, circa 1855. Bracelet of gold, turquoise, and carbuncle designed as a serpent, circa 1845. Link bracelet of engraved gold, enamel, ruby, and diamond designed as a belt and buckle.

Necklace and ear pendants of platinum, graduated pear-shaped turquoise and circular diamonds by Van Cleef and Arpels.

Zircon

Zircon is a gem commonly found in igneous rocks such as granite and metamorphic formations such as crystalline limestone and gneiss. It is insoluble and very tough allowing the stone around it to weather and break apart without affecting the zircon crystal inside. Zircon occurs naturally in both a blue and colorless state, but very often the stone is heat-treated to make it more colorful and therefore more attractive to the consumer. Heat-treated zircons may range in color from a greenish blue to a orangy red. Both hyacinth and jacinth are names used to describe zircons of a particular color, but this practice is subsiding. Sri Lanka is one of the oldest sources of zircon in the world and the mining techniques there remain very primitive. It is also found in quantity in Cambodia, Burma, France, Australia and the United States. Zircon is, along with turquoise, one of the birthstones of December and is under the zodiacal Virgo. It is recommended that those under the sign of either Taurus or Scorpio not wear the stone.

The zircon, with its variety of names, has many talismanic and medicinal powers associated with it. In India, it was worn as an antidote against poison, and to attract riches, honor and wisdom to the owner. It was also thought to be able to drive away evil spirits.

During the Middle Ages, the zircon was held to make the wearer welcome wherever he went and to stimulate the appetite and aid in digestion. The people of the time also used the zircon as a talisman against fever, dropsy and jaundice. Jacinth was also thought to protect the wearer from lightening and to have the power to induce sleep in the wearer.

In the twelfth century, St. Hildegard, Abbess of Bingen described the ceremony to rid oneself of evil spirits using a jacinth, a reddish-brown zircon: "If any one is bewitched by phantoms or by magical spells, so that he has lost his wits, take a hot loaf of pure wheaten bread and cut the upper crust in the form of a cross,—not, however cutting it quite through,—and then pass the stone along the cutting, reciting these words: "May God, who cast away all precious stones from the devil . . . cast away from thee, N., all phantoms and all magic spells, and free thee from the pain of this madness". Folowing the incantation, the affected was to eat the bread, and find himself free of evil spirits.

Camillus Leonardus, in 1750, wrote that the jacinth had the power to strengthen weak hearts, allay paranoia, prevent jealousy, protect travelers and prevent plague and pestilence. The jacinth, it was said, would turn pale and dull if anyone in the vicinity of the wearer had contracted the plague giving fair warning for escape.

In the early nineteenth century, Barrett, in *Natural Magic* wrote: "The jacinth possesses virtues from the sun against poisons, pestilences, and pestiferous vapors; likewise it renders the bearer pleasant, and acceptable; conduces also to gain money; being simply held in the mouth it wonderfully cheers the heart, and strengthens the mind."

In the American Museum of Natural History in New York City lies the largest zircon known which is a greenish blue specimen weighing more than 208 carats. The museum also contains several other zircons of one hundred carats or more.

Bracelet of gold, zircon and enamel designed in repeating links by C. and A. Giuliano, London, circa 1895.

Corsage ornament pin of diamonds designed as a flower with the head mounted *en tremblant,* circa 1820. Necklace of gold and garnets designed as a floral garland with pendant, circa 1820. Pin of gold, diamonds and rubies sym-metrically designed, circa 1880. Pin of diamonds with central oval stone, circa 1820. Finger ring of diamonds designed as a floral cluster, circa 1820. Finger ring of diamonds with large central stone, circa 1820.

Opposite page:
Pendant and earrings of gold and enamel, circa 1870; Pin and earrings of gold and Roman mosaic in Egyptian style, Italian, circa 1860; Pendant/pin of gold and crystal intaglio depicting a parrot, circa 1870.

The Power of Design

Anchors & Ships

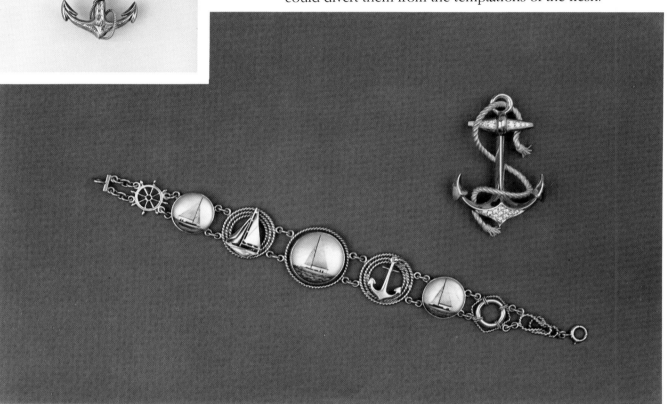

In Christianity, the anchor is the symbol of hope and steadfastness stemming from a verse of the Epistle to the Hebrews which says, "Which hope we have as an anchor to the soul, both sure and steadfast," referring to the goodness of God's guidance. The symbol of an anchor was often carved by Christians on gems. The anchor is associated with St. Clement who was cast into the sea bound to an anchor, and to St. Nicholas, the patron saint of seamen.

The ship has long been a symbol of the church, and its wearers believed that it could divert them from the temptations of the flesh.

Pin of sterling silver and agate in the form of an anchor, mid-nineteenth century.

Pin of silver and marcasite designed as a seventeenth century sailing ship, circa 1930. A pin of yellow gold and diamonds designed as an anchor, circa 1950. Bracelet of gold and intaglio carved round crystal with sailing motifs, circa 1950.

Angels

Angels are the messengers of God and symbolize several different virtues depending on their position in the three-tiered hierarchy of the angelic host. The Seraphim appear red, sometimes holding a burning candle, and are God's representatives of divine love. The Cherubim, in gold or blue garb and sometimes holding books, represent divine wisdom. Thrones wear the robes of judges and are the symbol of divine justice. These three angels, the Seraphim, Cherubim and Thrones of the first hierarchy, are believed to attain their glory directly from God, and pass it in turn upon the angels of the second hierarchy: Dominations, Virtues and Powers. The angels of the third hierarchy are Princedoms, Archangels and Angels.

Of the multitude of angels and archangels alluded to in the Bible, only three are given personal traits: St. Michael, St. Gabriel and St. Raphael. These three archangels plus one other, Uriel, are believed to uphold God's throne and represent beauty and divine fortitude.

Finger ring of gold, enamel, and foil-backed red paste in the Renaissance-revival style, mid-nineteenth century.

Pendant of enamel, diamond, ruby and emerald designed as an angel with lyre.

Pendant of enamel and diamonds depicting an angel and wings, mid-nineteenth century.

Pin of gold with pearls and grisaille enameled panel depicting an angel and Diana dressing, French, mid-nineteenth century.

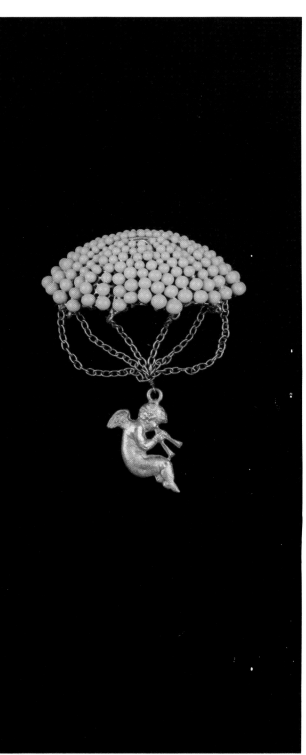

Pin of gold and turquoise depicting an angel and parachute, French.

Locket of sterling silver with relief design of an angel and woman "Love's Dream", by Unger Bros., Newark, New Jersey, circa 1900.

Necklace of gold and enamel depicting
two angels, French, circa 1840.

Bracelet of gold and enamel depicting a
Muse and two angels, circa 1870.

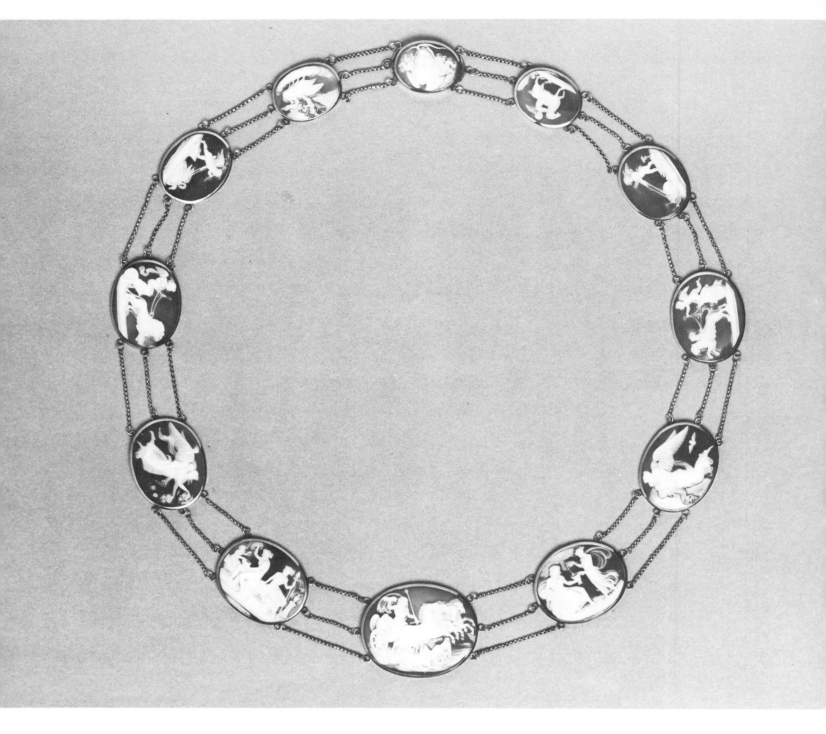

Necklace of gold chain and shell cameos
depicting angels and mythical figures,
English, circa 1820.

Earrings of gold and enamel depicting a
running horse, French, circa 1830.

Animals

Horse

The horse was symbolic of the sun in ancient mythology but during the Renaissance became symbolic of lust stemming from the Bible verse, "They were fed as horses in the morning: every one neighed after his neighbor's wife" (Jer. 5:8).

Pin of gold, sapphires and diamonds designed as a horseshoe. Locket of gold and enamel with engraving, Russian. Pin of gold depicting a horseshoe and bucket. Locket of gold and diamonds designed as a horseshoe. Pin of gold, ruby and diamond designed as a crop. Stick pin of gold and gems depicting a horseshoe. Stick pin of gold and a reverse intaglio crystal of a horse's head.

Watch fob of platinum and gold, sapphire and diamond depicting a horseshoe and horse's head, by Cartier, circa 1910.

Two pins of gold with reverse intaglio crystals of hunting scenes, circa 1920.

Fox

The fox is most commonly a symbol of cunning, but has also symbolized the devil.

Dog

The dog is a common symbol of fidelity and watchfulness but is also a symbol of faithfulness in marriage. When appearing, in Christian art, with a torch in its mouth it is a symbol of St. Dominic. In China, the dog, as well as being part of the diet, is an omen of good fortune and prosperity.

Cat

The *gatta della Madonna* or the cat of Madonna was believed to have given birth to a litter in the same stable in which Christ was born. She is usually pictured with the markings of a cross on her back. The cat also symbolizes laziness and lust at the suggestion of its habits.

Leopard

In China, the leopard is a symbol of bravery and skill in the martial arts.

Pig

Pigs are considered by many to be a good luck charm!

Pin of pavé diamonds and ruby depicting a running fox.

Pin of gold depicting a duck and retriever.

Pin of gold with a reverse intaglio crystal of a brown and white dog, backed with mother of pearl.

Pin of ivory carved as a running hound.

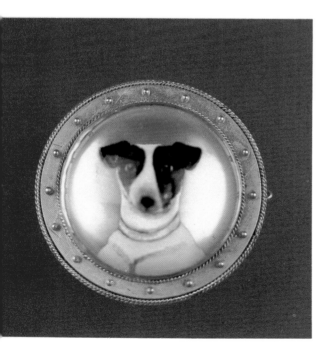

Three pair of gentlemen's cuff-links of gold, one with reverse intaglio crystals of four different game birds, circa 1890; one with enamel paintings of four Safari scenes, circa 1920; and one with enamel paintings of four different breeds of dogs, circa 1930.

Locket of gold and diamond depicting a panther, American, circa 1915.

Stick pin of gold and moonstone designed as a four-talon foot. Four stick pins of gold with reverse intaglio crystals depicting a horse and jockey, a duck, a bird's head with pearls, and a cat.

Pin of gold with a reverse intaglio crystal of a spaniel.

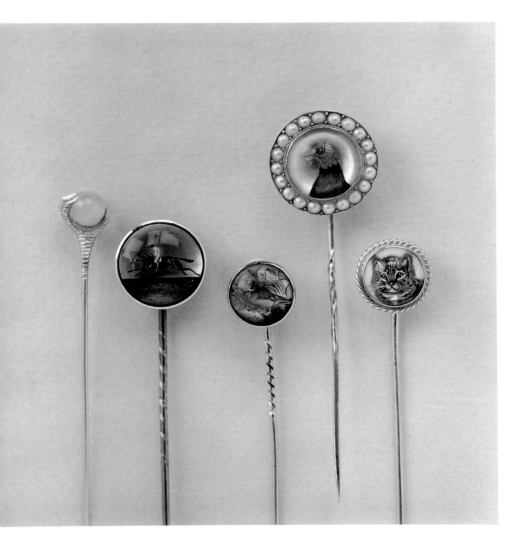

Lion

Strength, splendor and courage are the symbolic attributes of the lion. One legend associates the lion with the Resurrection as it was believed that lions were born dead and did not come to life until three days later when they were breathed upon by their father. Hence, the lion has come to symbolize Christ. The lion is also a symbol of watchfulness as it was believed at one point that the lion slept with its eyes open. The lion was also symbolical of the devil. In Buddhism, the lion came to symbolize a defender of the law and a guardian of sacred buildings. Statues of lions are often seen today guarding the entrances to buildings.

Bracelet of gold, coral, enamel, emerald and diamonds depicting lions' heads, by David Webb from his "enamel jungle" group, circa 1965.

Bracelet of gold, diamonds and rubies depicting three lions' heads and four oval panels, English, circa 1875.

Locket of gold and ruby depicting a lion's head, circa 1900.

Locket of gold, garnet and diamond depicting a lion's head, English, circa 1875.

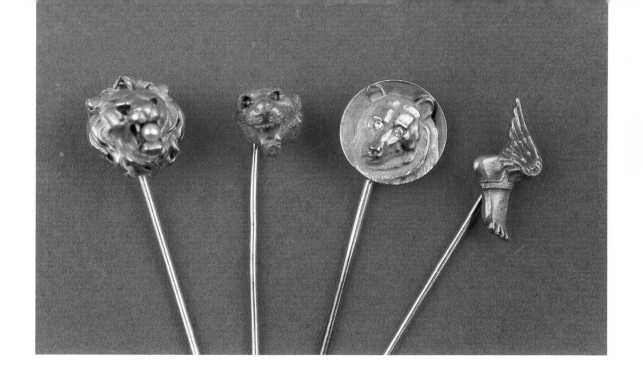

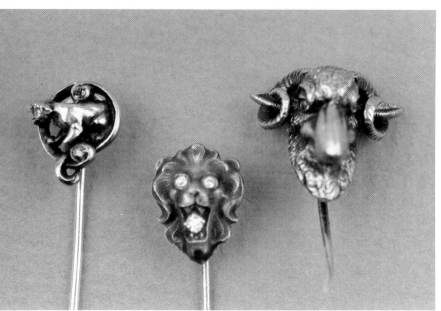

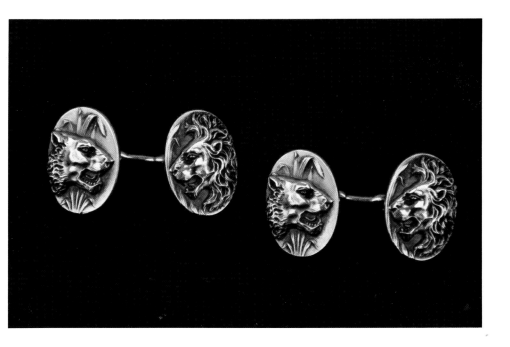

Four stick pins of gold depicting three lions' heads, one with a pearl and one with diamond eyes, and Mercury's winged foot.

Three stick pins of gold depicting a mountain lion, a lion's head, and a ram's head.

Cuff links of gold depicting a lion and a lioness, American, circa 1900.

Pin of gold with relief ram's head by Edwin W. Streeter, London, circa 1880.

Birds

Blackbird

The blackbird was symbolic of the darkness of sin and temptations of the flesh.

Crane

The crane is a Christian symbol of vigilance, loyalty and good life. It is associated with all the good virtues of leading a monastic life. One legend tells how cranes gathered together at night, and that certain cranes were required to stand watch for protection. To avoid falling asleep, each guard held a stone in his raised foot. If the guard fell asleep, the stone would drop and the crane would wake up.

Dove

The dove is a common symbol of purity and peace, an idea which has its origins in the biblical story of Noah. Noah sent a dove out from the ark, and the dove returned bearing an olive branch indicating that the waters had receded and the flood was over. In the days of Moses, the dove was offered as a symbol of purification upon the birth of a child. The dove is also a symbol of the Holy Ghost as a verse in the Bible recalls a vision, "And John bare record, saying, I saw the Spirit descending from heaven like a dove, and it abode upon him" (John I:32). The dove was a symbol of innocence to the ancient Egyptians, and a symbol of long life to the Chinese who believed the dove to be very stupid but endowed with the virtues of faithfulness and fairness.

Six pins of silver set with marcasite and designed as a starfish, two elephants, a deer, and two parrots with enamel details.

Four stick pins of gold depicting a pheasant set with diamonds, wings set with sapphires and diamonds, a dragon, and a fish with enamel.

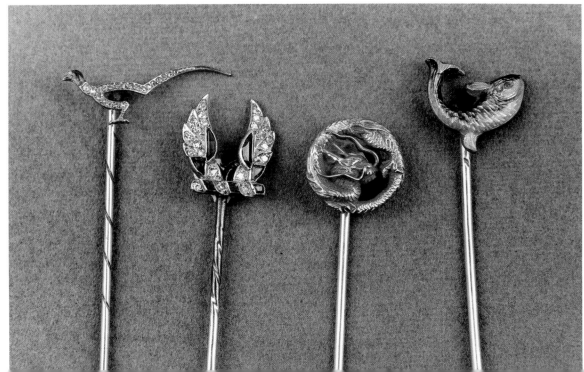

Pin of gold and micro-mosaic depicting a dove and radiant light, Italian, mid-nineteenth century.

Pendant of gold and micro-mosaic depicting a dove and flowers, and on the reverse PAX, Italian, mid-nineteenth century. Earrings of gold in the shape of Egyptian amphora and micro-mosaic depicting a dove and flowers, Italian, mid-nineteenth century.

Pin of gold and micro-mosaic in Etruscan revival style depicting doves and ram's heads, by Alessandro Castellani, Naples, mid-nineteenth century.

Bracelet of platinum, diamonds, rubies, emeralds, sapphires and onyx by Van Cleef and Arpels, Paris, #25064, circa 1925. The design was inspired by Egyptian jewelry and includes symbolic hieroglyphics, winged scarabs, owls, falcons and vases.

Pendant of gold depicting a heron with diamond, American, circa 1900.

Eagle

The eagle is also a symbol of the Resurrection stemming from the belief that it had the ability to renew its plumage and youth simply by flying near the sun and then plunging into the water. The eagle is also a symbol of generosity from the notion that it always left half of its prey to other birds no matter how hungry it was. The eagle, as a bird of prey, suggested to some that it symbolizes the devil as the devil preys upon people.

Griffin

The griffin, though an animal of fiction, is a powerful symbol of Christianity with a dual significance. While representing in its entirety, the Saviour, its components, the wings of an eagle and body of a lion, suggest the devil and the oppressors of Christ.

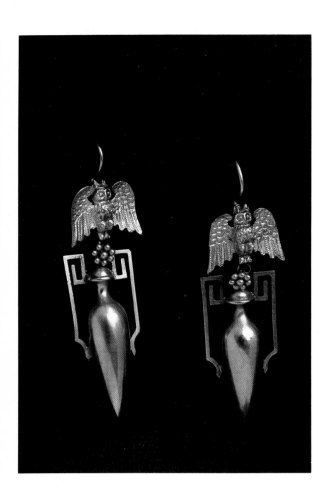

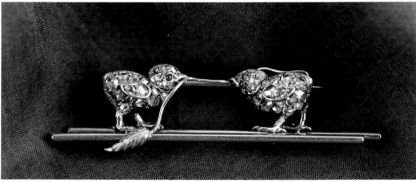

Earrings of gold depicting Egyptian style owls and amphora, English, circa 1820.

Watch pin of gold and diamond depicting a griffin, American, circa 1900.

Pin of gold, diamond and ruby depicting two chicks tugging at straw, English, circa 1880.

Four pins of gold, pearls, and gems depicting birds skiing, late 19th century.

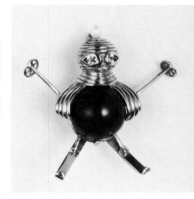

Owl

The Owl is symbolical of the devil in Christianity primarily because of its nocturnal habits, but also because the owl is known to deceive other birds as the devil deceives humans. The owl is also representative of the mission of Christ who gave His life, "To give light to them that sit in darkness and in the shadow of death" (Luke I:79). The owl sometimes symbolizes solitude in Christian art, and, of course, its most common symbolic virtue is that of wisdom.

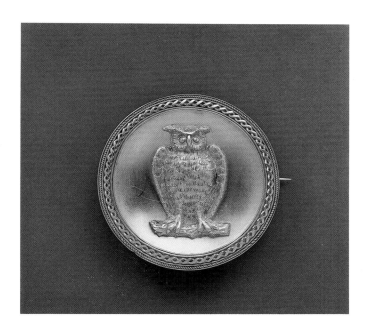

Pin of gold depicting an owl in high relief within a concave and rope designed frame, English, mid-nineteenth century.

Pin of gold, cabochon sapphire, diamonds, rubies and emeralds depicting a bird, English, circa 1960.

Pin of gold, emerald, and pavé diamonds designed as an ostrich by Van Cleef and Arpels.

Earrings of platinum with diamonds and calibre and cabochon rubies and emeralds in star design, circa 1920. Pin of platinum, onyx, ruby, sapphire and emerald depicting a parrot on a ring and with a trapezoid diamond as the water dish, circa 1920.

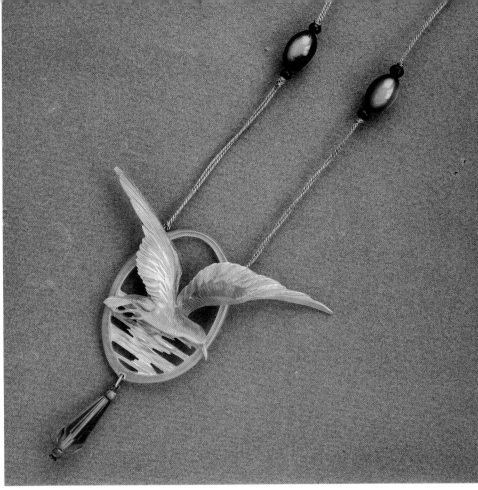

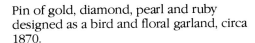

Pin of gold, diamond, pearl and ruby designed as a bird and floral garland, circa 1870.

Pendant necklace of silk cord with beads and carved horn depicting a seagull with briolette glass drop, circa 1900.

Pin of gold and silver, green onyx, carnelian, ruby, pearl and diamond depicting three birds and a nest, circa 1870.

Pin of gold, diamond, pearl, sapphire and ruby depicting four birds on a fence, circa 1870.

Peacock

The peacock is a symbol of immortality in Christianity stemming from the belief that its body does not decay after death. It is also a common symbol of pride and vanity for its habit of strutting and spreading its beautiful feathers. In China, the peacock is a symbol of beauty and dignity, and its tail feathers were used to designate official rank during the Ming dynasty.

Sparrow

The sparrow, to Christians, represented the poor who were, despite their lowly position, protected by God.

Swallow

The swallow, during the Renaissance was considered to be a symbol of the Incarnation of Christ.

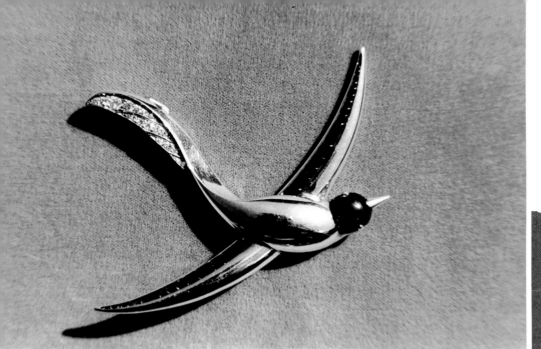

Pin of gold, sugarloaf cabochon sapphire, and diamonds, circa 1940.

Pin of silver, marcasite, and ruby designed as a swallow.

Pin of gold and diamonds designed as a swallow, mid-nineteenth century. Pin of opal, ruby and diamonds depicting a hummingbird. Pin of diamonds, gems and enamel designed as a tropical bird. Pair of clips representing butterflies and set with sapphire, ruby, emerald and diamond.

Butterflies

The Butterfly is a symbol of the resurrection not only of Christ, but of all men. The three stages of the butterfly's life; the caterpillar, the chrysalis, and the butterfly, correspond to the plight of man in life, death and resurrection. In China, the butterfly is a symbol of joy and summer, but is more interestingly depicted as a sort of Chinese cupid. An ancient legend tells how a young boy, chasing a beautiful butterfly, accidently ran into a private garden where he found the beautiful daughter of a retired magistrate. The boy fell in love with the girl and gained her hand in marriage.

Necklace of black silk cord and glass depicting a butterfly by Gabriel Argy-Rousseau, French, circa 1910.

Pin of gold, diamond, ruby and emerald designed as a butterfly and mounted *en tremblant*, French, circa 1900.

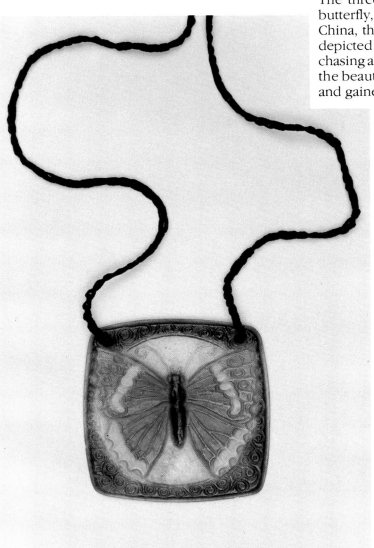

Pin of gold, *plique á jour,* opal, cabochon rubies, emeralds and diamonds designed as a butterfly, France, circa 1900.

Pin of gold and silver, *Plique á jour,* emerald and diamond designed as a butterfly, French, circa 1900.

Pin of silver and gold openwork set with cabochon ruby, baroque pearl, and diamonds, circa 1880.

Three pins of horn designed as butterflies, one with an oval turquoise, circa 1910.

Pin of cut steel designed as a butterfly, English, circa 1830.

Cloth ornament of black velvet and cut steel beads designed as a butterfly and intended to be sewn onto a garment, English, circa 1840.

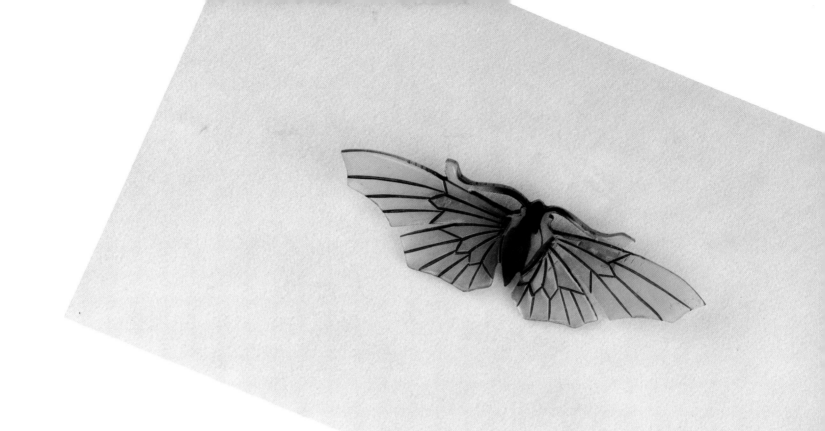

Pin of horn carved as a butterfly, circa
1900. Three pins of carved horn depicting
a cricket, a butterfly signed "GiP", and a
bee, circa 1900.

Crosses

The cross is the most important of Christian symbolic objects representing not only the Crucifixion, but Christianity itself. It signifies the Christian belief of atonement and symbolizes salvation and redemption. The Latin cross is seen most commonly and has a longer upright than crossbar.

The Greek cross has arms of equal length and the Egyptian cross, known also as Tau or the Old Testament cross, is in the form of the letter "T". The Tau cross placed upon the heart was a symbol of goodness and served as a talisman for protection against evil. It was also the monogram of Thoth, the Egyptian god of wisdom. When the Tau cross is accompanied by a circle, it represents eternal preservation of the world. St. Philip was said to have been crucified on a cross of this type.

The St. Andrew's cross is in the shape of an "X". At his execution, St. Andrew requested that he be crucified on a cross of a different form than the one on which Christ died because he felt unworthy to die in the same fashion as Christ. Thus, the St. Andrew's cross has become a symbol of humility in suffering.

The four arms of a cross symbolize to some the universe and the dominion of the spirit. The gesture of making the sign of the cross has been regarded as a protective measure against the devil and other evil spirits. Kings and nobles of the past used the cross as a symbol to bring them good luck. In the ancient Yucatan, the people prayed to the cross as the god of rain. In Scotland of old, similar practices were undertaken. When the people there needed rain, they would raise a cross to the sky. When enough rain had fallen, they would lower the cross again to the ground.

The rosary is a form of adoration of the Virgin Mary and is used during a series of prayers concerning events in the life of the Virgin Mary and Christ. Buddhist priests also employ a rosary in ceremony of 108 beads to assure the buddhist worshipper that he will repeat the sacred name of Buddha at least one hundred times. Three beads on the string represent the "Three Holy Ones" of the Buddhist trinity: Buddha, the Word, and the Priesthood. The string of the rosary, which is sometimes made of human hair, symbolizes the penetrating power of all the Buddhas.

Reversible pendant of gold and enamel in the form of a Christian cross, mark unknown, two views.

Necklace of pearls, diamond, and enameled gold including four strands of seed pearls and a pendant cross by C. Giuliano, London, circa 1880.

Pendant of gold and mosaic with dove design in the form of a cross, back with glass enclosed locket containing two curls of hair and the frame engraved "Angela Reyner died Decr 3rd, 1879/Emma Cheetham died Decr 10th, 1879", most probably made as a memorial, by C. Civilotti, Rome, circa 1880, two views.

Opposite page:

Pin of gold and enamel, diamonds, emeralds and pearl in a quatrefoil cross design in the Lombardic style of Castellani, Italian, mid-nineteenth century.

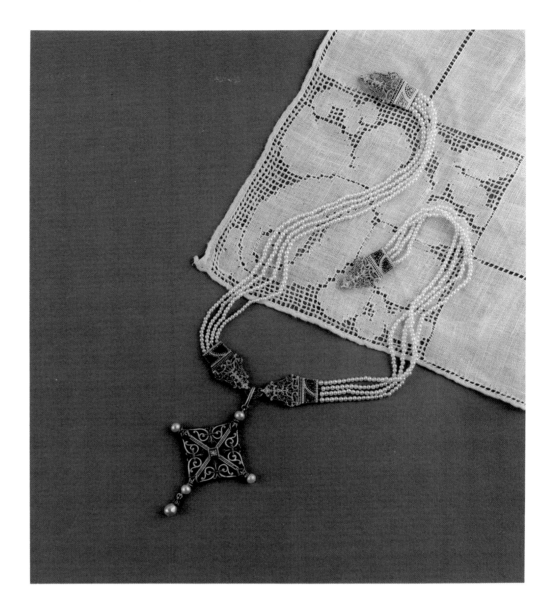

Necklace and pendant of gold, enamel, sapphire, ruby, diamond, emerald, and amethyst, the pendant in the form of a Christian cross, by C. Giuliano, London, circa 1880.

Pendant of gold, enamel and pearls in the shape of a Christian cross, by C. Giuliano, London, circa 1880.

Opposite page:

Necklace and bracelet of gold and enamel in the Egyptian-revival style, Swiss, circa 1925, two views.

Pin of gold and mosaic in the crossing forms of the Greek letters "chi" and "rho" by C. Castellani, Naples, mid-nineteenth century.

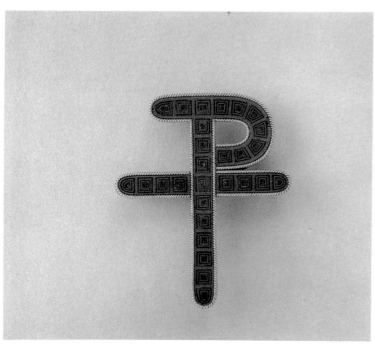

Finger ring and earrings of carved ivory,
diamonds and cabochon emeralds
designed as dolphins by M. Gerard, Paris,
circa 1980. Three pins of platinum and
white gold, star sapphire (the largest of
approximately 180 carats), cabochon
emeralds and diamonds designed as an
angel fish by Van Cleef and Arpels.

Opposite page:
Pin of gold, coral, obsidian, diamonds and
emerald designed as a sea horse emerging
from a couch shell, by Cartier, Paris.

Bracelet of gilded metal with cut-out and
raised fish design, French.

Fish

The fish was worn as a talisman in ancient Egypt as it represented the primeval creative principle and was believed to promote felicity, abundance and general prosperity. In China, because of its position as a primary food source, the fish has acquired great symbolic significance. The pronunciation of the word fish in Chinese closely resembles that of the word for "superfluity" and therefore is a symbol of wealth and abundance. The reproductive capability of the fish has made it a symbol of regeneration, and because it appears to be content in its environment, it is also a symbol of harmony and happiness. A pair of fish symbolizes the joyful union of a couple, and often a gift of fish is given to the family of the bride at a Chinese wedding. The fish, for its lifestyle, has also come to symbolize freedom. The carp is specifically a symbol of marital virtues and its struggles against currents suggest to the Chinese the quality of perseverance. The sturgeon of the Yellow River symbolize literary ability and the passing of tests with honor as they were believed to change into dragons as they swam up rapids. Other Chinese legends relate the fish to a king's subjects, and angling to a king's ability to rule. In Christianity, the fish has come to represent Christ originating, it is believed, because the letters forming the word "fish" correspond to the first letter of each word in the Greek phrase for, "Jesus Christ God's Son Saviour." The fish also symbolizes baptism as a fish acquires life from water, so does a Christian from the waters of baptism.

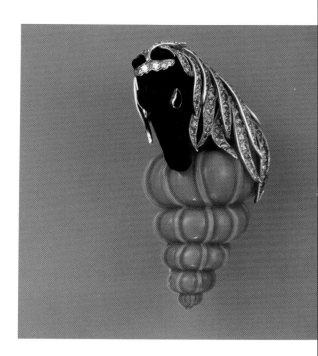

Flowers

There are as many legends and powers associated with flowers and plants as there are species throughout the world. The healing properties of plants and flowers are well known and are still believed by many to be the most effective means of leading a long and healthy life. The Doctrine of Signatures is an ancient healing philosophy which deems that the symptoms of a certain illness may be extinguished by using plants and flowers with physical characteristics resembling the illness. For example, the spotted leaves of the Pulmonaria was believed to be beneficial for tuberculosis with its symptoms of spotted lungs. Likewise, the yellowing of the skin by jaundice was held to be cured by tumeric which was the principal ingredient in yellow dyes.

Though plants and flowers are still used as ingredients in medicine and health foods, they are most popular as symbols of love and friendship. The traditional bridal bouquet symbolizes fertility and a healthy marriage, and the blooming flowers each Spring symbolize hope and rebirth.

Red Carnation
The red carnation is a symbol of pure love in Christianity. According to Flemish custom, the bride, on the day of her wedding, wore a pink carnation. The groom would then search her for it, and so the pink carnation became a symbol of marriage.

Daisy
The daisy, in all its simplistic beauty came to symbolize the innocence and purity of the Christ Child.

Hyacinth
The hyacinth was believed by the Ancient Greeks to have sprung from the blood of the beautiful young Hyacinthus after Apollo had struck and killed him with a discus. In Christianity, the hyacinth has come to symbolize petinence and humility.

Lily
The lily is perhaps the most significant of the flowers in Christian beliefs. It is a symbol of purity, and has long been associated with the Virgin Mary and the Immaculate Conception.

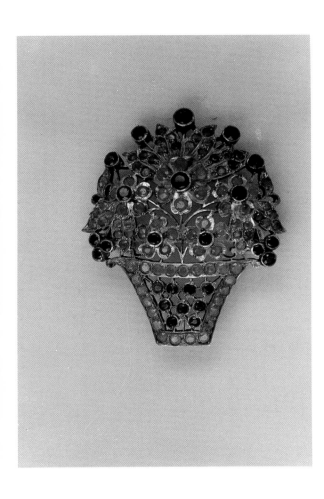

Pin of silver, emerald, ruby, and sapphire designed as a flower basket, India, circa 1920.

Pin of platinum, diamonds, fancy-shaped emerald and carved gems in a floral design, circa 1920. Pin of platinum, quartz, jade, diamonds, ruby and onyx designed as a bowl with flowers, French, circa 1930. Pin of platinum, diamonds, citrine, lapis lazuli, carnelian, and onyx designed as a rectangular panel enclosing a bowl with flowers, circa 1920.

Narcissus

The narcissus is a fierce symbol of self-love, dating from the ancient legend of Narcissus who fell so in love with his own beautiful image in a pool of water that he drowned while trying to embrace it. According to the legend, he changed into this beautiful flower when he died.

Rose

The rose symbolized victory, pride and love to the Romans and it was the flower of Venus, the goddess of love. In Christianity, the red rose is a symbol of martyrdom, and the white rose a symbol of purity.

In China, each flower has a significant meaning and purpose. China is often referred to as the "flowery land," and much of the decor and ornamentation in China is beautifully illustrated in floral patterns.

In China and in Europe, flowers are associated with each month of the year:

	In China	In Europe
January	prunus	snowdrop
February	peach	primrose
March	peony	violet
April	Cherry	daisy
May	magnolia	hawthorn
June	pomegranate	honeysuckle
July	lotus	water-lily
August	pear	poppy
September	mallow	morning-glory
October	chrysanthemum	hops
November	gardenia	chrysanthemum
December	poppy	holly

And so, as flowers are the perfect symbol of beauty, their design in magnificent gemstones may only enhance a piece of jewelry.

Pin of sterling silver and enamel depicting a floral bouquet, and with a marcasite-set butterfly in the stems.

Bracelet of gold, carbuncle, and diamonds by Hunt & Roskell, London, circa 1860. Pin of white gold and diamonds designed as a six-petal flower, eighteenth century. Pin of gold and diamonds designed as a six-petal flower, circa 1820. Two pins of gold and diamonds designed as six-petal flowers, eighteenth century.

Pin of sterling silver, carved jet and marcasite in the form of a rose, German, circa 1930.

Two necklaces of cut steel designed as graduated flowers and leaves, English, circa 1860.

Pin of glass and base metal, the domed glass frosted with a dogwood flower design by Rene Lalique, circa 1930.

Pin of gold and Florentine mosaic oval panel depicting white flowers, circa 1860.

Bracelet of gold, mosaic and pearls with floral design on one half and geometric design on the other half, Italian, circa 1860, two views.

Pendant and earrings of gold and micro-mosaic in a floral design, probably Italian, circa 1850.

Bracelet and locket of brushed gold, each with three diamonds in a small floral design, late nineteenth century.

Locket of gold, turquoise, cabochon amethyst and pearl with floral garland decoration, late nineteenth century.

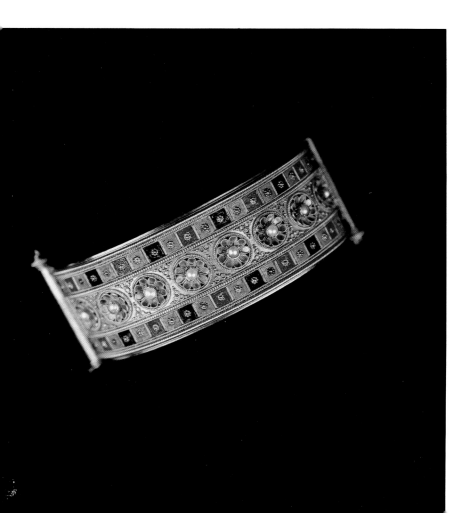

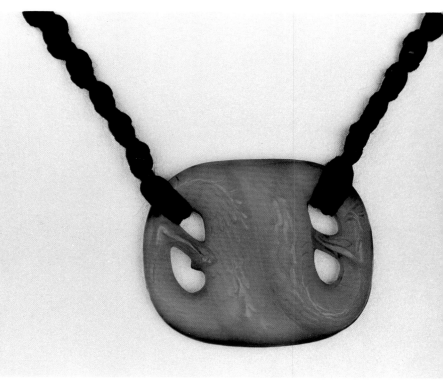

Pin of gold, enamel, pearl and diamond designed as a vine of ivy, English, circa 1885.

Pin of carved ivory depicting a violet, roses and leaves, circa 1860.

Pin and dress clip of ivory beads and carved jade designed to depict bunches of grapes, early twentieth century.

Necklace of black silk cord and a pendant of blue glass designed as the bark of a tree by Rene Lalique, circa 1930.

Bracelet of gold designed as six floral links by Castellani, circa 1860.

Earrings of gold and diamonds depicting flowerheads of Florentine gold work by Cartier.

Dress clip of gold and diamonds designed as a stylized bouquet of flowers with all the petals moveable, by Cartier, circa 1940.

Double clips of gold and diamonds designed as flower bouquets, circa 1945.

Hands

Pin of gold, diamonds and enamel depicting a woman's hand clutching a cross form, English, circa 1840.

Pin of gold, ruby and enamel depicting a hand clutching a rod entwined with a grape cluster, perhaps an heraldic device, nineteenth century.

Bracelet of three-colored gold, ruby and emerald designed as a pair of hands holding a floral bouquet, early 19th century.

The hand, in its various forms, has played a symbolic role in many civilizations and religions. One form dates back to 800 B.C. when hands were carved upon Etruscan tombs. The carvings showed the thumb placed between the first and second fingers with the hand clenched and pointing downward. It was considered great protection against all evil, in particular, the evil eye.

The varying positions of the hand give it significant and varying meanings. For example, the Romans used an open hand on their battle standards to represent justice and victory. The Devils' Horns, an Italian talisman, is formed by closing the second and third fingers with the thumb, and extending the first and fourth fingers.

Early Christians were hesitant to portray an actual picture of the Lord, and opted to indicate His presence by showing a hand reaching from the heavens. A hand with three fingers extended is a symbol of the Trinity and the hand extended with the palm toward the sky is symbolical of the blessing of God. An open hand symbolizes the slapping of the face of Christ in the Common Hall and a hand closed over straws recalls the tradition that lots were drawn to see whether Christ or Barabbas should be released. Hands exchanging money or holding a bag of money represent the betrayal of Judas, and hands over a basin recall Pilate's washing his hands of blame for the Crucifixion of Christ. The hand shown in combination with a cross was a powerful talisman for the evil eye, and it was considered bad luck to break a charm such as this.

To the Moslems, a hand with the thumb and fingers outstretched is known as the Hand of the Lady Fatima and is highly regarded as a sacred symbol of generosity, hospitality, power and divine providence. In its entirety, the Holy Family is represented by the hand. Mohammed is symbolized by the thumb, Lady Fatima by the first finger, her husband, Ali by the second, and their sons, Hassan and Hussein, by the third and the fourth. The hand, moreover reminds the Moslems of the five principal commandments: to keep the fast of Ramadan; to accomplish the pilgrimage to Mecca; to give alms; to perform the necessary ablutions and to oppose all infidels.

In China, the palm of the hand of Buddha, pointed out toward worshippers, represents his endless giving. When the left hand is laid upon the knees, palm up, and then the right hand placed upon it in the same manner with the points of the thumbs touching, it expresses the fusion in contemplation of the five material elements symbolized by the fingers: water, fire, metal, wood and earth. The unity of cosmic and individual souls in spiritual enlightenment is symbolized by the fingers of the right hand clasping the forefinger of the left.

Insects

The insects we encounter every day have, in the past symbolized a variety of ideas and beliefs. One of the oldest significant symbolic insects is the scarab as it was a powerful amulet to the ancient Egyptians signifying regeneration. The Egyptians believed that a green jaspar scarab engraved with certain verses from the Book of the Dead would not give unfavorable witness to its wearer after death. Such scarabs were placed on the heart of the mummy in order to ensure that the owner would enjoy eternal happiness in the after-life.

Spider

To the Etruscans, the spider was considered a good luck charm when engraved upon precious gems. It was held to be a talisman for business matters as it was shrewd and has remarkable quickness and sight. One ancient writer told how the future was predicted by examining the manner in which spiders spun their webs. It was also believed that if a little spider fell upon his clothes, a man would receive money.

The spider is also symbolically significant in Christianity. It represents the miser, as the spider bleeds a fly like the miser bleeds the poor. The spider symbolizes the devil as the spider's web represents the devil's trap. Finally, the spider symbolizes the wrong of evil-doers whose webs will break apart like those of a spider. Also in Christianity, the cobweb symbolizes the fragility of human life.

Bee

The bee in Christianity is symbolic of hard work, activity and diligence. It also represents sweetness and religious eloquence. For their elequence, the beehive is associated with St. Ambrose and St. Bernard de Clairvaux as their speech was considered to have been as sweet as honey. The beehive symbolizes a pious and unified community: the Christian being symbolically comparable to a bee, and the church to a hive. Honey is also a symbol of Christ and the bee has symbolized the virginity of Mary. The fly in Christianity has symbolized sin as it is considered the bringer of evil and pestilence.

In Chinese society, the bee symbolizes industry and thriftiness and often a crowd of people is referred to as a swarm of bee. Honey mixed with oil is symbolic of a false friendship.

Dragonfly

The dragonfly symbolizes summer, instability and weakness to the Chinese.

Ant

The ant symbolizes virtue, patriotism and self-interest to the Chinese.

Pendant of gold, banded onyx and green enamel, the onyx carved on the domed (front) side as a scarab beetle and on the flat (back) side with a man with bow and arrow inscribed IHTK, in Egyptian-revival style, Italian, circa 1860, two views.

Necklace of gold with a pendant of carved oval opal used as an Egyptian-revival style scarab beetle decorated with gold, sapphire, fancy yellow diamonds, colorless diamonds, synthetic rubies, synthetic sapphires, and simulated emeralds, circa 1905.

Pin of pearl, demantoid garnet, and diamond designed as a thistle, circa 1880. Pin of gold, ruby, and diamond designed as a bug, circa 1880. Pendant of ruby, emerald, and diamond designed as a heart, eighteenth century, and at the center a nineteenth century crystal intaglio of a bee. Two pins of gold and gems designed as bees, late nineteenth century. Pin of pear-shaped pink topaz, garnet, sapphires and diamonds depicting a swallow-tailed butterfly, circa 1890. Pin of sapphire, diamond and cabochon rubies designed as a moth, circa 1890. Pin of gold, pear-shaped peridot, and diamonds designed as a spider, circa 1890.

Pin of gold, enamel, demantoid garnet, and diamonds designed as a dragonfly by A. J. Hedges & Co., Newark, New Jersey, circa 1890. Earrings of gold, cabochon garnets and enamel in the forms of scarab beetles and cobra snakes by Robert Phillips, London, circa 1870.

Pin and earrings of gold depicting a spider and its web, late nineteenth century.

Pin of silver, enamel and marcasite in the form of a winged beetle clutching red disc, French, circa 1930.

Hair ornament of carved horn designed as a bee and tree bark, circa 1890.

Pin of gold, enamel, opal, ruby and diamonds designed as a butterfly, American, circa 1885. Pin of gold, garnet, diamonds, emerald, opal, demantoid garnet and pearl designed as a moth, French, circa 1880.

Finger ring of gold, cabochon garnet, ruby and diamonds designed to depict a cricket, late nineteenth century.

Necklace of silk cord and a pendant of horn and lapis lazuli carved as a moth, circa 1890.

Pin of gold and mosaic depicting a fly, English, circa 1870.

Pin of gold, emerald, diamond and ruby designed as a dragonfly, circa 1900.

Pin of freshwater pearl, rubies, diamonds and enamel designed as a dragonfly, English, circa 1900.

Pin of gold and silver, diamonds and enamel depicting a dragonfly.

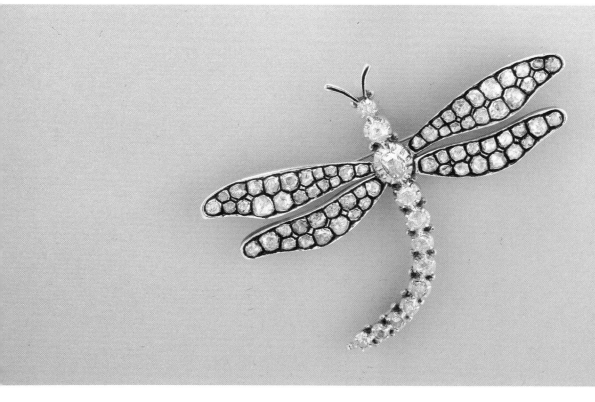

Moon, Stars & Arrows

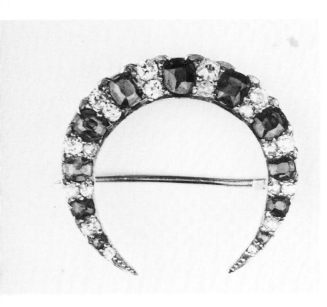

Pin of graduated diamonds and rubies designed as a crescent moon, English, late 19th century.

Moon

In China, the moon is believed to be inhabited by a hare which grinds the drugs of immortality beneath a cassia tree. The hare is accompanied by a three-legged female toad which had fled to this satellite to escape the wrath of her husband from whom she stole the Exilir of Immortality. The god of marriage, Chieh Lin is symbolized by the moon in China, and those who are to marry are believed to be connected to the moon by an invisible red thread.

In Christianity, the moon symbolizes the sorrow of all the world at the death of Christ.

Stars

The Chinese have long been fascinated by the stars, and they have based much of their philosophy and beliefs on the formations and movement of celestial bodies. The three star gods of China are symbolic of happiness, affluence and longevity.

The famous Christian Star of the East guided the three wisemen to the stable to witness the birth of Christ and stood of Bethlehem to symbolize the coming of the Saviour. Twelve stars symbolize the twelve tribes of Israel and the twelve Apostles in Christianity.

Arrows

The arrow in Christianity represents a spiritual weapon which is used in the favor of God. After Saint Sebastian survived being shot by many arrows, the arrow became symbolic of the plague, and he became the patron saint of all plague victims.

Pendant/pin of diamonds designed as a six-pointed star, late nineteenth century. Pendant/pin of diamonds designed as a sixteen-pointed star, late nineteenth century. Tiara of diamonds designed as five six-pointed stars, late nineteenth century. Necklace of graduated diamonds arranged in clusters, nineteenth century.

Hair ornament/pin of graduated diamonds designed as a sun rising, circa 1890. Pin of ruby and diamonds designed as a four-leaf clover, circa 1880. Pin of crimson enamel, diamonds and pearl, circa 1900. Pin of diamonds designed as an eight-pointed star, circa 1880. Pendant/pin of diamonds and a pear-shaped ruby designed as a heart, circa 1880. Locket of diamonds, ruby and emerald with monogram AG entwined, circa 1880. Pendant of graduated diamonds in openwork oval shape with central cross design, circa 1880. Pin of demantoid garnets and diamonds shaped as a star, circa 1885.

Three pins of graduated diamonds, one designed as a sunburst, one as a floral bouquet, and one as a butterfly, all English, 19th century.

243

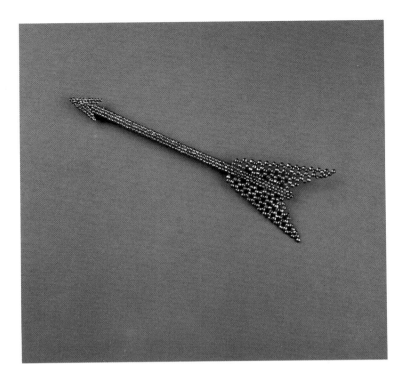

Pin of carved marcasite designed as an arrow, circa 1930.

Earrings, pin and pendant of sterling silver designed as men-in-the-moon faces, circa 1930.

Pin of silver in the form of a butterfly and an arrow, twentieth century.

Three pins of gold with pearls, two designed as stars and one as a crescent, circa 1900.

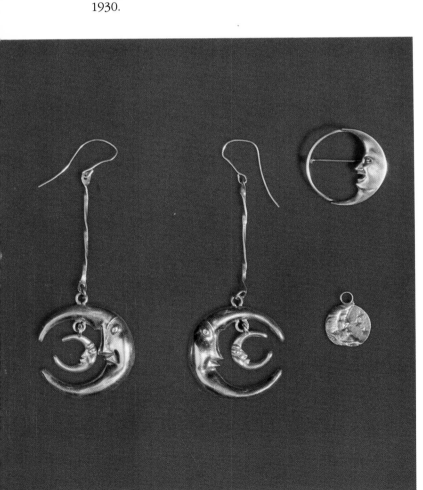

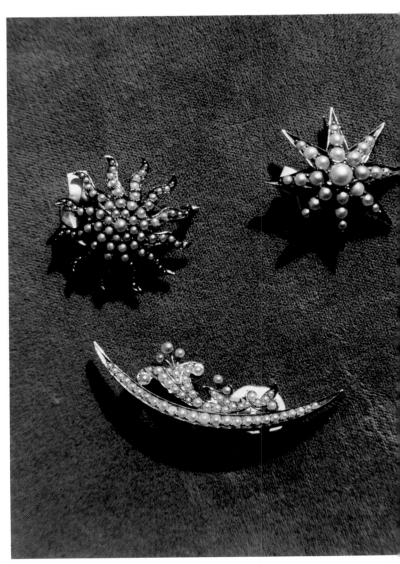

Necklace of platinum with pentagon and square sapphires. Two finger rings of yellow gold and diamonds, one with cabochon and calibre rubies, the other of cabochon and calibre sapphires. Jabot pin of ruby and diamonds in the shape of an arrow, circa 1935. Bracelet of platinum with forty-one square rubies.

People

Jewelry has often been made to commemorate powerful people whose contributions to society have been deemed exemplary and worthy of remembrance. These people may be nationally significant, such as a head of state, or even legendary, such as the ancient gods and Biblical figures whose powers made popular stories for generations. The people are sometimes more privately remembered, such as a loved one in the family, or a child whose powers were yet unrealized. Mourning jewelry was traditional for many centuries.

Portrait medallions and cameos may have depicted very specific people whose names and special deeds are now unknown. In modern times, some jewelry bears the image of a person whose uniform or costume signifies the importance, rather than the personality. Still, the special powers are communicated through the jewelry design.

Necklace and earrings of gold and mosaic in pendant medallions depicting Julius Caesar and unidentified classical Roman dignitaries, eagles, trophies of arms, lictor sticks and a dove, probably Italian, circa 1880.

Link bracelet of gold, gem stones
and Swiss enamel depicting girls in Swiss
cantonal dress, each identified on the
reverse: Basle, Soleure, Glaris, Zug,
Unterud, Schwyz, Uri, Lucerne, Zurich, and
Berne, mid-nineteenth century.

Pendant containing the mourning coin for Voltaire (Francois Marie Arouet, 1694-1778) surrounded with rubies and emeralds, two views.

Pendant of gilded silver depicting a woman embracing two children and inscribed "ORPHELINAT DES ARMEES", commemorating a parade on 20 June, 1915 by the society dedicated to ensuring orphans of the first world war maternal tenderness, a state education, a career appropriate to each child, and instruction in the religion of their parents, designed by Rene Lalique, French, 1915.

Pin of gold and silver, pearls, and porcelain placque painted with the portrait of England's Queen Elizabeth I, back inscribed "Elizabeth d'Angleterra Sirendt", two views.

Pendant seal of carved onyx and gold showing three faces of men.

Pendant of gold granulations depicting Bacchus in archaeological style probably by Castellani, Italian, last quarter of the 19th century.

Pendant/pin of gold and enameled placque showing Rebecca at the well in Greek-style dress, goldwork in Etruscan-revival style, by John Brogden, London, circa 1880

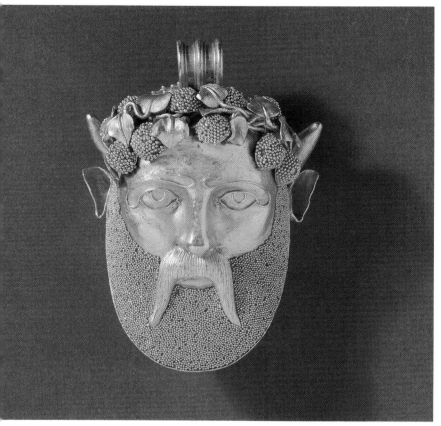

Pin of gold and diamonds depicting a Pharaoh's head, birds and flowers in Egyptian-revival style, circa 1925.

Pendant of gold, a stone carved in relief with the head of Minerva, enamel, emerald, ruby, and pearl by C. Civilotti, Rome, circa 1860.

Pendant of gold, jasper and enamel depicting a pilgrim carrying a staff, with pendant pearl, probably Spanish, late seventeenth century.

Bracelet of gold with grey and pink stone cameos depicting a sleeping child, man and woman's portraits, and angels strongly suggesting a mourning theme, circa 1820.

Two pins and earrings of gold and shell cameos depicting Aurora with horses, two classical women's portraits, and dancing girl, circa 1850.

Pin of gold and pearls with a chalcedony cameo of a woman's portrait including a bead necklace, English, circa 1880.

Pendant of gold with glass cameo of a man's portrait in Classical style, English, circa 1820.

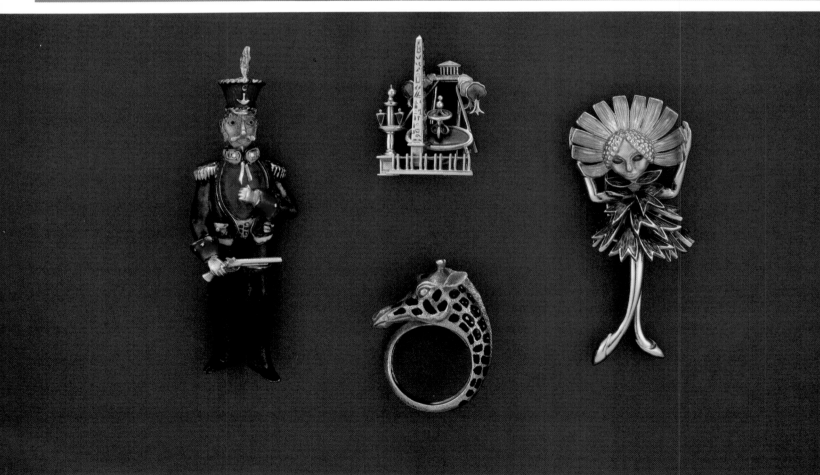

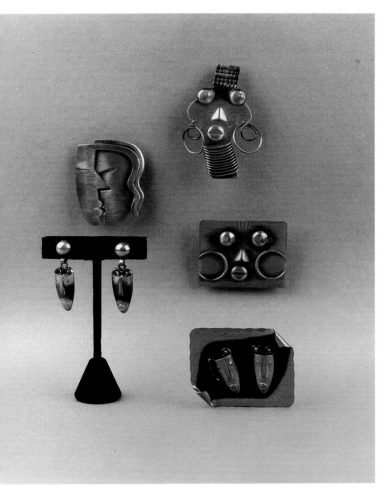

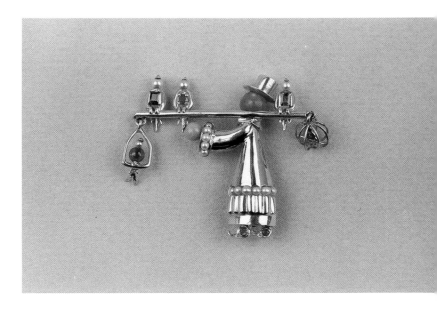

Pin of gold and gems depicting a circus clown and birds, American, circa 1945.

Four pins and earrings of copper depicting different face motifs, by Rebajez, New York, circa 1950.

Pendant of gold and enamel depicting a puppet, circa 1905.

Finger ring of silver, gold overlay, rubies and emeralds designed as a face, circa 1940.

Opposite page:

Pin of gold, carved coral, diamonds, pearls, cabochon ruby and emeralds, and turquoise designed as the head of Buddha with jewelry, by Cartier. Pin of gold, carved basalt, diamonds, coral, and abalone shell designed as a Blackamoor warrior, by Cartier, Paris.

Pin of gold and enamel designed as a French soldier. Pin of gold and enamel designed with Parisian landmarks by Fred, Paris. Pin of gold and enamel designed as a flower dancer by Fred, Paris. Finger ring of gold and enamel designed as a giraffe.

Serpents

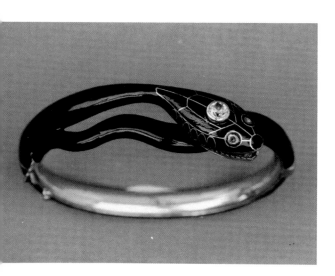

Serpents and snakes have long symbolized the concept of eternity and have been used as a talisman for longevity, health and vitality. To the Aztec Indians, the snake was a symbol of the sun and denoted the concept of perpetual time, without a beginning, giving life, causing death and existing forever. This was especially true of a snake depicted with its tail in its mouth to form an unending circle. A coiled snake signified the succession of the ages and a snake with its tail hidden, antiquity. It was a belief in primeval days that at death, the soul would pass into a serpent and regenerate as the snake shed its skin each year.

To the Chinese, the serpent is one of the symbolic creatures of the twelve terrestrial branches and denotes flattery, cunning and evil. However, because of supernatural powers attributed to the snake it is also highly respected. The Chinese believe that elves, demons and fairies have the power to transform themselves into snakes, and it is considered bad luck to harm a snake that has taken up residence underneath your house. The Columbrine is a harmless snake commonly found under the floorboards of houses in some parts of China.

Also in the East, the movement of the sun through the sky was connected with the snake as its path across the sky formed a curve similar to that of the body of a snake. The snake symbolized lightening and fire, with either the good virtue of having the power to give life, or the evil potential to take it away.

The serpent was an important symbol to the ancient Egyptians. A headpiece called the "uraeus" was worn to indicate royalty. The uraeus was believed to protect the wearer from the attacks of Rerek or Apep, the servant of Set, the god of evil. The servant of Set was represented as an evil serpent which, even when killed, had the power to change form and block one's passage to heaven. Regardless of its associations with evil, the serpent was thought to wield protective powers, and sculptured serpents have been found guarding the tombs of most Egyptian kings.

Egyptian divinities were depicted with snakes around their heads as a symbol of power. The son of the first man-god Ptah, was represented by a giant serpent and called Tem. Ptah was the god of the rising sun, and it was believed that a serpent would not die until after the setting of the sun.

In India, the serpent served as a talisman for knowledge, wisdom and understanding. The serpent is a symbol of eternity and is known as "anata." The creator Vishnu is depicted sleeping on anata with each of the snakes' several heads watching him carefully, awaiting new creations and a new order of things.

In Greek mythology, serpents were sacred to the great god of medicine, Aesculapius, from the idea that its life is renewed each time their skin is shed. Aesculapius carried a staff called a caduceus around which was entwined a serpent as a symbol of health. It was from the staff of Aesculapius that the modern symbol of medical science was derived. The serpent was also connected with the good qualities of Ceres, Mercury and Diana, but the python symbolized evil.

The serpent was the god of the household for the Romans. According to the writings of Livy, on the advice of the Delphic Oracle, a sacred serpent brought from the temple of Aesculapius put an end to pestilence in Rome. The Romans wore rings in the form of a coiled serpent as a talisman to preserve health.

Perhaps the most notorious symbolism of the serpent is that which embodies it as satan—the tempter of Eve in the Garden of Eden. The painters of the Renaissance chose the serpent or dragon to symbolize the devil, and it was often depicted at the foot of the cross to exemplify the power of Christ over evil. The dragon, in Revelation 12:7-9, is depicted as a fierce enemy of God which Micheal and his angels fought and cast from heaven and called the devil, and satan. The archangel Michael was often depicted with a dragon at his feet symbolizing his power over evil.

A rebirth of the serpent in jewelry came about when Albert presented a serpent engagement ring to Queen Victoria. The serpent was worn as a talisman of good luck, and was popular throughout the Victorian period.

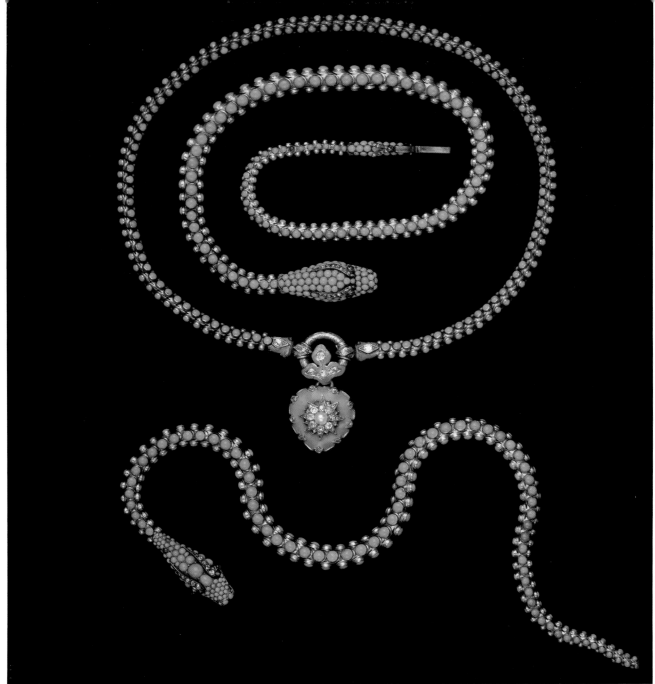

Necklace of gold, turquoise, enamel and diamonds with a heart-shaped locket set with a pearl, circa 1865. Two very similar necklaces of gold, turquoise and diamonds shaped as serpents, one with cabochon ruby eyes, the other with diamond eyes and garnet-set head, circa 1845.

Necklace of gold, enamel, baroque pearl, diamonds and cabochon rubies designed as a serpent, circa 1900.

Opposite page:

Bracelet of gold, enamel, aquamarine and diamonds designed as a serpent, English, circa 1800.

Necklace of gold, turquoise and ruby designed as a serpent holding in its mouth a pendant locket, circa 1885.

Bracelet of gold, enamel, diamonds, and cabochon rubies, English, circa 1860.

Pin of gold, pearls, emeralds and rubies shaped as a lizard, circa 1900.

Pin of white gold, diamonds and emeralds depicting a frog, English, circa 1960.

Bracelet of silver mesh in the form of a serpent, circa 1930.

Lizard

The lizard was often carved on rings in ancient Rome and was used to prevent the weakening of eyesight. It was also, because its green color resembles the emerald, spiritually respected. In Portugal, paintings of lizards on porcelain are hung on the walls of households to bring good fortune.

Frog

In ancient Egypt, it was believed that by wearing a frog, one could attract the favors of Isis, the goddess of nature. It was also a symbol of fertility and was worn to aid in recovery from disease, for general health and for a long life. In Burma, frogs of amber or metal were worn by children to protect them from sickness caused by the evil glance. A rain of frogs was one of the plagues of Egypt and has since acquired a symbolical association with the devil. Also in Christianity, it has come to represent one who snatches at pleasures in life and symbolizes worldly things in general.

In ancient Rome, the frog was worn as a talisman for fertility and abundance. Pliny wrote that the frog had the power to maintain constant affections and promote relations between lovers and friends. The frog was a symbol of Aphrodite, the goddess of love, who was said to have been born from the foam of the sea. The frog was a popular health amulet when carved in amber and was also worn by the Italians, Greeks and Turks as a talisman for protection from the evil eye.

In China, the eggs of a frog were believed to fall from heaven in the form of dew. The frog is referred to in the Chinese language as the "heavenly chicken," and a type of medicine was derived from a fluid taken from the warts of a toad and used as a heart remedy. One Chinese legend tells of a three-legged toad which exists only in the moon. This particular frog symbolizes the unattainable. The three-legged toad is also a symbol of making money and good fortune stemming from a legend describing an ancient Taoist magician who would bait frogs by dangling gold coins in front of them.

Picture Credits

Anne's Arts, Chestnut Hill, Philadelphia, 28 top, 28 bottom, 31 bottom, 50 top right, 54 top, 55 bottom, 106 bottom, 107 bottom, 112, 127 top, 133 bottom, 136 top, 136 center, 137 bottom, 150 top, 171 center, 176 top, 176 center, 193 top, 208 bottom, 212 top right, 212 bottom right, 220 right, 221 center, 230 top, 236 top, 244 bottom left, 248 bottom. Asprey & Co., London, 130 top left, 132 bottom right, 133 top, 135 top, 146 top left, 147 top right, 148 bottom, 210 bottom left, 233 bottom right, 256 center. Bizarre Bazaar, NY, 127 bottom, 186 top, 251, 256 top. Bentley & Co., London, 45 bottom, 50 top left, 52 top, 98 bottom left, 104, 124 top, 130 right, 134, 136 bottom, 144 bottom, 146 center right, 150 bottom, 151 bottom, 188, 190 top, 205 right, 210 top, 216 center, 225 top, 234 top left, 240 top right and bottom left, 241 left, 251 bottom left. Linnett Bolduc, 25, 28 right, 198 top, 199. Bonham's, London, 205 top left, 242 top. M. Carroll, Adamstown, 39 left, 55 top, 111, 219 center, 231 top. Christie's East, NY, 18 bottom, 24 bottom, 30, 62 top, 70 top, 86, 96, 100, 129, 181, 184 center, 194, 217 bottom left, 241 bottom, 252 bottom. Christie's, London, 23 bottom, 219 bottom. Christie's, NY, 41, 49, 52 bottom, 56, 57 58 top, 60, 61, 64, 65, 68, 69, 71, 72, 75, 76, 77, 78, 79, 80 top, 81, 82, 88, 90, 91, 92, 93, 94, 97, 99, 102, 103, 113, 118, 130 center left, 138, 139, 140, 141, 142, 143, 144 top, 145, 149, 151 top, 152, 155, 156 top, 157 bottom, 158, 159, 160 bottom, 161, 162, 163, 164, 165, 166 top, 167, 168, 170, 177, 178, 179, 182, 183, 184 left and right, 185, 196, 200, 212 top left, 221 bottom, 228, 237 left, 245, 250 top right, 252 top. D. Cogdell, Adamstown, 26 bottom. Norman Crider, NY, 204 top, 232 top left. Sandy DeMaio, Bryn Mawr, 27, 29, 33 top right, 33 bottom, 62 bottom right, 63 top, 83 bottom left, 83 top right, 119 bottom, 121 bottom, 122, 123 top, 131 bottom, 146 top right, 148 top, 160 top, 169 top right, 169 bottom left, 171 top, 171 bottom, 173, 174, 175, 180 bottom, 186 bottom left, 187 bottom, 204 center, 206 top and bottom, 209, 211 top left, 212 bottom left, 213 left, 214 bottom, 215 bottom left, 216 top right, 218 top left and bottom, 219 top, 235, 239 top right, 240 top left, 244 bottom right, 250 top center, 253 top right and center, 254 top. Jackie Fleischmann, Adamstown, 244 top right. Diana Foley, London, 20 bottom, 21 bottom, 28 middle, 46 top right, 110 top, 114, 116 top left, 116 bottom, 117 top right, 117 bottom, 121 top, 126 left, 147 top left, 222 center and bottom, 232 top right. Franny's, Adamstown, 51. P. Funt, NY, 116 top right, 244 top left. M. Greenberg, 21 top, 22 bottom, 24 top, 26 top, 36, 37, 38 bottom, 39 right, 44 top, 45 top, 46 top left, 53 top, 126 right, 192. Nicholas Harris, London, 4, 18 left, 35, 38 top, 40, 98 top, 109 bottom, 120 top, 123 bottom, 124 bottom, 125 top, 135 bottom, 154, 186 bottom right, 211 bottom, 213 right, 215 top, 217 top left, 218 top right, 224 left, 225 bottom, 226, 227 left, 237 right, 249, 250 top left. John Joseph, London, 19 bottom, 33 top left, 59 bottom, 83 top left, 106 top left, 108 top, 130 bottom left, 132 top, 132 bottom left, 147 bottom, 157 top, 180 top, 180 center, 190 bottom, 207 top, 210 center, 232 bottom left, 233 top right, 251 top. Muriel Karasik, NY, 23 top, 253 top left. M. Klein, Philadelphia, 119 top, 120 bottom, 169 top left, 169 bottom right, 220 left, 232 center, 234 bottom right, 248 center, 253 bottom left, 254 center. Angela Kramer, NY, 117 top, 206 left, 229 bottom. Maureen McEvoy, London, 19 top, 42, 47, 115, 146 bottom, 234 bottom left. Nigle Milne, London, 31 top, 125 bottom, 147 center left, 193 bottom, 241 top. Linda Morgan, London, 50 bottom, 110 bottom, 195, 204 bottom, 210 bottom right, 214 top, 216 top left, 222 top, 234 top right, 239 bottom right and left, 240 bottom right. Phillips, London, 62 bottom left, 74 top, 89, 101, 107 top, 131 top right. James Robinson, NY, 20 top, 22 top, 43, 53 bottom, 54 bottom, 80 bottom, 95, 109 top, 127 center, 156 bottom, 176 bottom, 201, 211 top right, 215 center, 215 bottom right, 217 bottom right, 221 top, 227 top and right, 230 bottom, 232 and 233 bottom, 233 top left, 239 top left. Terry Rodgers, NY, 46 bottom, 48. Sotheby's, Geneva, 66 bottom, 166 bottom, 255 bottom. Sotheby's, London, Title page, 8, 9, 12, 13, 16, 17, 32, 44 bottom, 58 bottom, 63 bottom, 66 top, 67, 73, 74 bottom, 84, 85, 87, 105, 106 top right, 108 bottom, 128, 137 top, 153, 172, 187 top, 189, 191, 197, 198 bottom, 202, 203, 205 bottom left, 207 bottom, 231 bottom, 235 top, 236 bottom right, 238, 242 bottom, 243 top, 246, 255 top. Wartski Ltd., London, 83 bottom right, 98 bottom right, 131 top left, 208 top, 224 right, 236 bottom left, 243 bottom, 247, 248 top, 250 bottom, 251 bottom right, 254 bottom.

References

References for The Powers That Be

Budge, Sir E.A. Wallis, KT. *Amulets and Talismans*. New York: University Books, 1961. Reprint. New York: Dover Publications, Inc., 1978.

Fernie, William T. *The Occult and Curative Powers of Precious Stones*. 1907. Reprint. New York: Rudolf Steiner Publications, 1973.

Gemological Institute of America. *The Gemological Institute of America Colored Stone Course*. 2 vols. New York: Gemological Institue of America, 1980.

Gregor, Arthur S. *Amulets, Talismans, and Fetishes*. New York: Charles Scribner's Sons, 1975.

Jones, William. *Finger-Ring Lore*. London: Chatto & Windus, 1890. Reprint. Detroit, Michigan: Singing Tree Press, 1968.

Kozminsky, Isadore. *The Magic and Science of Jewels and Stones*. New York and London: G.P. Putnam's Sons, 1922.

Kunz, George F. and Charles H. Stevenson. *The Book of the Pearl*. New York: The Century Co., 1908.

Kunz, George Frederick. *The Curious Lore of Precious Stones*. Philadelphia: J.B. Lippincott Company, 1913. Reprint. New York: Dover Publications Inc., 1971.

Sapir, Richard B. *Quest*. New York: E.P. Dutton, 1987.

Weinstein, Michael. *The Word of Jewel Stones*. New York: Sheridan House, n.d.

Whitlock, Herbert P. *The Story of Gems, A Popular Handbook*. New York: Lee Furman, 1936.

References for Agate

Budge, Sir E.A. Wallis, KT. *Amulets and Talismans*. New York: University Books, 1961. Reprint. New York: Dover Publications, Inc., 1978.

Fernie, William T. *The Occult and Curative Powers of Precious Stones*. 1907. Reprint. New York: Rudolf Steiner Publications, 1973.

Gemological Institute of America. *The Gemological Institute of America Colored Stone Course*. 2 vols. New York: Gemological Institute of America, 1980.

Gregor, Arthur S. *Amulets, Talismans, and Fetishes*. New York: Charles Scribner's Sons, 1975.

Kozminsky, Isadore. *The Magic and Science of Jewels and Stones*. New York and London: G.P. Putnam's Sons, 1922.

Kunz, George Frederick. *The Curious Lore of Precious Stones*. Philadelphia: J.B. Lippincott Company, 1913. Reprint. New York: Dover Publications Inc., 1971.

Kunz, George Frederick. *The Magic of Jewels and Charms*. Philadelphia and London: J.B. Lippincott Company, 1915.

Newman, Harold. *An Illustrated Dictionary of Jewelry*. London: Thames and Hudson Ltd., 1981.

Pavitt, William. *The Book of Talismans, Amulets and Zodiacal Gems*. Reprint. London: Stephen Austin and Sons, Ltd., 1914.   Whitlock, Herbert P. *The Story of Gems, A Popular Handbook*. New York: Lee Furman, 1936.

References for Amber

Fernie, William T. *The Occult and Curative Powers of Precious Stones*. 1907. Reprint. New York: Rudolf Steiner Publications, 1973.

Gemological Institute of America. *The Gemological Institute of America Colored Stone Course*. 2 vols. New York: Gemological Institute of America, 1980.

Pavitt, William. *The Book of Talismans, Amulets and Zodiacal Gems*. Reprint. London: Stephen Austin and Sons, Ltd., 1914.   Whitlock, Herbert P. *The Story of Gems, A Popular Handbook*. New York: Lee Furman, 1936.

References for Amethyst

Budge, Sir E.A. Wallis, KT. *Amulets and Talismans*. New York: University Books, 1961. Reprint. New York: Dover Publications, Inc., 1978.

Charubel. *Psychology of Botany, Minerals and Precious Stones*. Tyldeley, England: R. Welche Esq.

Fernie, William T. *The Occult and Curative Powers of Precious Stones*. 1907. Reprint. New York: Rudolf Steiner Publications, 1973.

Gemological Institute of America. *The Gemological Institute of America Colored Stone Course*. 2 vols. New York: Gemological Institute of America, 1980.

Gregor, Arthur S. *Amulets, Talismans, and Fetishes*. New York: Charles Scribner's Sons, 1975.

Kozminsky, Isadore. *The Magic and Science of Jewels and Stones*. New York and London: G.P. Putnam's Sons, 1922.

Newman, Harold. *An Illustrated Dictionary of Jewelry*. London: Thames and Hudson Ltd., 1981.

Pavitt, William. *The Book of Talismans, Amulets and Zodiacal Gems*. Reprint. London: Stephen Austin and Sons, Ltd., 1914. Whitlock, Herbert P. *The Story of Gems, A Popular Handbook*. New York: Lee Furman, 1936.

References for Aquamarine

Budge, Sir E.A. Wallis, KT. *Amulets and Talismans*. New York: University Books, 1961. Reprint. New York: Dover Publications, Inc., 1978.

Gemological Institute of America. *The Gemological Institute of America Colored Stone Course*. 2 vols. New York: Gemological Institute of America, 1980.

Newman, Harold. *An Illustrated Dictionary of Jewelry*. London: Thames and Hudson Ltd., 1981.

References for Beryl

Budge, Sir E.A. Wallis, KT. *Amulets and Talismans*. New York: University Books, 1961. Reprint. New York: Dover Publications, Inc., 1978.

Fernie, William T. *The Occult and Curative Powers of Precious Stones*. 1907. Reprint. New York: Rudolf Steiner Publications, 1973.

Gemological Institute of America. *The Gemological Institute of America Colored Stone Course*. 2 vols. New York: Gemological Institute of America, 1980.

Kozminsky, Isadore. *The Magic and Science of Jewels and Stones*. New York and London: G.P. Putnam's Sons, 1922.

Kunz, George Frederick. *The Curious Lore of Precious Stones*. Philadelphia: J.B. Lippincott Company, 1913. Reprint. New York: Dover Publications Inc., 1971.

Newman, Harold. *An Illustrated Dictionary of Jewelry*. London: Thames and Hudson Ltd., 1981.

Pavitt, William. *The Book of Talismans, Amulets and Zodiacal Gems*. Reprint. London: Stephen Austin and Sons, Ltd., 1914.

References for Bloodstone

Budge, Sir E.A. Wallis, KT. *Amulets and Talismans*. New York: University Books, 1961. Reprint. New York: Dover Publications, Inc., 1978.

Fernie, William T. *The Occult and Curative Powers of Precious Stones*. 1907. Reprint. New York: Rudolf Steiner Publications, 1973.

Gemological Institute of America. *The Gemological Institute of America Colored Stone Course*. 2 vols. New York: Gemological Institute of America, 1980.

Gregor, Arthur S. *Amulets, Talismans, and Fetishes*. New York: Charles Scribner's Sons, 1975.

Kunz, George Frederick. *The Curious Lore of Precious Stones*. Philadelphia: J.B. Lippincott Company, 1913. Reprint. New York: Dover Publications Inc., 1971.

Pavitt, William. *The Book of Talismans, Amulets and Zodiacal Gems*. Reprint. London: Stephen Austin and Sons, Ltd., 1914.

References for Carnelien

Budge, Sir E.A. Wallis, KT. *Amulets and Talismans.* New York: University Books, 1961. Reprint. New York: Dover Publications, Inc., 1978.

Fernie, William T. *The Occult and Curative Powers of Precious Stones.* 1907. Reprint. New York: Rudolf Steiner Publications, 1973.

Gemological Institute of America. *The Gemological Institute of America Colored Stone Course.* 2 vols. New York: Gemological Institute of America, 1980.

Gregor, Arthur S. *Amulets, Talismans, and Fetishes.* New York: Charles Scribner's Sons, 1975.

Kelynda. *The Crystal Tree.* West Chester, PA: Schiffer Publishing Ltd., 1987.

Kunz, George Frederick. *The Magic of Jewels and Charms.* Philadelphia and London: J.B. Lippincott Company, 1915.

Pavitt, William. *The Book of Talismans, Amulets and Zodiacal Gems.* Reprint. London: Stephen Austin and Sons, Ltd., 1914.

References for Cat's-eye

Budge, Sir E.A. Wallis, KT. *Amulets and Talismans.* New York: University Books, 1961. Reprint. New York: Dover Publications, Inc., 1978.

Gemological Institute of America. *The Gemological Institute of America Colored Stone Course.* 2 vols. New York: Gemological Institute of America, 1980.

Gregor, Arthur S. *Amulets, Talismans, and Fetishes.* New York: Charles Scribner's Sons, 1975.

Kelynda. *The Crystal Tree.* West Chester, PA: Schiffer Publishing Ltd., 1987.

Kunz, George Frederick. *The Magic of Jewels and Charms.* Philadelphia and London: J.B. Lippincott Company, 1915.

Pavitt, William. *The Book of Talismans, Amulets and Zodiacal Gems.* Reprint. London: Stephen Austin and Sons, Ltd., 1914.

Whitlock, Herbert P. *The Story of Gems, A Popular Handbook.* New York: Lee Furman, 1936.

References for Chalcedony

Budge, Sir E.A. Wallis, KT. *Amulets and Talismans.* New York: University Books, 1961. Reprint. New York: Dover Publications, Inc., 1978.

Gemological Institute of America. *The Gemological Institute of America Colored Stone Course.* 2 vols. New York: Gemological Institute of America, 1980.

Kunz, George Frederick. *The Curious Lore of Precious Stones.* Philadelphia: J.B. Lippincott Company, 1913. Reprint. New York: Dover Publications Inc., 1971.

Kunz, George Frederick. *The Magic of Jewels and Charms.* Philadelphia and London: J.B. Lippincott Company, 1915.

Newman, Harold. *An Illustrated Dictionary of Jewelry.* London: Thames and Hudson Ltd., 1981.

Whitlock, Herbert P. *The Story of Gems, A Popular Handbook.* New York: Lee Furman, 1936.

References for Citrine

Kunz, George Frederick. *The Magic of Jewels and Charms.* Philadelphia and London: J.B. Lippincott Company, 1915.

Newman, Harold. *An Illustrated Dictionary of Jewelry.* London: Thames and Hudson Ltd., 1981.

Whitlock, Herbert P. *The Story of Gems, A Popular Handbook.* New York: Lee Furman, 1936.

References for Coral

Charubel. *Psychology of Botany, Minerals and Precious Stones.* Tyldeley, England: R. Welche Esq.

Ferguson, George. *Signs and Symbols in Christian Art.* Reprint. London: Oxford University Press, 1974.

Fernie, William T. *The Occult and Curative Powers of Precious Stones.* 1907. Reprint. New York: Rudolf Steiner Publications, 1973.

Gemological Institute of America. *The Gemological Institute of America Colored Stone Course.* 2 vols. New York: Gemological Institute of America, 1980.

Kunz, George Frederick. *The Magic of Jewels and Charms.* Philadelphia and London: J.B. Lippincott Company, 1915.

Newman, Harold. *An Illustrated Dictionary of Jewelry.* London: Thames and Hudson Ltd., 1981.

Pavitt, William. *The Book of Talismans, Amulets and Zodiacal Gems.* Reprint. London: Stephen Austin and Sons, Ltd., 1914.

Seven Thousand Years of Jewellry. Edited by Hugh Tait. London: British Museum Publications, 1986.

Whitlock, Herbert P. *The Story of Gems, A Popular Handbook.* New York: Lee Furman, 1936.

Williams, C.A.S. *Outlines of Chinese Symbolism and Art Motives.* Tokyo: Charles E. Tuttle Company Inc. 1941. Reprint. Hong Kong: Kelly and Walsh, Ltd., 1974.

References for Crystal

Budge, Sir E.A. Wallis, KT. *Amulets and Talismans.* New York: University Books, 1961. Reprint. New York: Dover Publications, Inc., 1978.

Charubel. *Psychology of Botany, Minerals and Precious Stones.* Tyldeley, England: R. Welche Esq.

Gemological Institute of America. *The Gemological Institute of America Colored Stone Course.* 2 vols. New York: Gemological Institute of America, 1980.

Gregor, Arthur S. *Amulets, Talismans, and Fetishes.* New York: Charles Scribner's Sons, 1975.

Jones, William. *Finger-Ring Lore.* London: Chatto & Windus, 1890. Reprint. Detroit, Michigan: Singing Tree Press, 1968.

Kelynda. *The Crystal Tree.* West Chester, Pennsylvania: Schiffer Publishing Ltd., 1987.

Kozminsky, Isadore. *The Magic and Science of Jewels and Stones.* New York and London: G.P. Putnam's Sons, 1922.

Kunz, George Frederick. *The Magic of Jewels and Charms.* Philadelphia and London: J.B. Lippincott Company, 1915.

Kunz, George Frederick. *The Curious Lore of Precious Stones.* Philadelphia: J.B. Lippincott Company, 1913. Reprint. New York: Dover Publications Inc., 1971.

Newman, Harold. *An Illustrated Dictionary of Jewelry.* London: Thames and Hudson Ltd., 1981.

Pavitt, William. *The Book of Talismans, Amulets and Zodiacal Gems.* Reprint. London: Stephen Austin and Sons, Ltd., 1914.

Whitlock, Herbert P. *The Story of Gems, A Popular Handbook.* New York: Lee Furman, 1936.

References for Diamond

Budge, Sir E.A. Wallis, KT. *Amulets and Talismans.* New York: University Books, 1961. Reprint. New York: Dover Publications, Inc., 1978.

Fernie, William T. *The Occult and Curative Powers of Precious Stones.* 1907. Reprint. New York: Rudolf Steiner Publications, 1973.

Gregor, Arthur S. *Amulets, Talismans, and Fetishes.* New York: Charles Scribner's Sons, 1975.

Jones, William. *Finger-Ring Lore.* London: Chatto & Windus, 1890. Reprint. Detroit, Michigan: Singing Tree Press, 1968.

Kozminsky, Isadore. *The Magic and Science of Jewels and Stones.* New York and London: G.P. Putnam's Sons, 1922.

Kunz, George Frederick. *The Curious Lore of Precious Stones.* Philadelphia: J.B. Lippincott Company, 1913. Reprint. New York: Dover Publications Inc., 1971.

Kunz, George Frederick. *The Magic of Jewels and Charms.* Philadelphia and London: J.B. Lippincott Company, 1915.

Newman, Harold. *An Illustrated Dictionary of Jewelry.* London: Thames and Hudson Ltd., 1981.

References for Emerald

Budge, Sir E.A. Wallis, KT. *Amulets and Talismans*. New York: University Books, 1961. Reprint. New York: Dover Publications, Inc., 1978.

Charubel. *Psychology of Botany, Minerals and Precious Stones*. Tyldeley, England: R. Welche Esq.

Fernie, William T. *The Occult and Curative Powers of Precious Stones*. 1907. Reprint. New York: Rudolf Steiner Publications, 1973.

Gemological Institute of America. *The Gemological Institute of America Colored Stone Course*. 2 vols. New York: Gemological Institute of America, 1980.

Gregor, Arthur S. *Amulets, Talismans, and Fetishes*. New York: Charles Scribner's Sons, 1975.

Jones, William. *Finger-Ring Lore*. London: Chatto & Windus, 1890. Reprint. Detroit, Michigan: Singing Tree Press, 1968.

Kunz, George Frederick. *The Curious Lore of Precious Stones*. Philadelphia: J.B. Lippincott Company, 1913. Reprint. New York: Dover Publications Inc., 1971.

Kunz, George Frederick. *The Magic of Jewels and Charms*. Philadelphia and London: J.B. Lippincott Company, 1915.

Newman, Harold. *An Illustrated Dictionary of Jewelry*. London: Thames and Hudson Ltd., 1981.

Pavitt, William. *The Book of Talismans, Amulets and Zodiacal Gems*. Reprint. London: Stephen Austin and Sons, Ltd., 1914.

Whitlock, Herbert P. *The Story of Gems, A Popular Handbook*. New York: Lee Furman, 1936.

References for Garnet

Budge, Sir E.A. Wallis, KT. *Amulets and Talismans*. New York: University Books, 1961. Reprint. New York: Dover Publications, Inc., 1978.

Charubel. *Psychology of Botany, Minerals and Precious Stones*. Tyldeley, England: R. Welche Esq.

Ferguson, George. *Signs and Symbols in Christian Art*. Reprint. London: Oxford University Press, 1974.

Fernie, William T. *The Occult and Curative Powers of Precious Stones*. 1907. Reprint. New York: Rudolf Steiner Publications, 1973.

Gemological Institute of America. *The Gemological Institute of America Colored Stone Course*. 2 vols. New York: Gemological Institute of America, 1980.

Kozminsky, Isadore. *The Magic and Science of Jewels and Stones*. New York and London: G.P. Putnam's Sons, 1922.

Newman, Harold. *An Illustrated Dictionary of Jewelry*. London: Thames and Hudson Ltd., 1981.

Pavitt, William. *The Book of Talismans, Amulets and Zodiacal Gems*. Reprint. London: Stephen Austin and Sons, Ltd., 1914.

References for Jade

Budge, Sir E.A. Wallis, KT. *Amulets and Talismans*. New York: University Books, 1961. Reprint. New York: Dover Publications, Inc., 1978.

Fernie, William T. *The Occult and Curative Powers of Precious Stones*. 1907. Reprint. New York: Rudolf Steiner Publications, 1973.

Gemological Institute of America. *The Gemological Institute of America Colored Stone Course*. 2 vols. New York: Gemological Institute of America, 1980.

Gregor, Arthur S. *Amulets, Talismans, and Fetishes*. New York: Charles Scribner's Sons, 1975.

Kunz, George Frederick. *The Magic of Jewels and Charms*. Philadelphia and London: J.B. Lippincott Company, 1915.

Newman, Harold. *An Illustrated Dictionary of Jewelry*. London: Thames and Hudson Ltd., 1981.

Pavitt, William. *The Book of Talismans, Amulets and Zodiacal Gems*. Reprint. London: Stephen Austin and Sons, Ltd., 1914.

Seven Thousand Years of Jewellry. Edited by Hugh Tait. London: British Museum Publications, 1986.

Whitlock, Herbert P. *The Story of Gems, A Popular Handbook*. New York: Lee

Furman, 1936.

Williams, C.A.S. *Outlines of Chinese Symbolism and Art Motives.* Tokyo: Charles E. Tuttle Company Inc. 1941. Reprint. Hong Kong: Kelly and Walsh, Ltd., 1974.

References for Jet

Budge, Sir E.A. Wallis, KT. *Amulets and Talismans.* New York: University Books, 1961. Reprint. New York: Dover Publications, Inc., 1978.

Charubel. *Psychology of Botany, Minerals and Precious Stones.* Tyldeley, England: R. Welche Esq.

Fernie, William T. *The Occult and Curative Powers of Precious Stones.* 1907. Reprint. New York: Rudolf Steiner Publications, 1973.

Gemological Institute of America. *The Gemological Institute of America Colored Stone Course.* 2 vols. New York: Gemological Institute of America, 1980.

Jones, William. *Finger-Ring Lore.* London: Chatto & Windus, 1890. Reprint. Detroit, Michigan: Singing Tree Press, 1968.

Kunz, George Frederick. *The Magic of Jewels and Charms.* Philadelphia and London: J.B. Lippincott Company, 1915.

Newman, Harold. *An Illustrated Dictionary of Jewelry.* London: Thames and Hudson Ltd., 1981.

Pavitt, William. *The Book of Talismans, Amulets and Zodiacal Gems.* Reprint. London: Stephen Austin and Sons, Ltd., 1914.

References for Lapis lazuli

Budge, Sir E.A. Wallis, KT. *Amulets and Talismans.* New York: University Books, 1961. Reprint. New York: Dover Publications, Inc., 1978.

Charubel. *Psychology of Botany, Minerals and Precious Stones.* Tyldeley, England: R. Welche Esq.

Fernie, William T. *The Occult and Curative Powers of Precious Stones.* 1907. Reprint. New York: Rudolf Steiner Publications, 1973.

Gemological Institute of America. *The Gemological Institute of America Colored Stone Course.* 2 vols. New York: Gemological Institute of America, 1980.

Gregor, Arthur S. *Amulets, Talismans, and Fetishes.* New York: Charles Scribner's Sons, 1975.

Kunz, George Frederick. *The Curious Lore of Precious Stones.* Philadelphia: J.B. Lippincott Company, 1913. Reprint. New York: Dover Publications Inc., 1971.

Newman, Harold. *An Illustrated Dictionary of Jewelry.* London: Thames and Hudson Ltd., 1981.

Pavitt, William. *The Book of Talismans, Amulets and Zodiacal Gems.* Reprint. London: Stephen Austin and Sons, Ltd., 1914.

Whitlock, Herbert P. *The Story of Gems, A Popular Handbook.* New York: Lee Furman, 1936.

Williams, C.A.S. *Outlines of Chinese Symbolism and Art Motives.* Tokyo: Charles E. Tuttle Company Inc. 1941. Reprint. Hong Kong: Kelly and Walsh, Ltd., 1974.

References for Lava

Gregor, Arthur S. *Amulets, Talismans, and Fetishes.* New York: Charles Scribner's Sons, 1975.

Newman, Harold. *An Illustrated Dictionary of Jewelry.* London: Thames and Hudson Ltd., 1981.

References for Onyx

Budge, Sir E.A. Wallis, KT. *Amulets and Talismans.* New York: University Books, 1961. Reprint. New York: Dover Publications, Inc., 1978.

Charubel. *Psychology of Botany, Minerals and Precious Stones.* Tyldeley, England: R. Welche Esq.

Fernie, William T. *The Occult and Curative Powers of Precious Stones.* 1907. Reprint. New York: Rudolf Steiner Publications, 1973.

Gregor, Arthur S. *Amulets, Talismans, and Fetishes.* New York: Charles Scribner's

Sons, 1975.

Kozminsky, Isadore. *The Magic and Science of Jewels and*. New York and London: G.P. Putnam's Sons, 1922.

Kunz, George Frederick. *The Curious Lore of Precious Stones*. Philadelphia: J.B. Lippincott Company, 1913. Reprint.New York: Dover Publications Inc., 1971.

Pavitt, William. *The Book of Talismans, Amulets and Zodiacal Gems*. Reprint. London: Stephen Austin and Sons, Ltd., 1914.

Whitlock, Herbert P. *The Story of Gems, A Popular Handbook*. New York: Lee Furman, 1936.

References for Opal

Budge, Sir E.A. Wallis, KT. *Amulets and Talismans*. New York: University Books, 1961. Reprint. New York: Dover Publications, Inc., 1978.

Charubel. *Psychology of Botany, Minerals and Precious Stones*. Tyldeley, England: R. Welche Esq.

Fernie, William T. *The Occult and Curative Powers of PreciousStones*. 1907. Reprint. New York: Rudolf Steiner Publications,1973.

Gemological Institute of America. *The Gemological Institute of America Colored Stone Course*. 2 vols. New York: Gemological Institute of America, 1980.

Gregor, Arthur S. *Amulets, Talismans, and Fetishes*. New York: Charles Scribner's Sons, 1975.

Kunz, George Frederick. *The Curious Lore of Precious Stones*. Philadelphia: J.B. Lippincott Company, 1913. Reprint.New York: Dover Publications Inc., 1971.

Newman, Harold. *An Illustrated Dictionary of Jewelry*. London: Thames and Hudson Ltd., 1981.

Pavitt, William. *The Book of Talismans, Amulets and Zodiacal Gems*. Reprint. London: Stephen Austin and Sons, Ltd., 1914.

Whitlock, Herbert P. *The Story of Gems, A Popular Handbook*. New York: Lee Furman, 1936.

References for Pearl

Budge, Sir E.A. Wallis, KT. *Amulets and Talismans*. New York: University Books, 1961. Reprint. New York: Dover Publications, Inc., 1978.

Ferguson, George. *Signs and Symbols in Christian Art*. Reprint. London: Oxford University Press, 1974.

Fernie, William T. *The Occult and Curative Powers of PreciousStones*. 1907. Reprint. New York: Rudolf Steiner Publications,1973.

Gemological Institute of America. *The Gemological Institute of America Colored Stone Course*. 2 vols. New York: Gemological Institute of America, 1980.

Gregor, Arthur S. *Amulets, Talismans, and Fetishes*. New York: Charles Scribner's Sons, 1975.

Kozminsky, Isadore. *The Magic and Science of Jewels and Stones*. New York and London: G.P. Putnam's Sons, 1922.

Kunz, George F., and Charles H. Stevemson. *The Book of the Pearl*. New York: The Century Co., 1908.

Kunz, George Frederick. *The Curious Lore of Precious Stones*. Philadelphia: J.B. Lippincott Company, 1913. Reprint.New York: Dover Publications Inc., 1971.

Newman, Harold. *An Illustrated Dictionary of Jewelry*. London: Thames and Hudson Ltd., 1981.

Pavitt, William. *The Book of Talismans, Amulets and Zodiacal Gems*. Reprint. London: Stephen Austin and Sons, Ltd., 1914.

Whitlock, Herbert P. *The Story of Gems, A Popular Handbook*. New York: Lee Furman, 1936.

References for Peridot

Budge, Sir E.A. Wallis, KT. *Amulets and Talismans*. New York: University Books, 1961. Reprint. New York: Dover Publications, Inc., 1978.

Gemological Institute of America. *The Gemological Institute of America Colored Stone Course*. 2 vols. New York: Gemological Institute of America, 1980.

Newman, Harold. *An Illustrated Dictionary of Jewelry*. London: Thames and Hudson Ltd., 1981.

Whitlock, Herbert P. *The Story of Gems, A Popular Handbook*. New York: Lee Furman, 1936.

References for Ruby

Budge, Sir E.A. Wallis, KT. *Amulets and Talismans*. New York: University Books, 1961. Reprint. New York: Dover Publications, Inc., 1978.

Charubel. *Psychology of Botany, Minerals and Precious Stones*. Tyldeley, England: R. Welche Esq.

Fernie, William T. *The Occult and Curative Powers of Precious Stones*. 1907. Reprint. New York: Rudolf Steiner Publications, 1973.

Gemological Institute of America. *The Gemological Institute of America Colored Stone Course*. 2 vols. New York: Gemological Institute of America, 1980.

Gregor, Arthur S. *Amulets, Talismans, and Fetishes*. New York: Charles Scribner's Sons, 1975.

Kozminsky, Isadore. *The Magic and Science of Jewels and Stones*. New York and London: G.P. Putnam's Sons, 1922.

Kunz, George Frederick. *The Curious Lore of Precious Stones*. Philadelphia: J.B. Lippincott Company, 1913. Reprint. New York: Dover Publications Inc., 1971.

Newman, Harold. *An Illustrated Dictionary of Jewelry*. London: Thames and Hudson Ltd., 1981.

Pavitt, William. *The Book of Talismans, Amulets and Zodiacal Gems*. Reprint. London: Stephen Austin and Sons, Ltd., 1914.

Sapir, Richard B. *Quest*. New York: E.P. Dutton, 1987.

Whitlock, Herbert P. *The Story of Gems, A Popular Handbook*. New York: Lee Furman, 1936.

References for Sapphire

Budge, Sir E.A. Wallis, KT. *Amulets and Talismans*. New York: University Books, 1961. Reprint. New York: Dover Publications, Inc., 1978.

Charubel. *Psychology of Botany, Minerals and Precious Stones*. Tyldeley, England: R. Welche Esq.

Fernie, William T. *The Occult and Curative Powers of Precious Stones*. 1907. Reprint. New York: Rudolf Steiner Publications, 1973.

Gemological Institute of America. *The Gemological Institute of America Colored Stone Course*. 2 vols. New York: Gemological Institute of America, 1980.

Gregor, Arthur S. *Amulets, Talismans, and Fetishes*. New York: Charles Scribner's Sons, 1975.

Kozminsky, Isadore. *The Magic and Science of Jewels and*. New York and London: G.P. Putnam's Sons, 1922. Stones

Kunz, George Frederick. *The Curious Lore of Precious Stones*. Philadelphia: J.B. Lippincott Company, 1913. Reprint. New York: Dover Publications Inc., 1971.

Kunz, George Frederick. *The Magic of Jewels and Charms*. Philadelphia and London: J.B. Lippincott Company, 1915.

Newman, Harold. *An Illustrated Dictionary of Jewelry*. London: Thames and Hudson Ltd., 1981.

Pavitt, William. *The Book of Talismans, Amulets and Zodiacal Gems*. Reprint. London: Stephen Austin and Sons, Ltd., 1914.

Sapir, Richard B. *Quest*. New York: E.P. Dutton, 1987.

Whitlock, Herbert P. *The Story of Gems, A Popular Handbook*. New York: Lee Furman, 1936.

References for Shell

Ferguson, George. *Signs and Symbols in Christian Art*. Reprint. London: Oxford University Press, 1974.

Newman, Harold. *An Illustrated Dictionary of Jewelry*. London: Thames and Hudson Ltd., 1981.

Whitlock, Herbert P. *The Story of Gems, A Popular Handbook*. New York: Lee Furman, 1936.

References for Topaz

Budge, Sir E.A. Wallis, KT. *Amulets and Talismans.* New York: University Books, 1961. Reprint. New York: Dover Publications, Inc., 1978.

Charubel. *Psychology of Botany, Minerals and Precious Stones.* Tyldeley, England: R. Welche Esq.

Fernie, William T. *The Occult and Curative Powers of Precious Stones.* 1907. Reprint. New York: Rudolf Steiner Publications, 1973.

Gemological Institute of America. *The Gemological Institute of America Colored Stone Course.* 2 vols. New York: Gemological Institute of America, 1980.

Gregor, Arthur S. *Amulets, Talismans, and Fetishes.* New York: Charles Scribner's Sons, 1975.

Kozminsky, Isadore. *The Magic and Science of Jewels and.* New York and London: G.P. Putnam's Sons, 1922. Stones

Newman, Harold. *An Illustrated Dictionary of Jewelry.* London: Thames and Hudson Ltd., 1981.

Pavitt, William. *The Book of Talismans, Amulets and Zodiacal Gems.* Reprint. London: Stephen Austin and Sons, Ltd., 1914.

Whitlock, Herbert P. *The Story of Gems, A Popular Handbook.* New York: Lee Furman, 1936.

References for Tourmaline

Charubel. *Psychology of Botany, Minerals and Precious Stones.* Tyldeley, England: R. Welche Esq.

Gemological Institute of America. *The Gemological Institute of America Colored Stone Course.* 2 vols. New York: Gemological Institute of America, 1980.

Pavitt, William. *The Book of Talismans, Amulets and Zodiacal Gems.* Reprint. London: Stephen Austin and Sons, Ltd., 1914.

Whitlock, Herbert P. *The Story of Gems, A Popular Handbook.* New York: Lee Furman, 1936.

References for Turquoise

Budge, Sir E.A. Wallis, KT. *Amulets and Talismans.* New York: University Books, 1961. Reprint. New York: Dover Publications, Inc., 1978.

Charubel. *Psychology of Botany, Minerals and Precious Stones.* Tyldeley, England: R. Welche Esq.

Fernie, William T. *The Occult and Curative Powers of Precious Stones.* 1907. Reprint. New York: Rudolf Steiner Publications, 1973.

Gemological Institute of America. *The Gemological Institute of America Colored Stone Course.* 2 vols. New York: Gemological Institute of America, 1980.

Gregor, Arthur S. *Amulets, Talismans, and Fetishes.* New York: Charles Scribner's Sons, 1975.

Jones, William. *Finger-Ring Lore.* London: Chatto & Windus, 1890. Reprint. Detroit, Michigan: Singing Tree Press, 1968.

Kunz, George Frederick. *The Curious Lore of Precious Stones.* Philadelphia: J.B. Lippincott Company, 1913. Reprint. New York: Dover Publications Inc., 1971.

Newman, Harold. *An Illustrated Dictionary of Jewelry.* London: Thames and Hudson Ltd., 1981.

Pavitt, William. *The Book of Talismans, Amulets and Zodiacal Gems.* Reprint. London: Stephen Austin and Sons, Ltd., 1914.

Whitlock, Herbert P. *The Story of Gems, A Popular Handbook.* New York: Lee Furman, 1936.

References for Zircon

Budge, Sir E.A. Wallis, KT. *Amulets and Talismans.* New York: University Books, 1961. Reprint. New York: Dover Publications, Inc., 1978.

Charubel. *Psychology of Botany, Minerals and Precious Stones.* Tyldeley, England: R. Welche Esq.

Gemological Institute of America. *The Gemological Institute of America Colored Stone Course.* 2 vols. New York: Gemological Institute of America, 1980.

Kunz, George Frederick. *The Curious Lore of Precious Stones.* Philadelphia: J.B.

Lippincott Company, 1913. Reprint. New York: Dover Publications Inc., 1971.

Kunz, George Frederick. *The Magic of Jewels and Charms*. Philadelphia and London: J.B. Lippincott Company, 1915.

Newman, Harold. *An Illustrated Dictionary of Jewelry*. London: Thames and Hudson Ltd., 1981.

Pavitt, William. *The Book of Talismans, Amulets and Zodiacal Gems*. Reprint. London: Stephen Austin and Sons, Ltd., 1914.

Whitlock, Herbert P. *The Story of Gems, A Popular Handbook*. New York: Lee Furman, 1936.

References for Anchors and Ships

Ferguson, George. *Signs and Symbols in Christian Art*. Reprint. London: Oxford University Press, 1974.

Pavitt, William. *The Book of Talismans, Amulets and Zodiacal Gems*. Reprint. London: Stephen Austin and Sons, Ltd., 1914.

References for Angels

Ferguson, George. *Signs and Symbols in Christian Art*. Reprint. London: Oxford University Press, 1974.

References for Animals

Ferguson, George. *Signs and Symbols in Christian Art*. Reprint. London: Oxford University Press, 1974.

Pavitt, William. *The Book of Talismans, Amulets and Zodiacal Gems*. Reprint. London: Stephen Austin and Sons, Ltd., 1914.

Williams, C.A.S. *Outlines of Chinese Symbolism and Art Motives*. Tokyo: Charles E. Tuttle Company Inc. 1941. Reprint. Hong Kong: Kelly and Walsh, Ltd., 1974.

References for Birds

Ferguson, George. *Signs and Symbols in Christian Art*. Reprint. London: Oxford University Press, 1974.

Pavitt, William. *The Book of Talismans, Amulets and Zodiacal Gems*. Reprint. London: Stephen Austin and Sons, Ltd., 1914.

Williams, C.A.S. *Outlines of Chinese Symbolism and Art Motives*. Tokyo: Charles E. Tuttle Company Inc. 1941. Reprint. Hong Kong: Kelly and Walsh, Ltd., 1974.

References for Butterflies

Ferguson, George. *Signs and Symbols in Christian Art*. Reprint. London: Oxford University Press, 1974.

Williams, C.A.S. *Outlines of Chinese Symbolism and Art Motives*. Tokyo: Charles E. Tuttle Company Inc. 1941. Reprint. Hong Kong: Kelly and Walsh, Ltd., 1974.

References for Crosses

Ferguson, George. *Signs and Symbols in Christian Art*. Reprint. London: Oxford University Press, 1974.

Pavitt, William. *The Book of Talismans, Amulets and Zodiacal Gems*. Reprint. London: Stephen Austin and Sons, Ltd., 1914.

Williams, C.A.S. *Outlines of Chinese Symbolism and Art Motives*. Tokyo: Charles E. Tuttle Company Inc. 1941. Reprint. Hong Kong: Kelly and Walsh, Ltd., 1974.

References for Flowers

Ferguson, George. *Signs and Symbols in Christian Art*. Reprint. London: Oxford University Press, 1974.

Friend, Hilderic. *Flower Lore*. London, 1884. Reprint. Massachusetts: Para Research Inc., 1981.

References for Hands

Ferguson, George. *Signs and Symbols in Christian Art.* Reprint. London: Oxford University Press, 1974.

Pavitt, William. *The Book of Talismans, Amulets and Zodiacal Gems.* Reprint. London: Stephen Austin and Sons, Ltd., 1914.

Williams, C.A.S. *Outlines of Chinese Symbolism and Art Motives.* Tokyo: Charles E. Tuttle Company Inc. 1941. Reprint. Hong Kong: Kelly and Walsh, Ltd., 1974.

References for Insects

Ferguson, Geroge. *Signs and Symbols in Christian Art.* Reprint. London: Oxford University Press, 1974.

Pavitt, William. *The Book of Talismans, Amulets and Zodiacal Gems.* Reprint. London: Stephen Austin and Sons, Ltd., 1914.

Seven Thousand Years of Jewerllry. Edited by Hugh Tait. London: British Museum Publications, 1986.

Williams, C.A.S. *Outlines of Chinese Symbolism and Art Motives.* Tokyo: Charles E. Tuttle Company Inc. 1941. Reprint. Hong Kong: Kelly and Walsh, Ltd., 1974.

References for Moon, Stars and Arrows

Ferguson, George. *Signs and Symbols in Christian Art.* Reprint. London: Oxford University Press, 1974.

Williams, C.A.S. *Outlines of Chinese Symbolism and Art Motives.* Tokyo: Charles E. Tuttle Company Inc. 1941. Reprint. Hong Kong: Kelly and Walsh, Ltd., 1974.

References for Serpent

Bell, Jeanenne. *Answers to Questions About Old Jewelry.* Florence, Alabama: Books America, Inc., 1985.

Pavitt, William. *The Book of Talismans, Amulets and Zodiacal Gems.* Reprint. London: Stephen Austin and Sons, Ltd., 1914.

Williams, C.A.S. *Outlines of Chinese Symbolism and Art Motives.* Tokyo: Charles E. Tuttle Company Inc. 1941. Reprint. Hong Kong: Kelly and Walsh, Ltd., 1974.

Index

Abbey of Saint Denys 31
adamantine spar 10
Aesculapius 254
Aesopus 136
Afghanistan 34, 153
Africa 34, 56, 189
agate 4, 12, 14, 15, 18-23, 37, 39, 42, 43, 47, 192, 204
Aires 15
Ajax 4
Alaska 112
Albert, Prince 114, 254
Alexander the Great 6
Alexandria 6
alexandrite 11, 136, 137
Alfred, Lord Tennyson 90
Algeria 47
almandine 104
amber 6, 24, 25, 114
amethyst 10, 14, 15, 26-30, 39, 53, 87, 105, 192, 226, 233
amphora 216
Anakie 171
anchor 204
Andamooka 130
Andes Mountains 119
andradite 104
angel 205-208
Angelicus, Bartholemew 171, 176
ant 237
Antoinette, Marie 62, 63
Apep 254
Apollo 24, 172, 230
aquamarine 11, 30-34, 36,78
Aquarius 15, 129
Arabia 123
Archbishop of Mains 175
Argentina 34
Argy-Rousseau, Gabriel 220
Aries 26, 36, 56
Arizona 150, 195
ark 104
Arkansas 56
arrow 242, 244
Arthur, King 90
asteria 11
Athens 6
Audemars Piguet 184
Augustus 6
Aurora 251
Australia 52, 56, 129, 130, 130, 136, 141, 150, 153, 171, 183, 189, 195, 201,
Avon 198
Ayre and Taylor 167
Aztec 121, 195, 254

Bacchus 26, 249
Bahrain 136
Balthazar 150
Baltic 24
Barabbas 236
Barcoo River 129
Barrett, Frances 182, 201
Basle 247
Battle of Poitiers 154
bee 237
Belperron, Madame Suzanne 196
Benoni, Rabbi 48, 58, 190
Berenice 140
Bernardino Valley 150
Bernhardt, Sara 130
beryl 11, 14, 15, 31, 34, 35, 89
Bethlehem 242
Bishop Collection 113
Black Star 183
blackbird 214
blockamoor 12
bloodstone 14, 15, 31, 36, 37, 39, 192
blue rock 56
Blue Princess 170
Boer 56
Boivin, René 144
Book of the Dead 38, 237
Borneo 56
Botha, Louis 63
Boucheron 69, 166
Boyce Thompson Collection 113
Boyle, Robert 36
Brahma 63
Brahmans 136
Brazil 18, 26, 28, 31, 34, 38, 44, 56, 104, 123, 150, 189, 190, 193
Breastplate of Aaron 171
British Guiana 56
British Isles 114
Brogden, John 4, 125, 187, 249
Buddha 224, 236
Bulgari 79, 163
Burma 6, 112, 136, 141, 150, 153, 171, 189, 190, 193, 201, 256,
Burton, Sir Richard 183
butterfly 43, 128, 219-223, 231, 238, 243, 244,
Byzantine 19

caduceus 16, 254
Caesar, Julius 6, 18, 246
Cahn Dr. A.R. 139
cairgorm 22, 43, 53
California 42, 112, 136, 189, 193
Cambodia 153, 201

Canada 104, 114
Cancer 15, 41, 42, 52, 123, 136, 153
Capricorn 15, 41,123
carbon 12, 13, 56, 104, 105, 199
carnelian 12, 14, 15, 37-40, 42, 123, 192, 218, 230,
Cartier 48, 58, 74, 77, 78, 82, 87, 91, 92, 102, 120, 126, 142, 143, 152, 156, 173, 179, 209, 235, 253, 253
Caspar 150
Castellani 4, 98, 137, 215, 225, 226, 235, 249
cat's-eye 7, 11, 34, 35, 40, 41
cat 210
Catherine II 63
Catherine the Great 28
Caucasus 171
Celline, Benvenuto 121
Ceres 18, 254
Ceylon 6, 31, 171
chalcedony 38, 42, 43, 53, 99, 251
Charles V 176
Charlton 69
Charubel 190
Cherubim 205
Chile 119
China 6, 24, 47, 48, 112, 119, 136, 193, 195, 210, 218, 220, 229, 231, 236, 242, 254,
Chivo 89
Christ 4, 104, 216, 217, 218, 220, 230, 236, 237, 242, 254,
Christian 26
chrysoberyl 10, 34, 40
chrysolite 14, 15, 188
chrysophrase 42
citrine 21, 43, 44, 45, 46, 99, 230
Civilotti, C. 250
Claudius 89
Cleopatra 6, 136
Colorado 114, 189, 195
Columbia 89
Confucius 112
Connecticut 193
coral 6, 7, 10, 47-51, 126, 212, 253
Corsica 47
Cosquez 89
crane 214
cross 224-227
Crown of Russia 63
Crusades 19
Crucifixion 236
cryptocrystalline quartz 38
crystal 10, 52-55, 105, 147, 192, 210, 211
Cybele 114

Cyprus 89
Czechoslovakia 129, 150

Daisy 230
Dark Jubilee Opal 130
de Preston, Richard 176
de la Vega, Garcilaso 6
DeBoot, Boetius 198
Delphic Oracle 254
demantoid 104
Devonshire Emerald 91
Devonshire Opal 130
diamond 2, 6, 7, 9-14, 30, 32, 33, 36, 40,
     48, 50, 53, 56-88, 90-93, 95, 97-100,
     102, 103, 105, 107, 109, 113, 120,
     125, 131, 133, 134, 137, 139, 142,
     144, 146-148, 151-153, 155-157,
     159, 160-163, 166-168, 170, 173,
     175, 177-179, 181, 182, 184, 185,
     187, 190, 193, 194, 196, 197, 199,
     200, 202, 204, 205, 209-221, 225,
     226, 230, 233, 234, 235, 237-243,
     245, 250, 253, 255, 256
Diana 26, 205, 254
dog 210, 211
Donna Isabel II 62
Donne, John 198
dove 214, 215, 225
dragon 214
dragonfly 131, 237
Dreicer & Co. 70
Duke of Saxony 138
Duke of Devonshire 91

eagle 216
Earl of Essex 180
East Germany 24
Ebers Papyrus 119
Edith Haggin deLong Star Ruby 154
Edwardes Ruby 154
Egypt 6, 18, 89, 112, 229, 256
elephant 214
Elizabeth I 58, 138, 180, 248
Elizabeth of Roumania 12
emerald 2, 6, 8, 10, 11, 14, 15, 31, 34, 37,
     48, 53, 67, 69, 74, 87-103, 143, 147,
     152, 168, 177, 181, 190, 217, 219,
     221, 226, 230, 238, 240, 241, 248,
     250, 253, 256
Emperor Charlemagne 175
England 10, 28, 114, 130, 180, 186
Ephod 153
Epiphaneus 104, 171
Eridanus 24
essonite 11
Ethiopia 153
Eugenie, Empress 139
Eve 254

Fahrner, Theodore 126
falcon 2
Faraone, Raffaele 166
feldspar 11

Fenton 198
fish 214, 228, 229
Flame Queen 130
Florence 186
flower 2, 12, 32, 64, 66, 67, 74, 76, 84, 85,
     87, 120, 141, 159, 160, 163, 166,
     167, 178, 183, 185, 202, 215, 235
Forbes 89
fox 210
France 114, 186, 201
Fred 253
Freeman 34
frog 256

Galerie d'Apollon 62
Gallic Wars 18
Galuus, Marbodeus 36
garnet 10, 12, 14, 15, 43, 104-111, 132,
     194, 199, 201, 238-240, 255
Garrard & Co. Ltd.188
Gemini 15, 34, 193
geode 42
Gerard, M. 163
German Tyrol 123
Germany 104, 114, 195
Giuliano, Carlo 4, 13, 16, 40, 137, 201,
     226
Gnostics 36
Golden Reliquary 31
Gonelli 42
granite 34, 37, 192
Great Mogul 63
Greek Cross 224
Gregory XV 176
griffin 216
grossular 104
Guatemala 112
Gulf of Manaar 136
Gustavus the Third 154

Hadrian 6, 189
hand 236
Harlequin 129
Harrington, Sir John 48
Hassas 236
Hawaii 150
Hedges, A.J. & Co. 239
heliotrope 36
hematite 10
Hercules 123
Hermias 89
Hermoine, Baroness 130
heron 215
hessonite 11
Hill of Precious Stones 171
Himalayas 171
Hindu Kush 119
Hindu 7
Holbeinesque 13, 105, 137
Holy Grail 90
Holy City 26
Hope Collection 41
Hope Diamond 63

horse 209, 211
Hotz 175
hummingbird 219
Hungary 44, 129
Hunt & Roskell 231
Hussein 236
hyacinth 10, 11, 230
Hyacinthus 230

Iceland 42
Idar-Oberstein 18
idocrase 11
igneous 119
Immaculate Conception 230
Incas 195
India 6, 18, 34, 38, 48, 56, 104, 123, 130,
     153, 171, 189, 193
Indian Ocean 186
indicolite 11
Ireland 189
Island of Elba 193
Isreal 6, 242
Issachar 26
Istanbul 150
Italy 19, 186
ivory 6

jacinth 7, 10
jade 8, 38, 103, 112, 113, 235
jadeite 112
Jaipur 8
Japan 48, 112, 141, 189,
jasper 14, 36, 37, 53, 250
Jehovah 7, 171
jet 6, 48, 114-117
John II 154
Jonson, Ben 130
Judas 236
Judea 186
Jupiter 24, 26, 41

Kashmir 171
Kenya 150, 153
Kimberly Fields 56
King Solomon 171
King, Rev. C.W. 38
Ko Kei 112
Koh-i-Noor 62, 63
Koran 4, 19
kunzite 11

La Reine Pearl 139
labradorite 10
LaCloche-Freres 74
Lady Fatima 236
Lalique, Rene 235, 232, 248
Lambert Brothers 181
Landon, Miss 90
Lapidario of Alfonso X 38
Lapis lazuli 10, 11, 114, 118-120, 171,
     230, 240,
Latin Cross 114, 224
lava 121, 122

Leo 15, 123, 129
Leonardus, Camillus 28, 34, 38, 48, 61, 104, 190, 196, 201
leopard 210
Leyden papyrus 36
Libra 15, 47, 119, 129
Light of the World Opal 130
Lily 230
lion 212, 213
lizard 256
loadstone 61
Louvre 62, 63

Macedonia 119
Madagascar 31, 34, 44, 123, 186, 193
Madonna 210
Madras 63, 136
Magi 26
Magnus, Albertus 19, 190
Magus 37
Maimonides 6, 7
Maine 193
Marbodus 26, 38, 57, 130
marcasite 50
Mars 56, 123, 189
Mary, Queen 63
Mauboussin 97, 168
Mayans 121
Mecca 236
Medea 48
Medes 26
Medici, Catherine de 138
Mediterranean 47
Melchior 150
Menardes 36
Mercury 213, 254
Mexico 121, 129, 136, 195
Michael 254
Midnight Star 183
Mikimoto, Kokichi 139
Minerva 250
Mise, Tatsuhei 139
Mississippi River 136
Mogaung 112
Mogok 105, 153, 189
Monardes 113
Montana 153, 171
moon 242
moonstone 10, 11, 136, 198, 211
Moore, N.F. 52
Morgan Collection 150
Morganthau Topaz 190
Morgan, J. Pierpont 34
Morocco 47
Moscow 150
Moses 119
Mount Sinai 119
Movado and Tiffany & Co. 168
Muzo 89

Naharari 190
Nan-Ratan 190
Naoratna 7

Naples 186
Napoleon 12, 38, 62
narcissus 32, 231
Navajo 48, 199
Nechepsos 36
nephrite 11, 55, 112, 120
Nero 19, 89
Nevada 130
New York 31
New Zealand 112
New Mexico 150
New South Wales 130
New Testament Cross 224
New Hampshire 189
Nicander 114
Nicias 24
Nishikawa, Tokichi 139
Noah 104, 214
North Carolina 153
Norway 150, 190
Nova Scotia 114

obsidian 121
olivine 10
onyx 12, 13, 15, 42, 69, 78, 123-128, 143, 217, 230, 237, 249,
opal 10, 11, 13, 128-134, 219, 240
Orient 18, 53, 89, 182
Orloff 63
Orpheus 18
ostrich 217
owl 2, 216, 217

Pakistan 153
Panama 136
panther 211
Paracelsus 180
parrot 99, 214, 217
Parteal Mines 62
Patek Philippe 87
Pavitt, W. 175
peacock 218
pearl 4, 6-10, 13, 16, 23, 29, 50, 69, 70, 74, 82, 91, 95, 98, 102, 107, 108, 109, 135-149, 155, 190, 199, 206, 210, 216, 218, 221, 225, 226, 233, 234, 238, 240, 243, 244, 248, 250, 251, 253, 255, 256
Pedro I, Dom 91
pegemites 34
peridot 150-152, 238
Perseus 48
Persia 6, 18, 19, 26, 48, 171, 194
Persian Gulf 135
Peru 26
Peter the Great 154
Petochi 80
Petrarch, Francesco 154
Phaethon 24
pheasant 214
Phillips, Robert 4, 19, 239
pig 210
Pisces 15, 26, 47

Pitt, Thomas 62
Pliny the Elder 18, 24, 26, 47, 52, 56, 119, 123, 129, 154, 256
Poland 14, 24, 153
Pomet 136
Pompey 6
Pope Innocent III 175
Porta 176
Portugal 56, 256
Prince of Wales 28
Prometheus 171
Ptah 254
Pugin, A.W.N. 98
pyrope 104

quartz 10, 44, 52

Rabert & Hoeffer 168
ram 213, 215
Ramadan 236
Rambam 6
Rasser Reeves Ruby 154
Rebajez 23
Rebecca 249
Red Carnation 230
Red Sea 189
Regent of France 62
Regent 62
Renaissance 136, 209
Rerek 254
Resch 12
Reuben 153
Reza, Alexandre 60, 89, 140
Ring of Solomon 7
Roebling 130
Rohland, William 119
Rome 6, 254, 256
Roosevelt, Mrs. Franklin D. 31
rose 231
Rowland, Dr. W. 90
rubellite 11
ruby 2, 7-11, 13-16, 73, 80, 82, 84, 87, 89, 92, 93, 99, 100, 107, 118, 131, 144, 151-153, 155, 155, 156, 157, 159, 160-163, 166, 170, 201, 205, 209, 210, 212, 216-221, 226, 230, 237, 238, 240-243, 245, 248, 250, 253, 255, 256
Rulandus 48
Runjeet Singh 63
Ruser 80
Ruskin 129
Russia 28, 31, 36, 44, 89, 104, 112, 119, 150, 153, 154, 189, 193
Sagittarius 15, 195
Sinai Peninsula 195
Salmon, Dr. 24, 48
Sancy 63
Sanskrit 136
Santiago 186
Santo Domingo Pueblo 199
Sapir, Richard B. 6
sapphire 2, 7, 8, 10, 11, 14, 15, 40, 65, 67,

sapphire, continued
  69, 73, 80, 89, 92, 95, 99, 100, 137, 144, 171-185, 209, 217, 218, 219, 226, 230, 237, 238, 245
sard 11
sardonyx 10, 42, 123
Saxon topaz 44
scarab 2, 237
Schlumberge 161
Schroder, Dr. J. 38, 48, 136, 154
scoopstone 24
Scorpio 15, 18, 31, 34, 44, 189, 201
Scotland 52, 136, 189, 224
Scott, Sir Walter 130
Scrope, Lady 180
seagull 218
seastone 24
Seraphim 205
Serapion 61
Sergius, Russian Grand Duke 171
serpent 116, 199, 254-256
Set 254
Shakespeare, William 19
shale 6
Shaman 38
shell 6, 186-188, 251, 253
ship 204
Shrine of Juggernaut 63
Siberia 42, 119, 189, 193
Sicily 186
snake 48, 50, 183
South Africa 56, 63
Spain 44, 114, 186
spaniel 211
Spanish topaz 44
sparrow 218
Spaulding-Gorham Inc. 183
spessartite 104
spider 237
spinel 10
Sri Lanka 136, 150, 153, 189, 193, 201
Saint Ambrose 237
Saint Andrew's Cross 224
Saint Bernard de Clairvaux 237
Saint Clement 204
Saint Dominic 210
Saint Edward 183
Saint Gabriel 205
Saint George's Cross 154
Saint Helen 34
Saint Helena 62
Saint Hildegard 201
Saint James the Great 186
Saint Jerome 172
Saint John 26
Saint Michael 205
Saint Nicholas 204
Saint Paul's Church 176
Saint Petersberg 154
Saint Raphael 205
Saint Sebastian 242
Saint Valentine 26
Star of India 183

star 110, 187, 217, 242, 244
starfish 214
Sterlé 61
Streeter, Edwin W. 213
Strickland, Agness 180
Stuart Range 129
Stuart Sapphire 183
Sudan 198
swallow 26, 218, 219
Sweden 154
Swedenborg 139
Syria 19

Tahiti 136, 141
Tanzania 89, 153
Tau Cross 224
Taurus 15, 189, 201
Tavernier, Jean Baptiste 63
Tem 254
Teste, M. 48
Tetragrammaton 7
Thailand 153, 171, 189
Thrones 205
Tibet 195
Tiffany & Co. 35, , 161, 168, 173, 179
Titi, Julia 31
Titus 31
topaz 7, 9-11, 14, 15, 44, 53, 85, 105, 151, 188, 189-192, 238
tourmaline 9-11, 99, 193, 194
Transvaal 63
Trithemius of Spandau 7
turquoise 6, 10, 14, 16, 188, 195-200, 206, 221, 233, 253, 255

Udall & Ballou 103
Unger Bros. 206
Ural Mountains 26, 193
Uruguay 18, 26, 38, 44
United States 18, 34, 44, 56, 104, 112, 114, 150, 153, 171, 189, 193, 201
Utah 114, 189
uyarovite 104

Vall River 56
Van Cleef and Arpels 2, 68, 80, 95, 143, 156, 159, 160, 177, 200, 217, 228
Van Helmont 196
Venezuela 136
Venus 41, 89, 123, 231
vermielle 11
Victoria, Queen 63, 130, 254
Victorian 44
Vienna 19
Virgin Mary 224, 230
Virgo 15, 38
Voltaire 248
Von Helmont, J.B. 182

Wadi Maghara 195
Wander 87
Webb, David 173, 212
West Germany 18

William III, King 154
William of Paris 37
Winston, Harry 58, 75
Wyoming 112

Yard 103
yellow ground 56
Yucatan 224

Zabargad 150
Zambia 89
Zanskar 171
Zer, Queen 198
Zimbabwe 89
zircon 10, 11, 15, 16, 137, 201-203
zodiac 15